Experimentalist Governance

Experimentalist Governance

From Architectures to Outcomes

BERNARDO RANGONI

Great Clarendon Street, Oxford, OX2 6DP,
United Kingdom

Oxford University Press is a department of the University of Oxford.
It furthers the University's objective of excellence in research, scholarship,
and education by publishing worldwide. Oxford is a registered trade mark of
Oxford University Press in the UK and in certain other countries

Published in the United States of America by Oxford University Press
198 Madison Avenue, New York, NY 10016, United States of America

British Library Cataloguing in Publication Data
Data available

Library of Congress Control Number: 2023932530

ISBN 978-0-19-884991-9

DOI: 10.1093/oso/9780198849919.001.0001

Printed and bound by
CPI Group (UK) Ltd, Croydon, CR0 4YY

Acknowledgements

This book emerged over five years, starting from the PhD that I completed at the London School of Economics. It would not have been possible without the extraordinary support of Mark Thatcher and Jonathan Zeitlin, who, rightly or wrongly, I consider my intellectual parents and much more. I have benefited from stimulating discussions with Chuck Sabel, which have taken place in a variety of locations on both sides of the Atlantic ranging from Yale Law School to the European University Institute and am also grateful to two anonymous reviewers, who have provided very constructive comments. On telecoms and tech markets, I have learnt from Emmanuelle Mathieu and Giorgio Monti, respectively. I am grateful for collaborations with each of them, which provided the grounds for Chapter 4. I thank Niamh Moloney for conversations on financial regulation, especially for pointing me to the case study on retail investments analysed in Chapter 5. Sebastian Krapohl sharpened my analysis of pharmaceutical regulation in Chapter 6—especially where he disagreed with me. I am extremely grateful to all the interviewees that generously shared their precious time and expertise with me as all chapters heavily relied on their expert inputs. Last, but certainly not least, I would like to thank Dominic Byatt of Oxford University Press for his warm encouragement, staunch support, and considerable patience, as well as the whole editorial team for their excellent assistance—I hope that this will be just the first of many projects to come.

Over the life of the project, I have benefited from stimulating and hospitable environments at a number of academic institutions. Hence, I wish to gratefully acknowledge the European University Institute, Luiss University, the University of Amsterdam, the London School of Economics, and the University of York.

On a more personal level, I thank, with all my heart, my family, notably my mother and sister, Maria Victoria and Rachele, whose love and support goes well beyond my academic endeavours. Thanks to Rachele also for having provided the foundations for the book cover, which the OUP design team then finalised. I dedicate this book to someone who is increasingly dear to me: my younger self.

Contents

List of Tables

Introduction

Beyond Non-hierarchical Architectures

This book takes as its point of departure an observation about the current
state of regulatory governance: especially, though not exclusively, within the
European Union (EU), over the past two decades, an impressive array of
policy domains has witnessed the emergence of novel architectures of non-
hierarchical governance ranging from regulatory fora to networks of regulators
and networked agencies. This raises at least two sets of issues. One is how and
why such architectures arose. The other concerns their effects on processes and
outcomes. This book looks at the second set, which relates to central debates in
regulatory governance—itself a field stemming from political science, public
administration, and law—over whether, why, and how regulation is shift-
ing away from conventional hierarchical governance, defined by top-down
imposition of stable rules with which compliance is enforced.

The goal of this book is to explore, both empirically and theoretically,
the relationship between non-hierarchical architectures, actual processes, and
eventual outcomes. In tackling this broad issue, the book pursues several specific questions. What does non-hierarchical governance mean? Under what
conditions are key actors more likely to engage in non-hierarchical processes?
Which trajectories capture the evolution of non-hierarchical and hierarchical
processes in the long run? What mechanisms aid non-hierarchical processes
to overcome gridlock and deliver outcomes effectively?

To respond to these questions, the book draws on contemporary debates
on regulatory governance which have different *foci* and are rarely combined
but which speak directly to its theme. It builds on the influential interpretation of institutional arrangements such as fora, networks, and networked
agencies as the widespread emergence of a novel architecture of experimentalist governance, defined by the discretion of lower-level actors, review of
their implementation experiences, and rule-making and revision in its light
(Sabel and Zeitlin 2008, 2010, 2012a). But it also considers critiques that, while
acknowledging the emergence of such novel form of governance, question its
pervasiveness relative to other forms of governance with which it co-exists,
notably conventional hierarchical governance (Börzel 2012: 380; Eckert and
Börzel 2012: 374–375). Further, the book engages with the functional and

Experimentalist Governance. Bernardo Rangoni, Oxford University Press. © Bernardo Rangoni (2023).
DOI: 10.1093/oso/9780198849919.003.0001

legal scope conditions put forward for experimentalist governance (Sabel and Zeitlin 2008: 280, 2012a: 174–176). But it also appraises political factors, often understudied in the experimentalist discussion and presented as antithetical to functional demands in explanations of variously centralized regulatory networks (Dehousse 1997; Coen and Thatcher 2008; Eberlein and Newman 2008; Kelemen and Tarrant 2011). Furthermore, the book engages with rival predictions about the long-term trajectory of novel and hierarchical forms of governance: at one extreme, that eventually, non-hierarchical governance is doomed to endogenously exhaust its own primary fuel—uncertainty—and thus be self-limiting (Eberlein 2010: 70–74); at the other, that it is most likely to transform conventional governance and be self-reinforcing (Sabel and Simon 2006; Rangoni and Zeitlin 2021). Finally, the book connects to debates about what is required to overcome gridlock within non-hierarchical governance, concentrating, on the one hand, on the widely canvassed shadow of hierarchy and, on the other, on the penalty defaults presented as an alternative to it (Héritier and Lehmkuhl 2008; Sabel and Zeitlin 2008: 305–309).

The present study develops an analytical framework that builds on these debates on regulatory governance but also seeks to respond to their limitations. It goes beyond institutional structures to examine the currently less studied effects of experimentalist architectures on actual processes, thus assessing the real balance between novel and conventional hierarchical governance. It extends attention to, and provides operationalization for, functional and legal as well as political factors, thus allowing examination of the largely overlooked politics of experimentalist governance and of claims positioning functional and political factors in mutual conflict. Further, it looks at how these factors might change over time, hence permitting refinement and much-required empirical analysis of hitherto largely untested predictions about the long-term trajectory of novel governance. Finally, it offers operationalization of mechanisms that might help to overcome impasses within non-hierarchical governance, thus addressing the current concept stretching and allowing falsification of claims emphasizing the shadow of hierarchy or else penalty defaults. Overall, the book sees governance processes as resulting from actors' decisions rather than being automatic responses to available institutional structures, understands such decisions as possibly influenced by legal, functional, as well as political pressures, and treats the long-term evolution and the mechanisms underpinning unconventional, non-hierarchical governance as matters to be studied rather than merely assumed.

The study applies its analytical approach to five key policy domains in the EU—electricity, natural gas, communications, finance, and pharmaceuticals.

For each, it compares two sub-cases over time. Hence, it combines temporal, within-case, and cross-sectoral comparisons with process-tracing to draw out the relationship between non-hierarchical structures, processes, and outcomes.

In answering its questions about the relationship between non-hierarchical architectures, processes, and outcomes in these policy domains, the book has four broad objectives. First, it seeks to analyse the real spread of innovative non-hierarchical governance as opposed to conventional hierarchical governance. The book finds that although the now widespread non-hierarchical institutional arrangements did often lead to corresponding governance processes, this was not always the case, thus underlining the importance of also examining governance in action, not just on paper.

A second aim is to refine existing claims about the scope conditions for non-hierarchical governance. The book argues that distributions of legal powers were neither sufficient nor necessary for novel governance processes: at times, actors were able to favour more hierarchical processes despite legal constraints; at other times, they chose non-hierarchical processes in the face of centralized powers. By contrast, actors engaged in non-hierarchical processes under conditions of higher cognitive uncertainty and weaker readily available coalitions, which hindered them from using centralized powers even when these were legally available. But when they were more confident about the best rules, and they could rely on a stronger supporting coalition, they overcame constraints posed by multipolar distributions of power and pursued hierarchical processes instead. Hence, the findings challenge the importance of legal factors, respond to an over-narrow focus on functional factors giving due weight also to political factors, and suggest that far from being antithetical to one another, both functional and political factors may be supportive of non-hierarchical governance.

Third, the study seeks to test and refine diametrically opposed views about the long-term trajectory of unconventional governance. Whereas non-hierarchical processes seldom led up to hierarchical governance, more often, additional rounds in the next cycle followed. Thus, by looking at periods spanning multiple policy cycles, the study provides much-needed empirical testing. It shows that either trajectory can materialize, but on balance, its findings challenge the conservative view that novel forms of governance are destined to decline. Further, the study also refines existing claims by showing that the self-reinforcing evolution of non-hierarchical governance was fuelled by not only the regular re-emergence of uncertainty but also the recurrent need for fresh coalitions.

Finally, the book aims at advancing understanding of the mechanisms required by non-hierarchical governance to deliver policy outcomes effectively. It shows that while in no case were non-hierarchical governance processes underpinned exclusively by threats of specific positive rules and only in rare cases were they supported just by threats of negative sanctions and prohibitions, more robust evidence from most cases shows that neither positive nor negative mechanisms are the only game in town. Most commonly, one mechanism does not occur to the exclusion of the other. By addressing the extant concept stretching and related operationalization issues, the study thus shows that, typically, the mechanisms underpinning non-hierarchical processes are neither limited to the conventional shadow of hierarchy nor are they entirely captured by penalty defaults. Instead, even within the same policy domain, a mix of mechanisms rather than a single mechanism support non-hierarchical governance. Indeed, the combination of mutually compatible mechanisms regularly aids overcoming gridlock, even in domains characterized by well-entrenched interests.

Preview of Approach and Central Findings

The study conceptualizes non-hierarchical governance as experimentalist governance, defined by rule-making and revision based on the review of implementation experiences with lower-level actors' discretion. It contrasts it to conventional hierarchical governance, marked by fixed rules that are developed, imposed, and monitored from the top. It treats these distinct forms of governance as ideal-types that empirical developments may only partially approximate.

The study distinguishes between novel architectures, structures, and arrangements that offer the potential for non-hierarchical governance and actual governance processes as undertaken in action, practice, or operation, whereby such potential for non-hierarchical governance might be unleashed.

The study looks at three factors. One is functional: cognitive uncertainty; another is legal: formal powers; still another is political: readily available support. Each factor can give rise to pressures to engage in more or less hierarchical governance processes. Under conditions of greater uncertainty in which key actors are unsure about what the best rules might be, they may be more likely to engage in experimentalist processes to identify such rules compared to situations where key actors already (perceive to) know the best rules in advance. Yet, functional factors may also drive in the opposite direction towards more centralized governance. Further, actors may be more likely to refrain from hierarchical governance when they lack the legal powers to do otherwise; conversely, in contexts where the distribution of legal powers is more centralized, actors may be more likely to pursue hierarchical governance by virtue of those powers. Finally, in situations in which key actors (perceive to) face strong opposition and thus the need to mould additional political support, they may be more likely to engage in non-hierarchical governance in order to build coalitions, relative to situations where they can rely on such coalitions from the start. It is worth observing that while the extent to which legal powers are multipolar is arguably entirely objective, the degree of cognitive uncertainty and political support are, in part, the result of actors' own perceptions.

The study also looks at how the three factors might evolve over time and thus at the trajectories of novel and conventional governance. For example, actors might shift from novel to conventional governance once a first cycle of experimentalist processes has shed light on the best rules, thus reducing uncertainty. Nevertheless, they might also continue to engage in experimentalist processes in the face of new questions that might arise. Further, the distribution of legal powers might progressively become more centralized, hence eroding the incentives for higher-level actors to engage in non-hierarchical processes. Finally, actors might move from experimentalist to hierarchical processes once the former have already facilitated the creation of enough support for a given rule. However, they might also carry on with or come back to unconventional governance, should new questions demanding further agreement emerge.

Finally, the study examines two mechanisms. One is the conventional shadow of hierarchy. The other is penalty defaults, which are presented as an alternative. Each mechanism can be employed to induce participation and overcome gridlock within non-hierarchical governance processes. But while the former relies on the threatened imposition of specific positive rules, the latter involves threats of a negative nature such as sanctions and prohibitions.

Investigation of the relationship between non-hierarchical arrangements, processes, and outcomes reveals often surprising results. Four central findings from the cases can be underlined. While most often non-hierarchical structures did lead to non-hierarchical processes, this was not always the case. Whereas legal powers did not have a significant influence on the employment of non-hierarchical governance, both functional and political factors did, pushing in the same direction. Although non-hierarchical processes seldom led to hierarchical processes, most often, they extended over additional policy cycles. The mechanisms underpinning non-hierarchical governance typically involved both the shadow of hierarchy and penalty defaults.

A first finding is that although non-hierarchical institutional arrangements were present in all cases, at times, actors ignored such arrangements, or worse still, employed them hierarchically. In each of the five policy domains, experimentalist architectures such as regulatory fora, networks, and networked agencies were available. Each of the five policy domains did host experimentalist processes featuring lower-level discretion, review of implementation experiences with such discretion, and revision of rules in its light. But three of them—natural gas, communications, and pharmaceuticals—also saw, in one of their two sub-cases (or parts thereof), hierarchical processes marked by the development and imposition of rules by top-down fiat and the enforcement of compliance with them, regardless of the fora and networked agencies and, at times, even thanks to the regulatory networks available in the domain.

A second finding is that even exceptionally centralized powers did not hinder actors from using non-hierarchical processes, and at the same time, conversely, the lack of centralized powers did not always prevent hierarchical processes either. The three sub-cases in the natural gas, communication, and pharmaceutical domains in which hierarchical processes dominated were characterized by a rather multipolar distribution of legal powers, as typical of the EU. Conversely, a sub-case in finance and another in communications featured extraordinarily centralized powers, which higher-level actors nonetheless refrained from using.

In sharp contrast to legal powers, both functional and political factors had much greater influence on the type of governance processes used. In all the sub-cases in which the predominant governance process was experimentalist, there was both cognitive uncertainty about the best rules and lack of readily available political support for particular rules. By contrast, in the three sub-cases in the natural gas, communication, and pharmaceutical domains dominated by hierarchical processes, key actors were both confident that they knew the best rules beforehand and that they did not need additional support beyond that already provided by the readily available coalitions.

The third finding is that, after a first cycle of non-hierarchical processes, governance generally continued along non-hierarchical routes. There were exceptions. In one sub-case in the natural gas domain, after key actors had initially engaged in experimentalist processes during the late 1990s–early 2000s, they shifted to hierarchical processes once they had become convinced that they knew the best rules and that they could rely on a strong coalition to impose such rules on other recalcitrant actors. Similarly, in one sub-case in the pharmaceutical domain, key actors engaged in experimentalist processes in the early 2010s, but, a few years later, turned their backs on them, once the cognitive confidence they had acquired became coupled with a strong coalition. But the general pattern was as follows: in both sub-cases in the electricity domain and single sub-cases in the natural gas, communication, and pharmaceutical domains, key actors engaged in multiple cycles of experimentalism over time as they never perceived they had reached the definitive rules nor that they no longer needed to mould support.

However, similar non-hierarchical processes did not mean a single mechanism. Thus, a fourth finding is that in order to aid participation and overcome impasse, most cases relied on the threatened imposition of specific positive rules as well as of negative prohibitions and sanctions. There were exceptions in that the communication and pharmaceutical cases show that, occasionally, non-hierarchical processes might depend on negative fines only. But the other three cases suggest that this is an exception to the general rule. Moreover, there was no apparent temporal pattern, such as a growth of negative prohibitions and sanctions over time and a withering away of threats of specific positive solutions; in fact, the latter were cast also in recent periods.

Thus, overall, the book suggests that an approach problematizing the relationship between non-hierarchical architectures, processes, and outcomes is well suited to understanding the effects of fora, networks, and agencies on actual policy processes and eventual policy outcomes. It distinguishes between experimentalist structures that have the potential for rule-making and revision based on review of implementation experiences with lower-level discretion and experimentalist processes whereby such potential is actually unleashed. It examines political factors as well as legal and functional ones. Indeed, it argues that political and functional factors are more influential than legal ones because when key actors are constrained by cognitive and political limits, they favour non-hierarchical processes even in the face of centralized powers. Conversely, when they are confident and supported by a strong coalition, they can overcome multipolar distributions of legal powers, imposing and enforcing their own preferred rules on other unwilling actors. Non-hierarchical processes are not necessarily self-limiting, notably because the emergence of new issues can renew demands for learning and coalition building. Finally, non-hierarchical processes contribute to policy outcomes even in policy domains characterized by well-entrenched interests, commonly thanks to a combination of shadows of positive hierarchy and negative penalty defaults.

Research Design and Case Studies

The book uses a comparative historical research design to study five key policy domains in the EU over the past decade (communications, finance) or two (electricity, natural gas, pharmaceuticals) to generate wider arguments. Indeed, the book is variable-orientated: it aims to establish relationships between variables that may be generalized beyond the cases selected and analysed. The comparative historical research design allows combination of several methods to maximize analytical leverage (Mahoney and Reuschemeyer 2003; Gerring 2004; George and Bennett 2005). Each unit or case (where the unit or case is the policy domain) is broken down into two sub-units or sub-cases, thus permitting not only cross-sectoral and temporal but also within-unit or within-case comparison of actual governance processes; their evolution over time; different possible combinations of independent variables—legal, functional, and political factors; and—positive and negative—supporting mechanisms. The temporal, within-unit/case, and cross-sectoral comparisons are integrated with historical process-tracing (Beach and Pedersen 2013; Bennett and Checkel 2015). This identifies the key relevant actors and establishes the causal mechanisms linking legal, functional, and political factors to the strategies and choices of those actors on distinct types of governance processes as well as the mechanisms used to support non-hierarchical processes' effectiveness.

Five key policy domains have been selected for analysis. Two—electricity and natural gas—are subjected to more detailed analysis over relatively long periods to generate initial findings. Those findings are then tested and refined in three other major domains—communications, finance, and pharmaceuticals. Why are these policy domains interesting for examining the relationship between non-hierarchical structures, behaviour, and outcomes? First, they are important in themselves. The domains are economically and politically strategic and have horizontal cross-sectoral effects—on the supply of energy and data, the ownership and capital of firms, and people's ability to work and live. They thus lie at the heart of modern capitalist societies.

Second, the study focuses on these cases in the EU because previous research has identified well-developed experimentalist architectures in all the five policy domains and suggested that the polity where experimentalist architecture has institutionalized most is precisely the EU (Sabel and Zeitlin 2008). Indeed, in each of the domains selected, key actors could, in principle, use a variety of non-hierarchical arrangements, including multi-stakeholder regulatory fora, European networks of national regulators, and EU networked agencies.

Table 0.1 Major non-hierarchical structures in five key policy domains in the EU

Policy domain	Institutional structure	Entry into operation
Electricity	Florence Forum	1998
	ERGEG[a]	2003[c]
	ACER[b]	2011
Natural gas	Madrid Forum	1999
	ERGEG	2003
	ACER	2011
Communications	BEREC[d]	2010
	ECN[e]	2004
Finance	ESMA[f]	2011
	EBA[g]	2011
	EIOPA[h]	2011
Pharmaceuticals	EMA[i]	1995

Notes: [a] European Regulators' Group for Electricity and Gas;
[b] Agency for the Cooperation of Energy Regulators;
[c] dissolved in 2011;
[d] Body of European Regulators for Electronic Communications;
[e] European Competition Network. This is not a sector-specific arrangement such as the one for telecommunications but a key one for general competition regulation, which applies to all sectors. Its application to digital markets and specifically a big tech (Google) constitutes one of the communications sub-cases;
[f] European Securities and Markets Authority;
[g] European Banking Authority;
[h] European Insurance and Occupational Pensions Authority;
[i] European Medicines Agency.
Source: author.

Table 0.1 summarizes the chief non-hierarchical, experimentalist structures in the five domains.

Third, the cases and sub-cases allow analysis of different factors and various combinations thereof. In the vast majority of sub-cases, the distribution of legal powers was multipolar; sometimes, strongly so. This is because in order to adopt rules, the European Commission generally has to pass by the European Parliament and Council. Further, even after having acquired comitology powers, the Commission still has to get the approval of member states within comitology committees. Two exceptions stand out, however. One concerns credit rating agencies (CRAs), an area where the relevant EU agency, albeit networked, holds rare direct and exclusive powers. The other is competition policy, in which the European Commission has extraordinarily centralized powers—especially by EU standards; the application of this policy to digital markets and particularly tech giants constitutes one of the domain's sub-cases.

As for functional and political factors, in most sub-cases, the degree of perceived cognitive uncertainty was high and the readily unavailable political support was strong. Yet, in the regulation of access to natural gas networks after the mid-2000s, electronic communications (or more simply, telecommunications), and conventional medicine after the mid-2010s, key actors perceived neither high cognitive uncertainty nor the need for additional coalitional support beyond that available already. Table 0.2 summarizes variations in the strength and timing of legal, functional, and political factors across the five policy domains and their sub-cases. Strength refers to the degree of pressure for engaging in non-hierarchical governance processes.[1]

Table 0.2 Legal, functional, and political factors and their strength in five key policy domains in the EU

	Legal: Multipolar distribution of powers	Functional: Cognitive uncertainty	Political: Opposition
Electricity	Very strong until early 2000s; strong thereafter	High	Strong
Natural gas	Very strong until mid-2000s; strong thereafter	High; low on network access after mid-2000s	Strong; weak on network access after mid-2000s
Communications	Strong in telecommunications; very weak in competition regulation (incl. of tech giants)	Low on telecommunications; high on tech giants (Google)	Weak on telecommunications; strong on tech giants (Google)
Finance	Strong; weak in CRAs	High	Strong
Pharmaceuticals	Strong	High; low on conventional pharmaceuticals (HES solutions for infusion) in late 2010s	Strong; weak on conventional pharmaceuticals (HES solutions for infusion) in late 2010s

Source: author.

[1] Although Table 0.2 was drafted with the intention of aiding readability, it is worth making a few clarifications. First, while the literatures the book engages with offer only one set of expectations centred on legal and on political factors, they offer completely opposite expectations associated with functional factors; for simplification, this table reflects only one (but cf. with the more detailed discussion and Table 1.2 in Chapter 1). Second, albeit strengths are summarized in absolute terms (e.g. high, low) in the table, these are, in fact, better understood from a comparative perspective (i.e. higher, lower). Finally, the strength of a factor should be understood as applying to the entire case and period, unless otherwise specified (e.g. high cognitive uncertainty in natural gas means that this functional factor was strong in both sub-cases throughout the period analysed, except for the sub-case of network access after the mid-2000s, as explicitly mentioned in Table 0.2).

A fourth reason for choosing the cases is that they have been hosting non-hierarchical, experimentalist arrangements for significant periods, thus allowing study of the paths taken by governance processes over multiple policy cycles. This is particularly, though not exclusively, true for electricity, natural gas, and pharmaceuticals, where the book takes a longer temporal perspective spanning two decades or more.

Fifth, the cases offer a variety of positive and negative mechanisms that can be used to stimulate participation and overcome impasse. Some are common to all policy domains, notably the shadows of hierarchy that can be cast by threatening the imposition of positive EU legislation and the penalty defaults that can be threatened via negative fines and prohibitions or commitments proposed directly by regulated firms as distinctive of general competition regulation. Other mechanisms, instead, are sector-specific. For example, the sectoral frameworks in electricity and natural gas empower the European Commission to take over the process, should national regulators sitting on the board of the EU agency fail to agree, whereas in electronic communications, the Commission can only negatively veto remedies proposed by national regulators but cannot impose remedies itself. In pharmaceuticals, the Commission has the legal authority to deviate from opinions of the EU agency and thus can threaten to do so. But it can also menace to impose fines on pharmaceutical firms that do not respect the regulatory provisions they are subjected to, a threat that, in finance, can also be cast over CRAs. In short, the five central policy domains offer a plethora of positive and negative mechanisms—sometimes general across the EU, at other times idiosyncratic to specific domains. It thus permits analysis of which mechanisms (and possible combinations thereof) actors actually used to avoid stalemate.

Finally, the domains are unlikely cases for effective non-hierarchical processes. Indeed, they are notorious for the incredibly powerful firms they host, which range from energy and 'tech giants', through 'too-big-to-fail' financial institutions and the 'big three' CRAs, to 'big pharma'. What is worse, traditionally, many of these companies were very closely tied to—if not directly owned by—the state, which meant that they could often count on the support and protection of national governments to control completely closed and disconnected national markets (Hancher 1997; Haase 2008; Woll 2014; Bulfone 2019; Haurey et al. 2021). If non-hierarchical governance processes are able to overcome gridlock and deliver policy outcomes in these domains, then they can be expected to do that also in domains with less well-entrenched interests.

Although the book makes no claim to comprehensiveness, the cases covered encompass a broad spectrum of policy domains, chosen for the six reasons just outlined. Indeed, such a spectrum starts from commonly compared domains and then gradually extends to less alike ones. It begins from energy—namely, electricity and natural gas. It then proceeds with another 'network industry'—communications. Thereafter, it expands from network industries or utilities to financial services. Finally, it stretches from economic to risk regulation, looking in particular at pharmaceuticals. Within each domain, the book looks at two specific yet crucial issue areas. It does not examine all possible issue areas within each domain. Yet, this is based on the assumption that the issue areas analysed matter, both as objects of study in themselves and for the understanding of the domains more broadly.

It is worth noting that the book looks at experimentalist behaviour—marked by lower-level discretion, review of implementation experiences, and revisions in their light—within institutional architectures and at its policy outcomes. It takes institutional frameworks as given and as a starting point for governance processes. It does not look at governance processes that might precede the institutionalization of architectures, nor at how governance processes might feed back into the evolution of such institutional architectures, which would have been beyond the scope and length of the present work.

Thus overall, the five cases represent vital policy domains where non-hierarchical institutional structures have been available for significant periods. The differences in legal, functional, and political factors across the ten sub-cases and over time help to offer variable-orientated—rather than sector-specific—claims about the conditions under which key actors are more likely to engage in non-hierarchical governance processes. Comparison across several policy cycles allows examination of the self-limiting or self-reinforcing routes taken by such processes. The wealth of positive and negative mechanisms available permits study of how actors attempt to overcome impasse within non-hierarchical processes, including via the possible combination (or lack thereof) of such mechanisms. Using hard cases because of well-entrenched interests, finally, helps to offer stronger claims about the effectiveness of non-hierarchical processes that can be expected to travel from the specific examples studied to different domains and polities (Mahoney and Reuschemeyer 2003; Gerring 2004; George and Bennett 2005).

Plan of the Book

Chapter 1 sets out the analytical framework used in the book. It offers a critique of major contemporary literatures in regulatory governance that study non-hierarchical architectures, processes, and outcomes. It argues that while they offer valuable elements, they pay too much attention to (experimentalist) institutional architectures and underestimate the potential for agency. They either see political factors as necessarily antithetical to functional pressures or neglect them altogether. They put forward rival but largely untested claims about the self-reinforcing or else self-limiting trajectory of non-hierarchical governance. And they conceptually overstretch mechanisms supporting non-hierarchical governance, thus foreclosing falsification of the associated arguments. Instead, the chapter offers an analytical approach that pays attention to actors' choices on whether and how to use non-hierarchical, experimentalist structures. It defines and discusses three factors that are examined in the study: (distributions of) legal power, functional pressures (in this case, strategic uncertainty), and political factors (opposition). It then discusses two possible mechanisms aiding non-hierarchical processes to deliver policy outcomes effectively: the shadow of hierarchy and penalty defaults.

The empirical chapters are divided by first looking at electricity (Chapter 2) and then natural gas (Chapter 3), before turning to the communication, financial, and pharmaceutical domains (Chapters 4–6). For each domain, the chapter examines two sub-cases, from the mid–late 1990s to the current day in electricity, natural gas, and pharmaceuticals and from around 2010 to the present time in communications and financial services.

Chapter 2 analyses how and why actors used experimentalist structures— notably the Florence Forum—extensively to regulate European electricity market integration (namely, network access and tarification) from the late 1990s to the present date. It shows that far from gradually declining, experimentalist processes persisted across multiple policy cycles. It argues that functional and legal as well as political factors—specifically, steadily multipolar distributions of power and recurring uncertainty as well as opposition—placed major pressures on key actors to use experimentalist structures actively and continuously. To deliver policy outcomes effectively despite the notoriously well-entrenched interests characterizing the domain, finally, experimentalist governance did not exclusively rely on any single mechanism. Instead, its carriers threatened the imposition of both specific positive rules—as distinctive of the shadow of hierarchy—and negative prohibitions and fines—as characteristic of penalty defaults.

In contrast to electricity, Chapter 3 shows that to regulate the integration of European gas markets from the late 1990s to the present date, common experimentalist structures—notably the Madrid Forum—were used to a different extent across distinct issue areas, namely, less in network access than in network tarification. Further, it highlights that in the two issues, experimentalist governance followed diverse trajectories, gradually declining in the former while persisting in the latter. Distributions of legal power, which were identical and remained multipolar in both issue areas, cannot explain this variation in processes as well as trajectories. Instead, the chapter emphasizes the explanatory value of functional and political factors, which were far from antithetical to one another. In network tarification, re-emerging cognitive uncertainty and political opposition placed major pressures to use experimentalist structures steadily. In network access, by contrast, by the mid-2000s, the European Commission purported to know the best rules already and, thanks to the support of the Austrian and German authorities, could impose such rules hierarchically on other recalcitrant actors. In the attempt to overcome gridlock, finally, the Commission threatened to impose both specific positive rules—as distinctive of the shadow of hierarchy—and negative prohibitions and fines—as characteristic of penalty defaults instead.

Chapter 4 extends attention from energy to communications. It shows that, despite the presence of comparable experimentalist networks (Body of European Regulators for Electronic Communications, BEREC; European Competition Network, ECN), over the past decade, the regulation of European communication markets has witnessed sharply different governance processes. To regulate electronic communications, the European Commission embraced the hierarchical imposition and enforcement of stable rules regardless of, or even thanks to, BEREC. Nevertheless, to apply competition policy in digital markets, the Commission favoured experimentalist discretion for tech giants (namely, Google), combined with regular performance reviews and rule revisions. In the latter instance, furthermore, the Commission favoured experimentalist governance despite the extraordinarily centralized powers held in competition law. Rather than by distributions of legal power, functional uncertainty and political opposition, both of which have been greater in digital than in telecommunication markets, explain the variation in governance processes between the two sub-cases. When employed, experimentalism travelled across distinct policy cycles, thus exhibiting durability. In this case, finally, to enhance experimentalist processes' effectiveness, actors relied exclusively on negative penalty defaults.

Transcending utilities to examine finance, Chapter 5 analyses how and why, to regulate the European market for financial services over the last decade, actors have used experimentalist structures extensively, notably the European Supervisory Authorities (ESAs) comprising the European Banking Authority (EBA), the European Securities and Markets Authority (ESMA), and the European Insurance and Occupational Pensions Authority (EIOPA). It shows that actors pursued experimentalist processes even where they were equipped with strongly centralized powers, as in the regulation of CRAs. Rather than distributions of legal power, what explains actors' reluctance to favour hierarchical governance are functional as well as political pressures, namely, cognitive uncertainty and political opposition, which have been strong in the regulation of both CRAs and packaged retail and insurance-based investment products (PRIIPs). To aid their effectiveness in overcoming gridlock and delivering policy outcomes, finally, experimentalist processes relied on the threat of negative sanctions as well as positive rules. Far from being antithetical to one another, penalty defaults and the shadow of hierarchy have thus worked in tandem.

Extending attention to risk regulation by looking at pharmaceuticals, Chapter 6 shows that, to regulate European markets from the mid-1990s to the present date, the same experimentalist structure (the European Medicines Agency, EMA) has been used less for conventional medicines (namely, hydroxyethyl starch (HES) infusion solutions) than for innovative ones—including the COVID-19 vaccine most used in the EU. The chapter further highlights that once employed, experimentalist processes can take both self-limiting and self-reinforcing trajectories. This variation in processes as well as trajectories is inconsistent with distributions of legal power, which were identical and firmly multipolar. Instead, it is in line with both uncertainty and opposition, which varied. For innovative medicines such as COVID-19 vaccines, the European Commission recognized its uncertainty and sought consensus with the EMA and the national authorities composing it. For conventional infusion solutions containing HES, by contrast, by the late 2010s, the Commission could rely both on an earlier blueprint—which reduced uncertainty—and a strong coalition led by Germany, which ensured comitology approval despite deviation from the scientific opinion of the EMA and most of the regulators sitting therein. To avoid break down, finally, in this case, experimentalist processes depended exclusively on the penalty-default mechanism.

Tables 0.3, 0.4, and 0.5, respectively summarize the governance processes dominant in the five key policy domains and ten issue areas, the trajectories taken across multiple policy cycles, and the mechanisms aiding experimentalist governance to overcome gridlock (more detailed tables are provided in individual chapters).

The final chapter summarizes the findings of the book and relates them to broader debates about non-hierarchical institutions, processes, and outcomes. It presents an analytical approach that builds on but develops contemporary debates in regulatory governance, itself a field drawing from law, public administration, and political science. The framework put forward differs from current literatures by adopting a broader definition of non-hierarchical governance, one that includes agency and actual policy processes. It suggests that scope conditions for non-hierarchical governance are not multipolar distributions of legal power and not just functional demands but also political opposition. It suggests that non-hierarchical governance is likely to be

Table 0.3 Dominant governance processes in five key policy domains in the EU

Policy domain	Chief governance process
Electricity	Experimentalist
Natural gas	Experimentalist; hierarchical in network access after mid-2000s
Communications	Hierarchical in telecommunications; experimentalist in tech giants (Google)
Finance	Experimentalist
Pharmaceuticals	Experimentalist; hierarchical in conventional pharmaceuticals (HES solutions for infusion) in late 2010s

Source: author.

Table 0.4 Trajectories of non-hierarchical governance in five key policy domains in the EU

Policy domain (period)	Sequence	Trajectory
Electricity (1996–2021)	3 × experimentalist cycles in network access;	Self-reinforcing;
	2 × experimentalist cycles in network tarification	Self-reinforcing
Natural gas (1998–2021)	1 × experimentalist cycle, followed by 1 × hierarchical cycle, in network access;	Self-limiting;
	2 × experimentalist cycles in network tarification	Self-reinforcing
Communications (2009–2021)	2 × experimentalist cycles in tech giants (Google)	Self-reinforcing
Finance (2011–2021)	None: one cycle only	Not applicable
Pharmaceuticals (1995–2022)	8 × experimentalist cycles in innovative pharmaceuticals (BioNTech and Pfizer COVID-19 vaccine);	Self-reinforcing;
	1 × experimentalist cycle, followed by 1 × hierarchical cycle, in conventional pharmaceuticals (HES solutions for infusion)	Self-limiting

Source: author.

Table 0.5 Mechanisms underpinning non-hierarchical governance in five key policy domains in the EU

Policy domain	Shadow of positive hierarchy	Negative penalty defaults
Electricity	Legislation	Competition prohibitions, fines, commitments
Natural gas	Legislation; sector-specific network codes[a]	Competition prohibitions, fines, commitments
Communications	None	Competition prohibitions, fines, commitments
Finance	Sector-specific technical standards	Sector-specific fines
Pharmaceuticals	None	Competition prohibitions and fines; sector-specific fines

Note: [a] Ineffective.
Source: author.

self-reinforcing and thus sustainable, thanks to both functional and political drivers, which bolster one another. It argues that non-hierarchical governance affects policy outcomes through a range of mechanisms rather than any single one and highlights that positive and negative mechanisms can be compatible rather than mutually exclusive. Finally, it discusses promising avenues for testing the conclusions from the book's case studies more widely, expanding their scope both within and beyond the EU.

1

Analysing Non-hierarchical Structures, Processes, and Outcomes

The present study examines how non-hierarchical institutional arrangements affect actual governance processes and ultimately policy outcomes. This chapter engages with major literatures in regulatory governance that deal directly with non-hierarchical governance. They are chosen because they represent relevant, contemporary literatures providing competing and complementary arguments on currently contested questions on non-hierarchical governance. The book uses their critique to develop and then apply an analytical framework that problematizes the relationship between non-hierarchical structures, processes, and outcomes.

The chapter is organized in two main parts. First, it briefly sets out the key elements of regulatory governance analyses that relate most directly to non-hierarchical structures, processes, and/or outcomes. It then offers a brief critique of them, highlighting valuable elements and *lacunae*, notably concerning the definition, scope conditions, long-term trajectories, and supporting mechanisms of non-hierarchical governance.

Thereafter, building on the previous discussion, the chapter puts forward the analytical framework used in the present study. It argues that there needs to be an understanding of non-hierarchical governance broader than a new architecture, which has hitherto been the focus of comparative experimentalist governance studies. It therefore includes a distinction between non-hierarchical structures as institutionally designed and non-hierarchical processes as used in practice—more specifically in this study, between experimentalist arrangements and experimentalist processes. It suggests that non-hierarchical governance does not automatically flow from non-hierarchical architectures; instead, key actors are its carriers in actual governance processes. It considers a range of factors for the use of non-hierarchical governance that includes functional and legal pressures, such as cognitive uncertainty and multipolar distributions of power, but also more political pressures such as opposition. It develops a framework that can be applied across several policy cycles, hence allowing empirical examination of hypothesized governance

Experimentalist Governance. Bernardo Rangoni, Oxford University Press. © Bernardo Rangoni (2023).
DOI: 10.1093/oso/9780198849919.003.0002

trajectories. Finally, it distinguishes the shadow of hierarchy from an allegedly rival mechanism, penalty defaults, and justifies the utility of such separation to overcome the current concept stretching, thus allowing refutation of otherwise unfalsifiable claims. The final chapter develops a more detailed discussion of the findings from the case studies and the implications for analyses of non-hierarchical architectures, processes, and outcomes.

Analyses of Non-hierarchical Structures, Processes, and Outcomes

A host of studies have looked at non-hierarchical governance, of which the following section does not attempt to offer a complete review. Rather, drawing on major contemporary works that deal most explicitly with the relationship between non-hierarchical structures, processes, and outcomes or parts thereof, it focuses on debates concerning four currently contested issues: the definition of non-hierarchical governance, its scope conditions, its predicted trajectories in the long term, and mechanisms whereby non-hierarchical governance can deliver policy outcomes effectively.

Studies in the experimentalist governance literature provide a conceptualization of non-hierarchical governance that has become increasingly influential over the past two decades.[1] Defined as recursive rule-making and revision based on review of local implementation experiences, experimentalist governance is presented as an alternative to conventional hierarchical governance (Sabel and Zeitlin 2012a).

Experimentalist governance shares with new modes of governance the departure from old modes that tend to be less inclusive, more rigid, more prescriptive, and more committed to uniformity (de Búrca and Scott 2006). Yet, it is not necessarily confined to informal, non-binding tools (Sabel and Zeitlin 2008: 274) and thus should not be conflated with soft law and understood in contrast to binding law-making (Eberlein and Kerwer 2004; Bickerton et al. 2015: 707). Nor should it be defined along the public-versus-private actors divide used to distinguish new from old modes of governance (Bartolini 2011) or be understood as necessarily incompatible with synchronically uniform rules insofar as these are diachronically revisable in the light of local

---

[1] Experimentalist governance is largely equivalent to two notions—directly deliberative polyarchy, and democratic experimentalism—which, nevertheless, have slightly different emphases and have appeared earlier (Cohen and Sabel 1997; Dorf and Sabel 1998; for a very succinct overview of experimentalist governance *avant la lettre*, see Rangoni 2022: 592–593).

implementation experiences (Campbell-Verduyn and Porter 2014; Zeitlin 2016: 1075; Zeitlin and Rangoni 2023).

Experimentalist governance sanctions the local discretion seen as problematic in street-level bureaucracy (Lipsky 1980), shares the intuition that successful solutions tend to come from decentralized polycentric experiences (Ostrom 1990), and echoes the emphasis put by collaborative and adaptive governance on learning from implementation (Goldstein 2011). Yet, it differs from all these frameworks by emphasizing the role of central actors in pooling information on and generalizing the most promising local experiences, showing how such learning processes can be institutionalized (de Búrca et al. 2014: 478).

Indeed, experimentalist governance is labelled experimentalist precisely by reference to American pragmatism (Dewey 1927), marked by solutions systematically treated as provisional and by reciprocal readjustment of ends and means (Sabel and Zeitlin 2008: 276–277; see also Ansell 2011). It is thus also close to reflexive governance (Scott 2010), understood here as reciprocal redefinition of policymaking and implementation (Rangoni and Zeitlin 2021: 823). But again, relative to both, it provides a distinctive architecture structuring such reciprocal readjustments.

Conversely, experimentalist governance shares with multi-level and network governance the attention to networks involving actors at various levels of governance (Kohler-Koch and Eising 1999; Hooghe and Marks 2001; Sørensen and Torfing 2007) but highlights how such multi-level networks can facilitate learning (Sabel and Zeitlin 2008: 273; de Búrca et al. 2014: 479).

To be sure, finally, experimentalist governance is not the only alternative to hierarchical governance. A recent, promising framework underlines how 'governors' may voluntarily enlist 'intermediaries' possessing the capabilities needed to reach governors' targets (Abbott et al. 2015). Yet, experimentalist governance offers a more dynamic perspective, which goes beyond the mere identification of actors that already possess certain capabilities beforehand and that, once identified, can thus be leveraged (Sabel 2004; Sabel and Zeitlin 2012b: 411; Zeitlin 2017).

The crucial argument of the experimentalist literature is that, while, on the one hand, traditional hierarchical governance is increasingly under challenge, on the other, experimentalist governance, through a variety of institutional forms including fora, open methods of coordination, councils of regulators, and networked agencies, is emerging across an impressive array of policy domains and polities (Sabel 2004; Sabel and Zeitlin 2012a).

The documented widespread institutionalization of experimentalist architectures has supported the claimed diffusion of experimentalist governance.

In the United States (US) and other developed democracies, the literature has found evidence of experimentalist architectures both in the provision of social welfare services, such as education and child welfare, and in the regulation of health-and-safety risks such as nuclear power, food processing, and environmental pollution (Sabel and Simon 2011, 2012; Sabel and Zeitlin 2012a; Sabel et al. 2018).

On the international plane, the literature has likewise documented the emergence of transnational experimentalist regimes across a number of major issue areas such as disability rights, data privacy, food safety, the environmental sustainability of forests and fisheries, and climate policy (de Búrca et al. 2013, 2014; Overdevest and Zeitlin 2014, 2018; Zeitlin 2015; Sabel and Victor 2017, 2022; Zeitlin and Overdevest 2021).

However, it is in the European Union (EU), the literature suggests, where the experimentalist architecture has found its way more quickly and consistently. There, scholars have found such architecture in an almost boundless list of domains, including the re-regulation of privatized network infrastructure in sectors such as electricity, gas, and telecommunications; the protection of public health and safety through drug authorization and occupational health and safety; and social solidarity in employment and social protection. The list also encompasses regulation in response to catastrophe, for example in food, maritime, rail, and aviation safety; prudential regulation in advance of failure, namely, in financial services; and the rationalization of existing centralized regulation, specifically competition policy and state aid. It even stretches from rules to rights, notably fundamental rights, for example against race, gender, or disability discrimination (Sabel and Zeitlin 2008, 2010).

However, the sweeping claim advanced by the experimentalist literature has not been accepted uncritically. While acknowledging the possibility that experimentalist governance may be an important and until recently overlooked form of governance, critiques stress that experimentalist governance has not replaced, but rather co-exists with, other pre-existing forms of governance, including, notably, conventional hierarchy, thus calling into question its actual pervasiveness (Börzel 2012: 380, 382; Eckert and Börzel 2012: 374–375).

The critique questioning the actual spread of experimentalist governance relative to other forms of governance with which it cohabits—first and foremost, conventional hierarchical governance—is supported not just by earlier general works on the EU, which suggest that the Union is better understood as a governance mix than any single form of governance (Wallace et al. 2005; Tömmel and Verdun 2008; Börzel 2010; Héritier and Rhodes 2011). Also, more recent studies focusing specifically on experimentalist governance have revealed varying degrees of experimentalist and hierarchical governance, both across otherwise comparable domains like electricity and natural gas and electricity and telecommunications (Rangoni 2019; Mathieu and Rangoni 2019) and within a given domain and sector such as competition policy in digital markets (Monti and Rangoni 2022).

A second, currently contested question on non-hierarchical governance concerns its scope conditions. The experimentalist literature has identified two essential scope conditions for experimentalist governance: strategic uncertainty and a multipolar or polyarchic distribution of powers. The literature explains the alleged decline of hierarchical governance and concomitant rise of experimentalist governance as a result of increasingly volatile and turbulent environments, themselves associated with globalization, vertical disintegration of value chains, and rapid technological innovation. Under these widespread conditions of strategic uncertainty, actors do not know in advance their precise goals or the means to achieve them and must therefore engage in experimentalist governance in order to discover it. If they knew this beforehand, they would favour hierarchical governance instead (Sabel and Zeitlin 2008: 280, 2012a: 174–175, 2012b: 411–412; Sabel and Simon 2011: 56, 78, 82; de Búrca et al. 2014: 479, 483; Sabel et al. 2018: 371–372). The other major scope condition identified in the literature is a multipolar or polyarchic distribution of powers, under which no single actor can impose their own preferred solution on others without considering their views. Unless bound by such multipolar constraints, which are said to be firm especially in the EU, actors would not bother about others' views and would use their hierarchical authority instead (Sabel and Zeitlin 2008: 280, 2012a: 175–176, 2012b: 412; Overdevest and Zeitlin 2014: 26, 43–44; Zeitlin 2016: 1073–1074, 1091–1092).

For their part, studies on the more or less hierarchical design of different governance arrangements—specifically, regulatory networks—have focused more attention than experimentalist analyses on political factors, typically pitting them against functional ones. The international cooperation literature has identified a governance dilemma whereby functional demands for stronger international organizations to cope with rising interdependence are, in fact, rarely cleared due to nation states' resistance against reductions of their own sovereignty (Keohane 2001). This has led, the argument proceeds, to a proliferation of trans-governmental networks. In EU governance, a well-established and now thriving literature has compared institutional arrangements that vary in their degree of centralization at the EU level such as looser European networks of national regulators, on the one hand, and EU regulatory agencies on the other. It has sought to explain the observed institutional choices by contrasting two opposing forces: on the one hand, functional demands, commonly indicating greater EU centralization as desirable, for instance, to enhance technical expertise and credible commitment; on the other hand, political supply, whereby resistance from national actors such as governments as well as pre-existing regulatory authorities has generally mitigated such demands (Dehousse 1997; Coen and Thatcher 2008; Eberlein and Newman 2008; Thatcher and Coen 2008; Kelemen and Tarrant 2011; Thatcher 2011). Minor disagreements notwithstanding (cf. Tarrant and Kelemen 2017 with Blauberger and Rittberger 2017), what matters here is that, by looking at major examples across economic and social regulation as well as over time, a rich body of works has concentrated attention on the respective role of functional and political factors, showing that political considerations regularly condition functional imperatives.

A third contested issue on non-hierarchical governance concerns its long-term sustainability. One view is that, while for the moment new governance co-exists with conventional governance, in the end, the most likely trajectory is one whereby the former eventually transforms the latter (Sabel and Simon 2006). Empirically, this view is supported by a fresh study of EU electricity regulation in a number of issue areas, which has found evidence that the temporal evolution of experimentalist governance may be self-reinforcing, either because actors stumble upon the re-emergence of strategic uncertainty or because they eventually come to anticipate it (Rangoni and Zeitlin 2021).

Yet, an alternative view suggests precisely the opposite. Thus, critics are sceptical of the transformative argument just discussed (Börzel 2012: 381), suggesting that, by endogenously leading to a gradual reduction of uncertainty, experimentalist governance is bound to reduce its own importance over time (Eberlein 2010: 70–74). As its polar opposite, this argument also relies on the empirical back-up of an analysis of EU electricity regulation, where actors are said to have moved from initially completely uncharted territories to relatively more familiar ones (Eberlein 2010).

Finally, a fourth open question about non-hierarchical governance concerns its effectiveness. At one extreme, the experimentalist literature suggests that experimentalist governance has several virtues (de Búrca et al. 2014: 483–485; Overdevest and Zeitlin 2018: 66; Rangoni and Zeitlin 2021: 823). These include the ability to transform distributive bargaining into deliberative problem-solving (Sabel and Zeitlin 2010: 9), which, in turn, can 'disentrench settled practices and open for reconsideration the definition of group, institutional, and even national interests associated with them' (Sabel and Zeitlin 2008: 276).

At the other extreme, experimentalist governance has been accused of incrementalism and thus of incapacity to deliver radical changes (Dorf and Sabel 1998: 403–418) as well as of being a 'pussy-footed rolling-rule regime' with simply no chance of being as effective as hierarchical intervention by the state (Lowi 2000: 75). Beyond these bold claims and harsh critiques, what is perhaps more troubling is the current disagreement on the mechanisms required for non-hierarchical governance to work effectively.

An influential view suggests that, in order to effectively overcome gridlock and deliver policy outcomes, the shadow of hierarchy must support non-hierarchical governance (Héritier and Lehmkuhl 2008). Building on earlier works in the German federal context (Scharpf 1997), the argument begins from the observation that in many instances, rather than producing solutions directly itself, the state has an interest in letting other parties, including private actors, co-produce solutions, for instance because of their superior specialized or local knowledge. The problem, however, is that this also creates the risk of impasse, given the different interests of the parties involved and the redistributive implications and conflicts that commonly arise. The solution to this dilemma, this literature suggests, is provided by the shadow of hierarchy whereby non-state actors are endowed with authority to co-produce solutions for the public good, but they do so under the 'Damocles sword of direct state intervention' (Schmitter and Streeck 1985: 131). Legislators, governments, and courts, in particular, can threaten to enact adverse legislative, executive, or judiciary decisions unless the otherwise affected parties alter their behaviour and overcome gridlock. The shadow of hierarchy thus provides a powerful incentive to cooperate.

The argument that the shadow of hierarchy provides the mechanism necessary for non-hierarchical governance to effectively deliver policy outcomes has found empirical support in several policy domains, including the European social dialogue, competition policy, regulation of energy, telecommunications, financial markets, and environmental self-regulation. In all of these examples, studies have found that effective new modes of governance were rarely found without the involvement of state actors who had the capacity to make and enforce collective decisions should that have become necessary (Héritier and Lehmkuhl 2008; Héritier and Rhodes 2011). The same argument has then been extended to experimentalist governance (Börzel 2012: 380–381), with EU electricity regulation presented as a case whereby parties within the sectoral regulatory forum came to agree on common rules only after having been threatened by the European Commission with legislative and competition initiatives (Eberlein 2008, 2010).

For its part, the experimentalist literature does not deny that distributive conflicts may jeopardize non-hierarchical governance and threats are often necessary to induce actors' participation. But there is a counter-argument that rather than as the shadow of hierarchy, such threats are better interpreted as penalty defaults. The argument here builds on the notion of 'default rules' that may be intentionally devised as punitive, so as to steer otherwise affected actors towards desirable behaviour such as the disclosure of information that may be particularly valuable in contexts marked by strong information asymmetries but which actors would not have revealed voluntarily (Ayres and Gertner 1989; Karkkainen 2006). The experimentalist literature thus explains that, while the shadow of hierarchy prompts parties to participate by changing their rational calculations including considering probabilistic elements (Halfteck 2006; Héritier and Lehmkuhl 2008: 2), penalty defaults operate through the terror cast by clearly unworkable solutions (Sabel and Zeitlin 2012b: 413–414). It goes so far as to suggest that, in the contemporary world of pervasive uncertainty where higher-level authorities are clearly unable to develop rules unilaterally, the mere consideration of such a top-down route counts in and of itself as a penalty threat (Sabel and Zeitlin 2008: 305–309, 2010: 13–16, 2012b: 413–414; Zeitlin 2016: 3–4).

Accordingly, the experimentalist argument that non-hierarchical governance is underpinned by costly penalty defaults—rather than the shadow of hierarchy—has been discussed in examples such as the Montreal Protocol on the Ozone Layer, arrangements to protect dolphins from tuna fishing, and international financial regulatory cooperation (de Búrca et al. 2013, 2014: 479, 484; Posner 2015: 221–226). Reinterpretations of previous analyses, too, have substantiated it. For instance, the literature has suggested that the EU electricity regulation case, originally understood as an illustration of the shadow of hierarchy (Eberlein 2008), is, in fact, evidence of penalty defaults because the European Commission would not really have been able to retake control of the process should parties have failed to deliver common rules (Sabel and Zeitlin 2008: 306–307).

Comments on the existing analyses

Having set out key debates on non-hierarchical governance (namely, on its definition, conditions, trajectories, and mechanisms), the chapter now offers a brief critique of the extant works. Existing literatures in regulatory governance offer many valuable elements for studying non-hierarchical arrangements, processes, and outcomes. They provide a distinguishable conceptualization of non-hierarchical governance, set out several factors that might affect it, and put forward competing claims about its long-term trajectory and the mechanisms underpinning its effectiveness.

However, major criticisms can also be made. First, there is a paradox in the treatment of non-hierarchical governance. The experimentalist governance literature has, among its merits, those of having made local discretion explicit and of having transformed it from a liability into an asset from which it is possible to learn. But it has not paid enough attention to the risk that the institutionalized reviews of local experiences meant to be at the heart of the process may themselves become subject to discretion when it comes to using them in practice. Indeed, although the literature had anticipated that institutions do not always work as designed (Sabel and Zeitlin 2008: 280–281), thus far, the bulk of the experimentalist studies has concentrated on tracing the emergence of a novel governance architecture, as distinct from analysing it in action. This is especially true for comparative works, which have systematically demonstrated the widespread emergence of the experimentalist architecture in the EU, US, and globally (Sabel and Zeitlin 2010; Sabel and Simon 2011, 2012; de Búrca et al. 2013, 2014; Zeitlin 2015) but which are virtually absent with regard to the operation of such architecture in practice. This is all the more problematic because case studies that do exist on this latter aspect have recently shown that, at times, experimentalist architectures and actual processes do not equate to one another (de Búrca 2010a; Mathieu and Rangoni 2019; Rangoni 2019; Monti and Rangoni 2022). To advance this literature and address the question moved by one of its critiques about the real pervasiveness of experimentalist governance compared to other forms of governance with which it co-exists, more systematic work on the actual operation of non-hierarchical, experimentalist governance is therefore needed, especially from a comparative angle.

A second criticism is that while the experimentalist governance literature has usefully identified two crucial scope conditions, it has paid only scant attention to political considerations. The literature does not clarify how the multipolar or polyarchic distribution of powers identified as one of the scope conditions for experimentalist governance should be understood and operationalised (Sabel and Zeitlin 2008: 175–176, 2012a: 174–176, 2012b: 411–412). But assuming that this factor should be approached in legal terms, and understanding strategic uncertainty as an example of functional factor, then the literature's claim that strategic uncertainty is commonly rising while multipolar constraints are generally firm is not always corroborated empirically (cf. Mathieu and Rangoni 2019; Rangoni 2019; Monti and Rangoni 2022). More importantly perhaps, the experimentalist literature also leaves ample room for the conventional criticism that learning theories are excessively a-political, and that more attention should thus be devoted to the politics of learning, in this case, the politics of experimentalist governance. To the extent that a few partial exceptions have acknowledged politics, they have seen it as inimical to experimentalist governance (see, e.g. Radaelli 2008; de Búrca et al. 2013: 782–783).

For their part, studies of variously centralized regulatory governance arrangements have focused much attention on political—as well as functional—factors (Dehousse 1997; Coen and Thatcher 2008; Eberlein and Newman 2008; Thatcher and Coen 2008; Kelemen and Tarrant 2011; Thatcher 2011). Yet, their presentation of functional demand and political supply as typically antithetical to one another should not be accepted uncritically but verified empirically. After all, not only recent analyses on experimentalist governance (Mathieu and Rangoni 2019; Rangoni 2019; Monti and Rangoni 2022) but also seminal works on incrementalism (Lindblom 1959, 1965) suggest that cognitive challenges and political considerations may not necessarily conflict with one another but rather push towards the same form of governance.

A third criticism is that while the literature is valuable in presenting two rival claims about the long-term trajectory of non-hierarchical governance (Sabel and Simon 2006; Eberlein 2010: 70–74), these claims remain largely untested and might need further specification. The author is aware of only two works that have explicitly engaged with this issue. Moreover, both have focused on the same case study—EU electricity regulation—and yet they have reached diametrically opposed conclusions (cf. Eberlein 2010 with Rangoni and Zeitlin 2021). Furthermore, these studies have addressed the question of whether experimentalist governance is self-limiting or else self-reinforcing by focusing on its relationship with strategic uncertainty. Yet, it might also prove appropriate to investigate the temporal relationship of experimentalist governance with factors other than strategic uncertainty insofar as additional scope conditions for experimentalist governance arise.

Finally, the problem is even worse for claims on the mechanisms underpinning non-hierarchical governance, which now are not only untested but also untestable. The shadow-of-hierarchy literature has the merit of having revealed that, despite the wide spread of new forms of governance, the threat of hierarchy remains essential to induce participation and overcome gridlock. The experimentalist literature has acknowledged the need to incentivize parties to overcome their conflicts but has criticized the shadow of hierarchy—like hierarchical governance itself—as increasingly unworkable. It has thus suggested that penalty defaults now provide these crucial incentives because, in contrast to the shadow of hierarchy, these do not require higher-level actors to be able to develop specific positive solutions unilaterally, a capacity that, in the pervasive conditions of uncertainty that actors face today, is long gone. These literatures have thus problematized what it takes for non-hierarchical governance to be effective despite the distributive conflicts that regularly arise. To that effect, each has put forward a distinct mechanism.

Yet, both the shadow of hierarchy and the experimentalist literature suffer from concept stretching. They do not clarify what the boundaries of their chief notions are, and as a result, it remains unclear how one can distinguish these from neighbouring concepts and probe and possibly falsify the associated claims. Thus, the shadow of hierarchy appears to know few boundaries except that for areas of limited statehood (Börzel and Risse 2010). Similarly, penalty defaults are claimed to even encompass unilateral retaliation by powerful actors on the international plane (de Búrca et al. 2014: 482, 484). Moreover, both mechanisms depend primarily on state authority (Héritier and Lehmkuhl 2008; Sabel and Zeitlin 2012b). When they do not, both manifest in the same alternative manners such as through consumer boycotts (cf. Börzel and Risse 2010 with de Búrca et al. 2014: 484). Furthermore, penalty defaults are said to induce actors by reducing control over their own fate (Sabel and Zeitlin 2012a: 177), but it is hard to see why this should not apply to the shadow of hierarchy, too. And if for the experimentalist argument, the rules that can be produced directly by higher-level actors are clearly unworkable (Sabel and Zeitlin 2012a: 176), the shadow-of-hierarchy argument begins precisely by recognizing that such rules are inferior to those that can be delivered by parties through non-hierarchical governance (Héritier and Lehmkuhl 2008). For these and other reasons, the shadow of hierarchy has been accused of being more a metaphor than a consistent theory (Töller 2017: 52–54); similar criticisms seem plausible for penalty defaults too. Finally, recent work has also uncovered the existence of functional equivalents to the shadow of hierarchy (Börzel and Risse 2010), putting additional pressure on the literature.

Accordingly, there is a need for operationalization allowing for empirically distinguishing the shadow of hierarchy from penalty defaults. Specifically, this is essential to the empirical examination of whether the two mechanisms are really mutually incompatible and whether one is indeed replacing the other as either implied or claimed in the shadow-of-hierarchy and experimentalist literatures. More generally, clearer boundaries are necessary to advancing understanding of the various mechanisms that might help non-hierarchical governance to work effectively as well as of the rival or complementary relationship between such mechanisms.

A Framework for Analysing Non-hierarchical Architectures, Processes, and Outcomes

Several contemporary literatures in regulatory governance look at the relationship (or parts thereof) between non-hierarchical arrangements, processes, and outcomes. They offer both strengths and weaknesses. The experimentalist literature offers a distinctive conceptualization of non-hierarchical governance and traces the widespread diffusion of its architecture but is weaker on analysis of its effects on actual governance processes. As a result, it downplays the role of agency and says little about the actual balance between hierarchical and non-hierarchical governance and how this might vary across and within policy domains. It identifies functional and legal scope conditions for experimentalist governance but pays scarce attention to political considerations. These are instead a central focus of studies of regulatory networks whereby, nevertheless, political supply is typically presented in contrast to functional demands. The experimentalist literature and one of its critiques provide useful rival claims about the long-term trajectory of non-hierarchical governance, yet these claims remain largely untested empirically. To the extent that exceptions exist, these devote attention only to strategic uncertainty and not to other factors that may influence experimentalist governance too. The shadow-of-hierarchy literature problematizes what non-hierarchical governance requires to deliver policy outcomes effectively and offers one such mechanism. Yet, this mechanism does not seem to know many boundaries, either conceptually or—consequently—empirically. The same applies to the experimentalist literature's response, the penalty defaults proposed as an alternative that is replacing the traditional shadow of hierarchy. As such, both literatures suffer from concept stretching, making their claims irrefutable. As an ironic result, scholarly debates dealing with how to overcome gridlock in governance find themselves in a state of impasse.

This book draws on the strengths of these contemporary approaches and seeks to respond to some of their weaknesses. It offers an analytical framework that treats the effects of non-hierarchical structures on actual governance processes as part of actors' choices. It assumes that governance processes are not merely an inevitable reflection of institutional architectures but have at least some autonomy from them. This means that processes can shape (the use of) institutions as well as being shaped by those institutions. The book thus treats responses of key actors to the institutional structures available as matters to be explained rather than automatic responses to them. It looks at the political coalitions of key actors as well as their functional needs and legal powers. It takes an approach encompassing several policy cycles to study the temporal evolution of non-hierarchical governance in practice and allows for the possibility that factors other than strategic uncertainty might matter for such evolution. It proposes operationalization to allow distinguishing between the shadow of hierarchy and penalty defaults, thus making their respective claims on the mechanisms required by non-hierarchical governance to deliver policy outcomes effectively amenable to falsification.

This section sets out the key elements of the analytical framework. The final chapter relates the empirical findings to it.

Non-hierarchical governance

Building on the experimentalist literature, the study defines non-hierarchical governance as experimentalist governance. It contrasts experimentalist with hierarchical governance (Sabel and Zeitlin 2012a). It treats these two forms of governance as ideal-types in the Weberian sense, which empirical developments can only approximate partially. It thus breaks with either/or dichotomies.

Compared to the existing experimentalist literature, however, the study draws a clearer boundary between institutional architectures that offer the potential for experimentalist governance and governance processes whereby such potential is realized in practice. It distinguishes, in other words, between institutional design and actual operation, or put in still another way, between structure and behaviour.

The study distinguishes between more hierarchical and experimentalist governance—both in design and in practice—based on three indicators, drawn directly from the experimentalist literature (Sabel 2004; Sabel and Zeitlin 2008, 2012a; Sabel and Simon 2011, 2012; de Búrca et al. 2013, 2014). A first indicator concerns the extent to which lower-level actors enjoy discretion to propose and experiment with solutions as opposed to solutions developed and imposed directly by higher-level actors on lower-level ones. Lower-level actors can be both public and private. In the EU, obvious examples of the former would be member states and national regulatory authorities, while an example of the latter would be regulated firms. In the same context, higher-level actors would instead be EU-level authorities such as the European Commission.

A second indicator concerns the extent to which reviews of implementation focus on assessing the performance of local experiences or else on ensuring local compliance with the rules previously adopted. While, in the former case, reviews aim at facilitating learning from lower-level implementation experiences, in the latter, they are instead more concerned with controlling compliance of lower-level actors with the rules mandated from the top.

A third indicator is the extent to which rules are conceived as revisable and are indeed revised based on reviews of local implementation experiences as opposed to rules that are supposed to be fixed and that, if altered at all, are revised only marginally and directly by hierarchical fiat rather than in the light of local implementation experiences.

It is worth underlining that, in line with recent clarifications, experimentalist governance is far from incompatible with binding law-making and thus should not be assessed based on the binding or voluntary nature of rules (Sabel and Zeitlin 2008: 274). Nor is experimentalist governance necessarily at odds with uniform rules as long as such rules are developed also based on lower-level inputs and are revisable in the light of performance reviews of lower-level implementation experiences (Campbell-Verduyn and Porter 2014; Zeitlin 2016: 1075). Indeed, whilst not its primary analytical focus, the book will reveal the widespread emergence of a general pattern in line with, but well beyond, fresh findings in banking and electricity (Zeitlin and Rangoni 2023). It will show that EU regulation regularly involves rules that are binding, uniform, and increasingly detailed but which are, nevertheless, informed by lower-level actors and jointly revised based on reviews of lower-level implementation experiences as opposed to being developed once-and-for-all exclusively by higher-level actors and being accompanied by compliance enforcement monitoring.

As summarized in Table 1.1, while non-hierarchical, experimentalist governance emphasizes lower-level actors' contribution to the development of rules that are regularly revised based on feedback from local implementation experiences, hierarchical governance stresses instead top-down development of stable rules, with which lower-level compliance is subsequently enforced.

Table 1.1 Indicators to distinguish hierarchical and non-hierarchical governance

	Hierarchical governance	Non-hierarchical governance
1. Rule-making	1a. Rules imposed by higher-level actors (e.g. European Commission)	1b. Rules proposed by lower-level actors (e.g. national authorities, regulated firms)
2. Monitoring	2a. Compliance monitored	2b. Performance of implementation experiences reviewed
3. Revision	3a. Rules stable	3b. Rules revised in the light of performance reviews

Source: author.

Scope conditions for non-hierarchical governance

By drawing on the literatures on experimentalist governance and on regulatory networks, the study considers three major factors that create pressures to engage in non-hierarchical governance: (multipolar distributions of) legal power, functional pressures (strategic uncertainty), and political factors (opposition). It thus analyses the effects of legal, functional, and political factors. As the more hierarchical or non-hierarchical forms of governance, these explanatory factors should also be understood in comparative perspective, focusing attention on their relative strength.

As seen earlier in the chapter, the experimentalist literature understands the widespread emergence of experimentalist governance as being jointly stimulated by strategic uncertainty—said to be generally rising—and polyarchic constraints—claimed to be commonly firm (Sabel and Zeitlin 2008: 175–176, 2012a: 174–176, 2012b: 411–412; Sabel and Simon 2011: 56, 78, 82; de Búrca et al. 2013: 725–726, 743, 2014: 479, 483; Overdevest and Zeitlin 2014: 26, 43–44; Zeitlin 2016: 18–19; Sabel et al. 2018: 371–372). Strategic uncertainty is understood as actors recognizing that they cannot rely on their general strategic dispositions (e.g. more market vs more state) to guide action in a particular domain, in contrast to what they would normally do when they do not know exactly how to tackle a given problem. Put another way, actors do not know *how* to achieve their declared goals. The argument is that 'in the absence of strategic uncertainty, actors are convinced that they know how to pursue their ends, so joint exploration of possibilities is superfluous'. By contrast, under conditions of uncertainty 'the official decision maker does not know how to respond to current or emergent situations, but neither do the primary actors.

The response, correspondingly, is [...] to organise joint exploration of the situation and possibilities for responding to it' (Sabel and Zeitlin 2012b: 411–412). Thus, the expectation is that the greater the strategic uncertainty, the more actors will engage in experimentalist governance processes and vice versa.

Yet, empirically assessing strategic uncertainty as when 'actors by definition have to learn what their goals should be, and while learning determine how to achieve them' (Sabel and Zeitlin 2010: 9) risks conflating cognitive uncertainty and experimentalist processes. Equally, assessing uncertainty as 'the need to address complex policy problems which have not shown themselves to be readily amenable to resolution whether through hierarchy, market, or otherwise' (de Búrca 2010b: 232) raises the issue of what observable implications could be used to distinguish between policy problems that are readily amenable to resolution from those that are not.

The book thus takes an alternative approach. In line with the conceptual definition offered in the experimentalist literature, it assesses uncertainty inversely, based on the specificity of key actors' preferences about how to achieve policy goals. Thus, it considers uncertainty greater when the preferences of the relevant actors are more general. Conversely, it considers it lower when these preferences are more precise.

The other major scope condition for experimentalist governance identified in the literature is a multipolar or polyarchic distribution of powers in which 'no single actor has the capacity to impose her own preferred solution without taking into account the views of the others' (Sabel and Zeitlin 2008: 280). The claim here is that 'in the absence of polyarchy, one actor is dominant, or there is a struggle for dominance, and the powerful prefer to impose outcomes, rather than pursue them cooperatively with others' (Sabel and Zeitlin 2012b: 412). The expectation, therefore, is that the more multipolar or polyarchic the distribution of powers, the more actors will favour experimentalist processes and vice versa.

However, the current experimentalist literature does not clarify how analysts should assess polyarchy empirically, nor exactly how they should understand it conceptually. Indeed, recent works on experimentalist governance have suggested that polyarchic distributions of power, just as power more generally, can be understood not just in *de jure* but also in *de facto* terms (Mathieu and Rangoni 2019; Rangoni 2019; Monti and Rangoni 2022).

Building on this distinction, the study understands distributions of power in legal terms and thus assesses this factor by looking at legal powers. Specifically, the more centralized the distribution of legal powers, the weaker the constraints on the exercise of hierarchical governance. Conversely, the more multipolar the distribution of legal powers, the stronger the constraints on hierarchical governance.

Finally, as discussed, studies of regulatory networks have devoted greater attention than the extant experimentalist literature to political factors and have pitted such factors against functional demands. Accordingly, they have explained the widespread rise of non-hierarchical networks as a response to the following dilemma. While increasing interdependence demands greater centralization of tasks in the hands of traditional international organizations, this regularly clashes with the political impossibility of greater upward delegation due to national actors' resistance (Dehousse 1997; Keohane 2001; Coen and Thatcher 2008; Eberlein and Newman 2008; Thatcher and Coen 2008; Kelemen and Tarrant 2011; Thatcher 2011). The expectations that the book derives from this literature are twofold. First, in direct contrast with the expectation drawn from the experimentalist literature, the greater the functional demands (of which strategic uncertainty is a specimen), the less actors will favour non-hierarchical governance and vice versa. Second, the stronger the political opposition, the more actors will engage in non-hierarchical governance and vice versa.

The book understands political support (opposition) in terms of coalitions already (un)available and empirically assesses it by looking at the similarity (diversity) of key actors' preferences. Thus, political opposition is greater when the preferences of relevant policy actors are more diverse. Conversely, opposition is weaker when the preferences of key actors are more similar.

To be sure, the study assumes neither who the key actors are nor what their preferences should be. Instead, it empirically identifies the crucial relevant actors and traces their preferences mostly based on primary sources of evidence, combining a wide range of expert interviews with European and national policy actors with extensive review of publicly available official documents.[2]

It is also worth noting that while legal powers are an arguably entirely objective factor, cognitive uncertainty and political support are, in part, also a result of actors' own perceptions. This implies that, for example, actors might be reluctant to acknowledge their actual state of cognitive uncertainty or underestimate the political opposition they actually face.

Table 1.2 summarizes the three species of factors considered, the specimens examined, their empirical assessment, and the associated theoretical expectations derived from the relevant literatures.

---

[2] A complete list of expert interviews, anonymized where requested by the interviewees, can be found in the appendix. References to this material are indicated in the body of the text by unique codes.

Table 1.2 Scope conditions for non-hierarchical governance

Species	Specimen	Assessment	Expectation(s)
Functional	Strategic uncertainty	Generic (specific) actors' preferences	The higher the uncertainty, the more the non-hierarchical governance and vice versa The higher the uncertainty, the less the non-hierarchical governance and vice versa
Legal	Polyarchy	Multipolar (centralized) distribution of legal powers	The more multipolar the distribution of powers, the more the non-hierarchical governance and vice versa
Political	Opposition	Diverse (similar) actors' preferences	The stronger the opposition, the more the non-hierarchical governance and vice versa

Source: author.

Trajectories of non-hierarchical governance

By focusing attention on its relationship with one of its key scope conditions (namely, strategic uncertainty), the experimentalist literature and one of its critiques have put forward rival claims about the long-term sustainability of non-hierarchical, experimentalist governance (Sabel and Simon 2006; Eberlein 2010: 70–74). However, these claims have hitherto remained untested (for exceptions, see Eberlein 2010; Rangoni and Zeitlin 2021). Furthermore, legal and political factors must also be considered as they, too, might influence the use of non-hierarchical governance.

Hence the study examines periods that may encompass more than one policy cycle, allowing empirical testing both of the claim that, by facilitating a gradual reduction of uncertainty, experimentalist governance endogenously leads to its own decline and of the opposite claim that, thanks to the regular re-emergence of uncertainty, experimentalist governance is self-reinforcing.

Moreover, the study extends attention from strategic uncertainty to multipolar distributions of legal power and political resistance. It thus offers the opportunity to examine whether the long-term trajectory of experimentalist governance might be sustained—or undermined—not just by functional but also by legal and political factors as well as to analyse whether, and how, the use of experimentalism might itself endogenously affect not only functional but also legal and political conditions.

Mechanisms of non-hierarchical governance

As seen, the shadow-of-hierarchy literature has revealed that, in order to effectively overcome impasse resulting from redistributive conflicts and thus eventually deliver policy outcomes, non-hierarchical forms of governance, such as new and experimentalist governance, still heavily rely on the support of traditional hierarchy (Héritier and Lehmkuhl 2008; Héritier and Rhodes 2011). The experimentalist literature has responded that, although there is indeed the need for an incentive device, actually, this is better interpreted as penalty defaults because, in the currently pervasive conditions of uncertainty, authorities are no longer potentially capable of developing rules unilaterally as the shadow of hierarchy presupposes (Sabel and Zeitlin 2008: 305–309, 2010: 13–16, 2012b: 413–414).

However, as also discussed, it is currently hard to distinguish the shadow-of-hierarchy and the penalty-defaults mechanisms empirically and thus ultimately judge the validity of their respective theoretical claims. It is not possible to make such a distinction by looking at the threatened use of authority or at other manifestations such as consumer boycotts since both are common to the two mechanisms (cf. Héritier and Lehmkuhl 2008 and Börzel and Risse 2010 with Sabel and Zeitlin 2012b and de Búrca et al. 2014: 484). Equally, judging whether rules developed by higher-level actors would be 'clearly unworkable' or just inferior to those that could be produced via non-hierarchical governance (cf. Sabel and Zeitlin 2012a: 176 with Héritier and Lehmkuhl 2008) clearly poses fierce methodological challenges. Such challenges do not disappear if one attempted to distinguish situations in which parties decide to participate because of their cost–benefit calculations or else because of *in terrorem* (cf. Héritier and Lehmkuhl 2008: 2 and Halfteck 2006 with Sabel and Zeitlin 2012b: 413–414).

Bearing in mind these dead ends, the study takes an original route by distinguishing the shadow of hierarchy from penalty defaults based on the positive or negative character of the threats cast by higher-level actors. This echoes the influential distinction between negative and positive European integration (Scharpf 1999) and builds on recent insights in the experimentalist literature (Zeitlin 2016: 1076; Rangoni and Zeitlin 2021: 823). Crucially, it captures the heart of the shadow of hierarchy and penalty defaults in that the former requires hierarchical authorities to be able to retake control of the process and impose rules, should that turn out to be necessary, whereas the latter's starting point is that such a capacity is now gone. Thus, the study considers being before the shadow of hierarchy when a mechanism involves threats of specific positive rules. By contrast, it considers being before penalty defaults when such a mechanism counts on threats of a negative character, such as fines and prohibitions or, at most, obligations for lower-level actors to repropose solutions themselves.

Concluding comments

Contemporary literatures in regulatory governance offer valuable elements to analyse the effects of non-hierarchical structures on actual processes and policy outcomes. A critique of them has uncovered their strengths as well as limitations. Building on that critique, an analytical framework has been set out that encompasses both non-hierarchical arrangements and non-hierarchical behaviour. It allows functional and legal as well as political considerations to be drivers for non-hierarchical governance, including over multiple policy cycles. It evaluates both positive and negative mechanisms that can aid non-hierarchical governance to deliver policy outcomes effectively.

The empirical chapters now use the analytical framework to show that non-hierarchical structures did not invariably lead to non-hierarchical behaviour. Functional and political factors had more influence than legal factors on actors' choices to employ non-hierarchical arrangements. They did so because, when actors had only a generic idea of the best rules and faced strong resistance, they could not pursue hierarchical governance despite being equipped with centralized powers. Conversely, when actors did have both confidence about the best rules and the support of a major coalition, they could impose their own preferred rules on others despite the constraints provided by multipolar distributions of legal power. While this was not always the case, functional and political pressures to engage in non-hierarchical governance often resurfaced as new issues demanding the identification of novel solutions and the creation of fresh coalitions arose, thus helping the long-term sustainability of non-hierarchical governance. Most commonly, these processes were able to influence policy outcomes despite the well-entrenched interests distinctive of the domains analysed thanks to a combination of threats of specific positive rules and negative sanctions, which were far from mutually exclusive. The final chapter of the book discusses the implications for the contemporary literatures on non-hierarchical governance.

2

Experimentalist Architectures, Processes, and Outcomes

European Electricity Markets 1996–2021

Electricity is so vital to our lives that we might take it for granted. The light we use to illuminate our offices and homes, the computers and mobile phones we employ for work and pleasure, and the trains and metros we use to travel within and across cities: these are only some of the several possible illustrations of how pervasive electricity is to our professional and personal lives. In the next few decades, moreover, the societal importance of electricity will only grow. The most obvious reasons are the efforts to decarbonize our societies, which put electricity centre stage, especially to fulfil our transport and energy requirements.

Yet, the electricity domain also poses significant challenges. Not only are we reminded on an almost daily basis that the efforts to fight climate change should be accelerated, as evidenced *inter alia* by natural disasters that occur with unprecedented frequency and intensity, but also, far from having declined as expected from more competitive markets, electricity prices have been soaring across the whole of Europe (ACER & CEER 2020: 18–19) and indeed worldwide, thus triggering popular discontent and associated political reactions.[1] The 2022 Russian invasion of Ukraine has only made such matters worse. It is not clear, furthermore, that the opening up of national markets to competition and their progressive European interconnection from the late 1990s onwards has really weakened the historically state-owned, vertically integrated monopolists that traditionally dominated the sector. In fact, market liberalization and integration has accompanied the transformation of such 'national champions' into even larger, arguably more powerful 'European champions' (Thatcher 2014a, b).

---

[1] See, e.g. *The Guardian*, 16 February 2017; *The Week*, 2 August 2017; *BBC News*, 25 November 2018; *The Atlantic*, 8 December 2018; *El Nacional*, 19 August 2021; *Politico*, 20 August 2021.

Experimentalist Governance. Bernardo Rangoni, Oxford University Press. © Bernardo Rangoni (2023). DOI: 10.1093/oso/9780198849919.003.0003

Besides being intrinsically important, the electricity domain hosts experimentalist architectures that open up the possibility for experimentalist processes, marked by rule-making and revision based on review of implementation experiences which lower-level actors such as national authorities and firms have discretion to pursue. The European Commission created the European Electricity Regulatory Forum, better known as the 'Florence Forum', in 1998, to aid market integration by facilitating exchange of views and experiences, especially on the issues of network access and tarification, the two sub-cases on which the chapter concentrates. For that purpose, the Florence Forum is expected to bring together, twice a year, a variety of public and private actors at different levels of governance. These include European Union (EU)-level associations of electricity producers and transmission system operators (TSOs), national regulatory authorities (NRAs), and their progressively formalized European networks (Council of European Energy Regulators, CEER; European Regulators' Group for Electricity and Gas, ERGEG), and more recently, the EU networked agency (Agency for the Cooperation of Energy Regulators, ACER). Indeed, these European regulatory networks and the EU regulatory agency may themselves be interpreted as experimentalist arrangements since they are EU-level institutions composed by NRAs and tasked to support the European Commission in the creation of rules for the internal market (Eberlein 2008, 2010; Sabel and Zeitlin 2008: 282–283).

Further, the electricity domain allows analysis of the evolution of experimentalist governance processes across multiple policy cycles because experimentalist institutional structures like the Florence Forum have been present for long periods, namely, two decades. It thus permits testing and refinement of rival claims about the long-term sustainability of non-hierarchical governance.

The electricity domain is also characterized by factors that, according to the literatures on experimentalist governance and on regulatory networks, should affect non-hierarchical governance. When the market integration process began in the late 1990s, there was virtually no EU regulation governing cross-border networks but rather a patchwork of asymmetric national rules (Hancher 1997, 1998). The definition of common rules on both network access and tarification was therefore 'virgin territory' (Eberlein 2008). As this chapter will show, such uncertainty has not declined over time. Under these conditions of great cognitive uncertainty, the experimentalist literature would expect actors to engage in experimentalist governance. On the contrary, studies in EU and global governance that see functional demands—of which uncertainty is a specimen—as drivers for increased centralization would expect hierarchical governance. The domain also features polyarchic or multipolar distributions of legal power, in which no single actor could impose their own preferred solution without taking into account others' views. Even though, since the early 2000s, the European Commission has been empowered to adopt rules without having to get the approval of both the Parliament and Council as in the ordinary legislative procedure, it has remained constrained by the member states representatives sitting in the committees governing the comitology procedure. Because of these multipolar distributions of legal power, the experimentalist literature would thus expect actors to engage in experimentalist governance. Finally, analyses of regulatory networks suggest that political resistance often hinders an otherwise functional centralization. Since member states have jealously safeguarded their sovereignty on a sector they consider strategic (Padgett 1992: 55; Hancher 1997; Bocquillon and Maltby 2020; Solorio and Jörgens 2020) and—as the chapter will illustrate—key actors have repeatedly found themselves without the support of a strong political coalition, the expectation here would be favourable to non-hierarchical governance.

The electricity case, finally, offers various mechanisms that higher-level actors might use to support the operation of non-hierarchical governance. Should gridlock happen within the Florence Forum due to redistributive conflicts among the involved parties, the European Commission could, for example, try to unblock the situation by threatening to use its competition law powers, and/or its legislative powers. The case thus allows studying whether the shadow of hierarchy and the experimentalist penalty defaults are really rival, as suggested by the literatures.

The construction of the integrated electricity market thus offers a fascinating case for examining the relationship between non-hierarchical architectures, processes, and outcomes. First, it allows probing whether experimentalist architectures such as the Florence Forum actually result in experimentalist behaviour. Second, it enables exploration of the trajectory of non-hierarchical governance over time, thus testing and refining rival claims about its long-term sustainability. Third, it permits analysing the explanatory value of functional, legal, and political factors, which are expected to influence the use of more or less hierarchical governance. Finally, it provides for the study of which mechanisms actors actually employed to aid the effectiveness of non-hierarchical governance, hence allowing probing the competing arguments about shadow of hierarchy and experimentalist penalty defaults.

With respect to the general questions of the book, the chapter allows development of four key arguments. First, it demonstrates that non-hierarchical architectures can, indeed, lead to non-hierarchical processes. In both the sub-cases analysed, actors employed experimentalist arrangements such as the

Florence Forum, the ERGEG, and the ACER extensively to compare the performance of local implementation experiences and to develop and revise EU rules on that basis. While the case of finance (Chapter 5) will confirm this finding, the cases of gas, communications, and pharmaceuticals (Chapters 3, 4, and 6, respectively) will highlight that experimentalist architectures do not result in experimentalist behaviour always and inevitably.

Furthermore, non-hierarchical governance persisted over time. In the regulation of network access, from the late 1990s to the present day there were no less than three cycles of experimentalism, which led to progressively more efficient and detailed rules on how to manage the use of interconnections across countries. In the regulation of network tarification, similarly, two cycles of experimentalism facilitated the elaboration of common rules ensuring the compensation of TSOs for the costs they incur in hosting cross-border electricity flows on their networks and that electricity producers located in different countries compete on a level playing field. While sub-cases from natural gas and pharmaceuticals (Chapters 3 and 6) will show that this is not always the case, others from the same two domains, plus another one from communications (Chapter 4), will lend further support to such a self-reinforcing trajectory.

Moreover, the chapter shows that actors continuously engaged in non-hierarchical processes due to pressures from constantly multipolar distributions of legal power as well as re-emerging cognitive uncertainty and political opposition. Thus, one reason why the European Commission favoured the identification and revision of rules through the regular comparison and debate of different approaches experimented across borders had to do with the complexity of elaborating common rules on network access and tarification, rules that did not previously exist. Importantly, the Commission and other actors continued to recognize their state of uncertainty also in later phases. Functional pressures were thus favourable to non-hierarchical governance, not inimical to it.

Another reason for experimentalist governance is that the Commission needed the approval of the Parliament and Council, or at least of the member states represented in the comitology committee. Multipolar distributions of legal powers thus also contributed positively to experimentalist governance.

However, a third reason that pushed the Commission to favour non-hierarchical processes was that it could not rely on a readily available coalition to impose its own preferred rules. On the contrary, the Commission acted in a field populated by multiple actors with different interests, starting from the historical resistance against integration by incumbent firms often allied with national governments (Hancher 1997; Eberlein 2010: 62) and then extending to other divides at more recent regulatory crossroads.

All subsequent chapters will corroborate the finding about the positive influence on non-hierarchical governance of functional factors (namely, strategic uncertainty) and of political ones—specifically lack of readily available coalitions. Instead, the value of multipolar distributions of legal powers as a scope condition for non-hierarchical governance will be challenged. Sub-cases in natural gas, communications, and pharmaceuticals (Chapters 3, 4, and 6) will demonstrate that polyarchy is not enough to prevent actors from engaging in hierarchical processes as long as these actors perceive that they know the right rules already and can count on a strong coalition allowing them to impose such rules on others despite the legal multipolar constraints. Conversely, a sub-case in communications (Chapter 4) and another in financial services (Chapter 5) will show that, under conditions of high uncertainty and weak coalitions, actors engage in non-hierarchical governance even if they hold exceptionally centralized powers that, in principle, would allow them to pursue hierarchy.

Finally, the chapter reveals that non-hierarchical governance was supported by both positive and negative threats and thus by both the shadow of hierarchy and penalty defaults rather than by one or the other mechanism alone. While in the early and the late 2000s, Florence Forum participants respectively agreed on network tarification and network access rules under explicit threats of EU legislative proposals to advance on both issues, the European Commission also used—or threatened to use—its competition law powers extensively. Yet, a close examination shows that, in fact, virtually all competition cases—or potential cases—were characterized by negative fines and prohibitions (e.g. against long-term reservations of network capacity) or, at most, by commitments that were offered directly by the lower-level firms (e.g. amending the German tarification agreement to avoid the prohibition of a major merger) rather than being imposed from the top by higher-level actors like the Commission. Although in rare instances, non-hierarchical governance will be found to rely exclusively on a single mechanism (Chapters 4, 6), most cases will corroborate the finding that, generally, the effectiveness of non-hierarchical governance is harnessed by both the shadow of hierarchy and negative defaults, thus suggesting that the two mechanisms are far from mutually exclusive.

The chapter begins by briefly introducing the key experimentalist architectures identified in the electricity domain and outlining their potential of leading to experimentalist behaviour, marked by discretion for lower-level actors to pursue different approaches, comparison and debate of their implementation experiences, and definition and revision of common rules in the light of this. The chapter then compares the governance processes actually employed to regulate network access and tarification, underlining their similarity across the two sub-cases as well as their persistence over time. It goes on to account for such a similarity and continuity, arguing that it was due to functional (cognitive uncertainty), legal (multipolar distributions of power), and political (lack of readily available coalitions) factors. Thereafter, the chapter examines the mechanisms that helped to overcome impasses in experimentalist processes, underscoring the role played by both shadows of positive hierarchy and negative penalty defaults. It concludes by offering more general implications for experimentalist governance.

Experimentalist Structures

As in every policy domain analysed in the book, institutional architectures that create the possibility for experimentalist processes have also spread in electricity (Eberlein 2008, 2010; Sabel and Zeitlin 2008: 282–283; Mathieu and Rangoni 2019; Rangoni 2019; Rangoni and Zeitlin 2021). The chief illustration is the Florence Forum for Electricity Regulation. Organized by the European Commission immediately after the first round of EU liberalization legislation and hosted by the European University Institute, since 1998, its key task has been to provide a neutral and informal framework for discussion of issues and exchange of experiences concerning the implementation of EU legislation and the creation of the internal electricity market, beginning from two issues that were identified at the outset as crucial, namely, network access and tarification. Over the past two decades or so, the Florence Forum has been bringing together, twice a year, the European Commission, European regulatory networks and EU agencies; national ministries and NRAs; TSOs, electricity producers, traders, and exchanges as well as their EU-level associations; plus a variety of additional stakeholders such as representatives of consumers and academic experts.[2] The Florence Forum is thus an experimentalist architecture because, by design, it aims to harness the wealth of experiences of its participants—including the lower-level ones—to make and revise EU rules.

For the very same reasons, the European regulatory networks and the more recent EU networked agency contributing to the Florence Forum might

---

[2] See https://commission.europa.eu/events/meeting-european-electricity-regulatory-forum-rome-2022-06-09_en (last accessed March 2023).

themselves be considered experimentalist arrangements. Initially organized informally in 2000 thanks to the initiative of a few NRAs seeking to exchange views and experiences on market liberalization and integration, in 2003, the CEER saw the establishment of a more formalized regulatory network (the ERGEG), created directly by the European Commission as its advisory group (European Commission 2003a). Thereafter, in 2011, the ERGEG evolved into the ACER,[3] whose key task is the elaboration of non-binding framework guidelines on a variety of issue areas, on which basis the European Network of Transmission System Operators for Electricity (ENTSO-E) then develops detailed network codes, which the European Commission eventually makes binding through comitology procedure (European Parliament and Council 2009a, b: art. 6). But despite the binding nature of the network codes (as distinct from the non-binding guidelines produced by the ERGEG) and the ACER's status as an EU agency (as opposed to the ERGEG's one as a regulatory network), the ACER actually remains networked since its board is composed of the heads of European NRAs, just as was the case for the CEER and the ERGEG, and analogously to the ENTSO-E, whose board consists of the heads of national TSOs. Furthermore, the ACER, together with the ENTSO-E and the Commission, has recently created informal groups to monitor the implementation of the network codes, identify possible problems that might be emerging in their actual operation, and consider revisions accordingly (ACER and ENTSO-E 2015; European Commission et al. 2017; Rangoni 2020: 30–33; Rangoni and Zeitlin 2021: 832–833).

Thus, both the Florence Forum and the European networks—including of national regulators—populating it create the potential for the comparison and debate of experiences that national actors have discretion to experiment with and for the development and revision of common rules in their light. However, to what extent has such potential been realized in practice? The chapter now proceeds to address this question.

Experimentalist Processes across Sub-cases and Time

Comparison of the governance processes used to regulate network access and tarification reveals a striking similarity. Far from being marked by the hierarchical development, imposition, and enforcement of rules, the regulation of both sub-cases has been characterized by discretion for local actors such as

---

[3] While the ERGEG ceased to exist when the ACER became operational in 2011, the CEER continues to exist alongside the ACER.

NRAs and TSOs to propose and experiment with a variety of solutions; regular comparison and debate of their experiences, especially in the Florence Forum; and elaboration and revision of common rules on that basis. The dominant type of governance process has been, therefore, experimentalist.

Furthermore, these experimentalist processes proved sustainable over time, given that network access regulation witnessed three distinct cycles of experimentalist governance, and network tarification regulation saw two of them.

Regulating network access with experimentalism, three times

A first cycle of experimentalist governance, late 1990s–early 2000s

The first indication that processes to regulate network access were experimentalist is that national public authorities and regulated companies had leeway on how to address the issue. From the 1990s onwards, the European Commission began to extend EU regulation, notably through a series of liberalizing and re-regulatory directives. After the first set of legislation on price transparency and energy transits in the early 1990s and over five years of negotiations in the Council, the resulting legislation accepted the general principle of an open market and the need for common rules within a European market. But as a political compromise, it was weak in terms of providing a coherent set of EU-level rules. The first 1996 Electricity Directive only prescribed limited market opening and granted member states a wide margin of discretion on key regulatory issues, including the regime of access to the natural monopoly of transmission wires. Further, it simply failed to establish common rules for the interconnection of national grid systems at the heart of cross-border trade (European Parliament and Council 1996).

The second indication of experimentalist processes is that actors used the Florence Forum extensively to compare and debate the experiences arising from local discretion. At the first meeting in 1998, the Director General for Energy of the Commission, Pablo Benavides, explained that 'the "cross-fertilisation" of experience between the member states is extremely useful and important'. Jonathan Green, who spoke on behalf of the United Kingdom (UK) Presidency of the EU Council of Ministers, pointed out that while 'particular national solutions cannot be taken as straight "blueprints" for other Member States [. . .], mistakes may be made which should be recognised and learned from'. British, Nordic, and Spanish representatives brought information about the most experienced markets. Roger Urwin of the British TSO gave an overview of developments in the UK since the power industry had been restructured in 1990. Jan Magnusson of the Swedish TSO emphasized what he presented as 'key factors' for the successful regulatory reform of national electricity markets, based on key examples from Norwegian and English and Welsh markets and also stressing the main elements of the Nord Pool, a pioneering joint trading exchange between Norway and Sweden that had opened all networks to access by third parties since 1996. Maria Luisa Huidobro y Areba of the Spanish wholesale market operator gave an overview of the Spanish liberalization experience beginning in 1997, including how her company matched up bids from the demand and production sides of the market, which, at that time, was a groundbreaking electricity pool. Participants from outside the EU, too, enriched the comparison of different approaches with network access. David Smol of ILEX Energy Consulting, for example, presented the New Zealand case and argued that one of the main lessons to be learned from it was that 'there are two key steps to reform: separation of transmission from generation and supply, and establishment of open and transparent wholesale trading arrangements'. James Barker of the United States (US) law firm Barker, Dunn and Rossi drew upon examples from California, Alberta, the New England Power Pool (NEPOOL), the Pennsylvania, New Jersey, Maryland Power Pool (PJM), New York, Canada, England and Wales, New Zealand, and Australia. He suggested that 'while regulatory reform in the EU should seek to avoid the pitfalls and disadvantages of the US regulatory framework, it should also recognise the critical factors underpinning the successful aspects and advantages of the US model' (Florence Forum 1998a: 2–10).

These debates and comparisons, third, informed agreement on rules. With a view to the increasing convergence of actors' positions, the Commission summarized that 'rules and mechanisms regarding cross-border congestion management [should] be based on the principles of cost-reflectiveness, transparency and non-discrimination' (Florence Forum 1998a: 3–5). Against these criteria, experts pointed to the superiority of auctions compared to the previously dominant methods (BUS 7a). In particular, Professor Ignacio Perez-Arriaga, Commissioner at the Spanish NRA and one of the main experts on auctions in the late 1990s, underlined the benefits of this method in order to allocate scarce interconnection capacity (Florence Forum 1999a: 3). This was contrasted to the 'administered' methods dominant at that time, which notably included pro rata rationing, used, for example, in Italy, whereby all the requested transactions were carried out but each transaction quantity was cut by the same percentage; and first come, first served, employed, for instance, in France, where requests were accepted until the capacity limit was reached (EUI 3a). After two years of discussions and comparisons of different approaches adopted by member states and companies, at the Florence Forum meeting of November 1999, participants agreed that network access 'should be based on market solutions that give proper and justified incentives to both market parties and transmission system operators to act in a rational and economic way [...] In this light, the draft agreement towards a transparent auctioning-based allocation mechanism at the French–Spanish interconnector was noted' (Florence Forum 1999b). It was also agreed that at the following meeting, the Commission, in collaboration with NRAs, member states, the European association of TSOs (ETSO) and all other appropriate market players would have outlined proposals (Florence Forum 2000a: 5–6). At the meeting of November 2000, the Commission, member states, NRAs, and TSOs as well as producers, consumers, traders, power exchanges, and other market players agreed on common Guidelines. These recommended that network congestion problems be addressed with market-based solutions, particularly auction systems, and be designed in such a way that all available transport capacity be offered to the market (Florence Forum 2000b: 4–8).

Shortly after, the agreement brokered in the Florence Forum was codified and given binding power. In March 2001, just a few months after the establishment of Guidelines on network access in November 2000, the Commission used the legislative procedure to propose a regulation to the European Parliament and the Council on conditions for accessing the network for cross-border exchanges in electricity (European Commission 2001a). The substantive content of the Commission's proposal was literally identical to the voluntary Guidelines, which were annexed to it. Without adding any substantial change to the Commission's proposal, in June 2003, the European Parliament and Council adopted Regulation (EC) No. 1228/2003 on conditions for accessing the network for cross-border exchanges in electricity, providing the first set of common rules for cross-border trade in electricity. At its core, it mandated that scarce interconnection capacity be managed through auctions because these are non-discriminatory, market-based solutions (European Parliament and Council 2003).

It is worth stressing that, as explained in Chapter 1, the book breaks away from automatic equations of binding law with hierarchical processes or soft law with experimentalist processes. Instead, it distinguishes governance processes into more experimentalist or hierarchical ones depending on the following three indicators: how far rules are proposed by local actors or developed from the top; whether monitoring focuses more on reviewing the performance of local implementation experiences or instead on ensuring compliance; and whether rules are designed as revisable and are, indeed, revised based on performance reviews or, by contrast, are stable. The mere fact that the agreement developed in the Florence Forum was given binding power, therefore, does not constitute evidence of hierarchical processes.

This does not mean that processes were completely experimentalist, though. As also explained in Chapter 1, the book treats experimentalist and hierarchical processes as ideal-types that empirical manifestations may only partially approximate. In the example at hand, there were a few hierarchical traits, such as reviews occasionally focusing mostly on compliance monitoring. In 2002, as a result of a discussion paper reviewing experience with the implementation of the voluntary Guidelines, Florence Forum participants noted that, although there had been improvements in the ways in which congestion was handled at cross-border lines, 'certain congested interconnections remain without a market-based allocation mechanism for scarce capacity. With respect to some interconnectors, therefore, the guidelines adopted by the Forum are not applied' (Florence Forum 2002: 4). The Commission and the CEER then presented a detailed status report of congestion management mechanisms operating throughout the Community, which argued that the delay in implementing market-based congestion management systems had created a very unclear situation at certain borders and had seriously prevented non-incumbent market parties from competing on the market. Market parties had complained against practices at the interconnectors still using non-market-based methods such as first come, first served. The report thus concluded that the Guidelines were only halfway implemented, with most of the interconnectors with the highest economic value, especially those at the borders of Italy, without market-based methods in place yet (Florence Forum 2002: 4). Despite this circumscribed evidence of hierarchy, however, overall governance processes were, as just shown, experimentalist.

A second cycle of experimentalist governance, early 2000s–late 2000s
Although, by making market-based auctions binding on all actors, Regulation (EC) No. 1228/2003 reduced local discretion at a certain level of granularity, at another level, it left unspecified what type of auction should be used, let alone through which detailed arrangement. In particular, it left open the choice between explicit auctions, where commodity and transport rights are explicitly traded through separate auctions, and implicit auctions, where transport rights are traded implicitly while trading commodity, through a single auction (European Parliament and Council 2003). As a result, member states and regulated companies continued to enjoy discretion to pursue different approaches, namely, alternative types of auctions.

Throughout the mid-2000s, actors kept using the Forum to compare and debate different implementation experiences. Immediately after the adoption of Regulation (EC) No. 1228/2003, the Commission asked consultants to analyse cross-border congestion management approaches (Frontier Economics and Consentec 2004). Equally, the ETSO and the Association of European Energy Exchanges (Europex) were invited to elaborate a joint proposal (ETSO and Europex 2004). Thereafter, the debate was broadened to additional actors, notably generators and suppliers represented by Eurelectric (2004). Forum participants decided to set up a number of mini fora, having the same participants and a similar composition to the Florence Forum but a macro-regional rather than pan-European dimension and an exclusive focus on network access. Each mini fora had to provide a plan and detailed timetable for the introduction of market-based auctions but had discretion on how to do so (Florence Forum 2004). In 2006, with the support of the Commission, the ERGEG launched the Regional Initiatives, which built on the mini fora and 'represent a bottom-up approach to completion of the internal energy market, in the sense that they bring all market participants together to test solutions for cross-border issues, carry out early implementation of the EU *acquis* and come up with pilot projects that can be exported from one region to others'.[4] The distinct types of auctions adopted by the Regional Initiatives were compared through the ERGEG monitoring reports and regularly discussed at the Florence Forum over a number of years. This revealed that some regions preferred to move from the previously dominant administered methods to explicit auctions, for example, the Italian interconnections with Slovenia (September 2007) and Switzerland (January 2008). Others, by contrast, favoured a transition straight to implicit auctions, including the 'trilateral market coupling' (TMC) project connecting France, Belgium, and the Netherlands (since November 2006), the Iberian electricity market project integrating Spain and Portugal (July 2007), and a project interconnecting continental Europe and Nordic countries through Germany and Denmark (then scheduled for June 2008) (see, e.g. ERGEG 2007a, 2008a).

These comparisons and debates, finally, aided development of reforms. By 2007, key authorities and market participants had expressed their preference for implicit rather than explicit auctions. For instance, the Directorate-General for Competition of the Commission declared that, 'Although explicit auctioning is theoretically and with perfect foresight an efficient mechanism

---

[4] See http://www.acer.europa.eu/en/electricity/regional_initiatives/Pages/default.aspx (last accessed February 2023).

and is compatible with Regulation 1228/2003, it has efficiency deficits compared to implicit auctioning' (European Commission 2007a). Equally, the Directorate-General for Transport and Energy stated that:

> in the future, more capacity will be allocated through implicit auctions. The so-called market coupling method, developed by ETSO and Europex, has the highest potential of truly integrating the European electricity market through implicit auctions. On the contrary, explicit auctions as currently practised often lead to inefficient use of interconnection capacity and prevent market integration.
>
> (European Commission 2007b: 5)

The ERGEG claimed that 'it is now widely recognized that [. . .] implicit allocation methods are more efficient than explicit auctions and should be the target mechanism for all regions' (ERGEG 2007b). And Eurelectric explained its change of preferences from explicit to implicit auctions by arguing that 'it is now appropriate to restate our position as regards the preferred solution and the way forward' (Eurelectric 2005: 7). After most actors reached agreement in favour of implicit auctions, however, still another cycle of experimentalist processes began.

A third cycle of experimentalist governance, late 2000s–mid-2010s

Although by the late 2000s actors had decided to eliminate local discretion on the type of auction to use, they still had discretion over the specific arrangements to employ. Indeed, member states and regulated companies had been experimenting with different subtypes of implicit auctions. France, for example, was involved in four parallel projects at the same time: the first with Germany, Belgium, Luxembourg, and the Netherlands; the second with Germany, Austria, Greece, Italy, and Slovenia; the third with Spain and Portugal; and the fourth with the UK and Ireland. The French NRA expressed concerns about the compatibility of these distinct projects and raised the issue of 'interregional coherence' (CRE 2008). Similarly, the ERGEG published coherence and convergence reports warning that, although most regions had been moving towards implicit auctions, attention was needed to their detailed design and implementation to ensure regions' compatibility (ERGEG 2008b: 10). These concerns were echoed by generators and suppliers, with Eurelectric stressing that different paces of market integration across Europe were leading to a 'patchwork of different solutions' and that there were too many, sometimes overlapping initiatives, going in different directions or not fully compatible. In order to 'start keeping track systematically of which regions are not meeting their targets', it thus suggested the next step to be the development of a 'master plan that includes specific targets for concrete issues'.

Similarly to three years earlier, in the context of the Florence Forum, the Commission requested a consultant to look at what had to be done within and between regions to move towards a single European electricity market. It then asked the ETSO and the Europex to write a common discussion paper addressing the challenges highlighted by the consulting study (Florence Forum 2007: 4). Thereafter, the ERGEG was invited to create an informal Project Coordination Group (PCG) of experts with participants from interested parties, tasked to develop a model to harmonize interregional and EU-wide coordinated congestion management and to propose a roadmap with concrete measures and a detailed timeframe, taking into account progress achieved by the Regional Initiatives (Florence Forum 2008: 2). Through debates within the PCG, its participants compared different approaches. Informed by the joint ETSO–Europex paper, actors identified two main alternative implementation arrangements. On the one hand, a less harmonized volume coupling, in which only the flows between markets are initially determined and national power exchanges calculate prices subsequently; on the other, a more harmonized price coupling whereby a single pattern-matching algorithm establishes both prices and volumes across all borders at the same time (ETSO and Europex 2008, 2009).

By reviewing the concrete experiences of the Regional Initiatives, PCG participants came to consider the volume-coupling arrangements less efficient because in the Danish–German project, they had delivered economically incoherent results (i.e. energy flowing from higher- to lower-priced areas) and had created problems of market power by allowing transport capacity to be often booked but unused. Volume coupling was producing incorrect results and came to be considered unpredictable, as explained by the Chairman of the Electricity Committee of the traders' association (BUS 7a). Indeed, the Danish–German volume-coupling project 'was a disaster' as it failed to launch twice, as confirmed by the ACER's Director, Alberto Pototschnig (EUI 3a). By contrast, reflecting in particular on the TMC project connecting France, Belgium, and the Netherlands, PCG participants concluded that price-coupling arrangements had proven their ability to operate efficiently since 2006 (PCG 2009a). A few months afterwards, PCG participants also reached consensus on the progressive extension throughout Europe of the price coupling arrangements (PCG 2009a, b, c). In December 2009, after one year of comparisons and deliberations within the PCG, the European Commission, regulators, TSOs, power exchanges, generators, suppliers, and traders successfully proposed to the Florence Forum a Target Model for congestion management based on implicit price coupling and a roadmap for its progressive extension from the TMC region to neighbouring regions (Florence Forum 2009).

The Target Model was eventually codified via comitology, after extensive involvement of the Commission, the ACER, and the successor of the ETSO (the ENTSO-E) plus several rounds of consultations with stakeholders as foreseen by the network codes procedure introduced in 2009. At its core, Commission Regulation (EU) No. 2015/1222 establishes that congestion management be addressed through implicit price coupling (European Commission 2015), thus giving binding power to the Target Model agreed within the Florence Forum. Even after this third round, experimentalist processes do not appear to be withering away.

A fourth cycle of experimentalist governance? Mid-2010s onwards

Although it is too early to provide a full assessment, a fourth cycle of experimentalist governance appears on the horizon. Commission Regulation (EU) No. 2015/1222 anticipated the possibility of revising the existing network access rules and specifically the current bidding zones—the geographical areas within which market participants can trade energy without having to buy transport capacity (European Commission 2015: arts. 32–34).

Such possible revisions built on discretion of lower-level actors like NRAs and TSOs and on the review of their own implementation experiences. Prompted by a technical and a market report on the early implementation of the Commission Regulation issued respectively by the ENTSO-E (2014) and the ACER (2014a), the Agency identified inefficiencies in the current bidding zone configurations. In 2016, it thus requested the TSOs of several member states (i.e. Austria, Belgium, the Czech Republic, Denmark, France, Germany, Hungary, Italy, Luxembourg, the Netherlands, Poland, Slovakia, and Slovenia) to review their current configurations (ACER 2016a). By the end of the following year, all those TSOs developed the methodology and assumptions as well as alternative configurations to be used in the review process and submitted them to the concerned NRAs for possible amendments. In the meantime, the ACER also requested the ENTSO-E to draft a report covering the whole EU during the period 2015–2017 (ACER 2017a). In 2018, the ENTSO-E, on behalf of all the TSOs involved, submitted to all relevant NRAs and to the EU Agency a report on the first review of the bidding zones, accompanied by technical reports (ENTSO-E 2018). During 2019–2020, the ACER also commissioned a study (DNV GL 2020) and held a public consultation.[5]

---

[5] See https://extranet.acer.europa.eu/Official_documents/Public_consultations/Pages/PC_2020_E_08.aspx (last accessed February 2023).

'Taking stock of lessons learnt from previous bidding zone reviews', at the end of 2020, the ACER adopted a decision on the methodology and assumptions that are to be used in the bidding zone review process and for the alternative bidding zone configurations to be considered (ACER 2020).

In summary, then, even though revisions of existing bidding zones, and hence of network access rules, have not yet been adopted, it can already be appreciated that such rules were meant as revisable by design and that the likely revisions are being based on reviews of implementation experiences with lower-level actors' discretion, as typical of experimentalist governance.

Having shown that actors addressed the regulation of network access by extensively employing experimentalist architectures such as the Florence Forum over multiple policy cycles, the chapter now illustrates very similar findings on the governance processes used to regulate network tarification.

Regulating network tarification with experimentalism, two times

A first cycle of experimentalist governance, late 1990s–late 2000s

The first indicator that governance processes were experimentalist rather than hierarchical is that member states and regulated companies had discretion to pursue tarification regulation through different approaches. As mentioned, the liberalization and re-regulation of European electricity markets began with the first Electricity Directive adopted by the European Parliament and Council in 1996, which established some common rules but set out a very broad framework that offered an exceptionally wide margin of discretion regarding crucial issues, including the pricing for accessing monopolistic networks (European Parliament and Council 1996). At the national level, it left the freedom to choose between regulated access, giving eligible customers and their suppliers a right of access on the basis of a published tariff, and negotiated access whereby the would-be supplier/eligible customer and the grid operator had to negotiate in good faith and on the basis of indicative prices. This allowed any combination of tariff principles and structures, hence leading to cross-national differences (Hancher 1997: 96). At the cross-border level, the Directive simply did not address issues arising from the very idea of cross-border trade in an integrated European market such as the pricing of cross-border transmission networks (Eberlein 2005: 64).

Second, actors employed the Florence Forum extensively to compare and debate the variety of approaches with which lower-level actors were experimenting. Roger Urwin of the UK National Grid Company explained that transmission prices in the UK were controlled by a pioneering incentive regulation developed by Professor Stephen Littlechild, Director General of the British NRA. Rudiger Winkler of Vereinigung Deutscher Elektrizitatswerke informed participants that, in Germany, a proposal for distance sensitive tariffs was subject to strong criticism. Jan Magnusson of Svenska Kraftnat grid utility argued for yet another approach, namely, nodal tariffs. Tim Russell of British National Power revealed trade-offs between economic efficiency, fairness, and political acceptability and thus that 'there is no single, particular pricing methodology (e.g., postage stamp, contract, MW Mile, Long Run Marginal Pricing) that can be considered the "intrinsically right" solution for all' (Florence Forum 1998a: 5–6). Christof Bauer of Degussa presented the view of industrial consumers, suggesting that Germany had left important aspects open to negotiation between a powerful incumbent and a much weaker new entrant, hence arguing against such a negotiated approach. David Smol from ILEX Consulting suggested that the New Zealand case underlined the importance of transparent pricing. James Barker of the US law firm Barker, Dunn, and Rossi argued that 'the EU states, at a relatively early stage in developing the structures and principles of such market regulation, could learn much from identifying the various advantages and disadvantages of the existing US framework and should consider carefully how to avoid its failures and pick the elements of success', stressing in particular the role of the regulator in establishing transparent tariffs (Florence Forum 1998a: 9-11). Debates also involved round-table discussions of NRAs (Florence Forum 1998a: 13). To identify the different types of transmission pricing under development at the national level and the conditions under which cross-border trade could take place, a study was carried out upon request of the Commission (Florence Forum 1998b: 2). It offered a qualitative and quantitative comparison of tarification approaches adopted in nine European countries (i.e. Austria, England/Wales, Finland, Germany, the Netherlands, Norway, Portugal, Spain, and Sweden), and reviewed cross-border arrangements in electricity (i.e. the US, Scandinavia, England/Scotland, Germany, the Union for the Coordination of Production and Transmission of Electricity (UCPTE) transit agreement) and other sectors, that is, postal services and telecommunications. The study showed that in most member states, tarification systems were non-transaction-based and thus recommended to generalize such an approach. It also considered different approaches to ensure that TSOs could recover the costs for hosting cross-border flows on their network, recommending appropriate compensation (Haubricht et al. 1999; Florence Forum 1999a: 2).

These comparisons and debates, finally, offered the foundations for agreement on three distinct rules. In accordance with the recommendations of the study, the Commission expressed a clear preference for a non-transaction-orientated tarification system. Dr Jorge Vasconcelos, Chairman of the CEER and of the Portuguese NRA, and Professor Ignacio Perez-Arriaga, Commissioner of the Spanish NRA, presented the common views of the Italian, Portuguese, and Spanish regulators, which largely coincided with those of the Commission. With the goal of increasing convergence in actors' positions and to outline a working programme for the following months, the Commission summarized that any tarification system had to be non-transaction-based: it did not have to impose different charges depending on different contract paths (Florence Forum 1999a: 2–4). At the Florence Forum in November 1999, participants considered that 'the voluntary approach developed so far has produced a common understanding of the main problems and processes involved in cross-border electricity trade, as well as a common view about possible solutions' (Florence Forum 1999b). Following the principles and the working programme established at the previous meeting, they agreed on the fundamental principle that each TSO's network costs be recovered through charges imposed upon local network users. Thus, these charges provided access to the whole interconnected EU network, 'independent of the commercial transactions that the network users may engage in' (Florence Forum 1999c: 1). This reform deviated from the then dominant system of transit fees or export charges, which hindered competition and cross-border trade. Indeed, all transit or export tariffs were eventually eliminated.

On the basis of the aforementioned comparisons and discussions, Forum participants also agreed on a mechanism to allow compensation for TSOs. Actors recognized that the existence of cross-border transactions could cause individual electricity systems to incur extra costs and agreed that TSOs that suffered extra costs caused by cross-border transactions had to receive payments from other TSOs (Florence Forum 1999c: 2). Although the Commission could have brought forward proposals directly itself, it took the view that such an issue 'would preferably be dealt with, at least at an initial stage, by the newly developing transmission system operators under the control of regulators' (Florence Forum 1998b: 4). Thus the ETSO, created upon invitation of the Commission, proposed a scheme designed to provide compensation to the TSOs that incurred costs related to cross-border transactions while, at the same time, charging this compensation to the TSOs responsible for such costs. As suggested by Professor Pippo Ranci Ortigosa, co-founder and Vice-President of the CEER and President of the Italian NRA, the main issues were how to quantify the transits (i.e. the flows of energy) and how to assess which costs had to be compensated for, that is, average or marginal (REG 1a). In order to address these issues, Forum participants set up a working group, bringing together the Commission, NRAs, member states, and the ETSO (Florence Forum 1999c: 1–2). The Commission, NRAs, and member states recognized the important progress and efforts made by the ETSO in coming forward with an unanimous proposal on the methodology to be applied and the amount of money to be recovered for an initial one-year period (Florence Forum 2000a: 1–2). To refine the cost calculations, an additional working group chaired by the Commission was established. Forum participants then reached an agreement on a provisional scheme that was to be implemented for the following year (Florence Forum 2002: 1). At the next meeting, the ETSO proposed a revision of the existing mechanism to be put into effect from 2003 onwards, which was regarded by the CEER, the Commission, and member states as an improvement relative to the existing approach, notably because it provided a more robust description of the network affected by transits (Florence Forum 2002: 1–2). This reform established a tarification system and trade-facilitating mechanism that, according to the actors themselves, 'will enable the single market to become a reality' (Florence Forum 1998b: 3).

On the same basis, Forum participants came to agree on a third reform. The association of the European power producers and suppliers (Eurelectric) highlighted that, as a complement to non-transaction-based tariffs and the compensation mechanism for TSOs, the rapid harmonization of transmission charges within national systems was also very important. NRAs, member states, the ETSO, and the other market players represented at the Forum echoed this message and invited the Commission to forward proposals. Participants then asked the CEER, in close collaboration with the Commission, member states, the ETSO, and other relevant stakeholders, to continue such work (Florence Forum 2002: 3–5). At the Forum meeting in 2003, participants agreed on the harmonization of transmission charges levied on producers by determining an allowed range, going from zero to a certain positive figure, within which all national charges would have to be (Florence Forum 2003: 4). Thus, this third reform contributed to the creation of a level playing field, avoiding distortions of competition between generators located in different countries and thus possibly charged more or less severe network tariffs.

The reforms agreed in the Florence Forum were then codified and made binding. The Commission tabled a legislative proposal (2001) which the European Parliament and Council adopted two years later without any major change (2003). Regulation (EC) No. 1228/2003 mandated non-transaction-based tariffs and an inter-TSO compensation (ITC) mechanism for TSOs incurring costs due to the hosting of cross-border flows of electricity on their national networks, precisely as agreed in the Florence Forum (European Parliament and Council 2003: arts. 3–4). Further, it provided for the future adoption of more detailed guidelines on the ITC mechanism and on the harmonized charges applied to generators under national tariff systems (European Parliament and Council 2003: art. 8). Upon request of the Commission, in 2005, the ERGEG thus proposed harmonization of the transmission charges levied on generators through a harmonized range of charges defined between zero and a specific positive value (ERGEG 2005), exactly as it had been agreed upon years before in the Forum. Analogously, with respect to ITC mechanism, in 2006, the ERGEG suggested specific methods for calculating the costs that TSOs incurred because of hosting cross-border flows. However, these methods reflected those already agreed upon by the Commission and the other Forum participants since developing a provisional mechanism in 2002 and then progressively refining it on an annual and voluntary basis thanks to an increasing number of TSOs (ERGEG 2006). As a result, the Guidelines annexed to Commission Regulation (EU) No. 774/2010, which reflect the draft guidelines produced by the ERGEG, effectively built on the voluntary agreements reached in the early 2000s in the Florence Forum. Commission Regulation (EU) No. 774/2010 thus codified and gave binding power to the other reforms previously developed in the Forum, as also confirmed by interviewees from both the Commission and the ENTSO-E (EUI 1a; BUS 3). As explained for the case of network access regulation, therefore, one should not necessarily read codification as being evidence of hierarchical governance.

To be sure, governance processes were not completely experimentalist either. Thus in a typically more hierarchical fashion, the ERGEG monitoring reports in the late 2000s focused more on enforcing compliance than on reviewing the performance of local implementation experiences. The ERGEG noted some lack of compliance with Regulation (EC) No. 1228/2003. It pointed out that, in contrast to what was previously agreed in the Forum, the temporary ITC mechanism that had been applied on a voluntary basis since 2002 did not cover all European countries, and deviation from specific individual network charges on individual transactions had not always been followed through. On that basis, it recommended making the Forum agreements binding (ERGEG 2007c: slides 5–7, 2007d). But these hierarchical traits notwithstanding, governance processes were, overall, mostly experimentalist. Indeed, this also applies to the period from the late 2000s to the present day, showing that experimentalist governance endured across distinct policy cycles.

A second cycle of experimentalist governance, early 2010s onwards

A first indication that a new cycle of governance processes continued to be primarily experimentalist is that lower-level actors kept retaining discretion. As seen, Regulation (EC) No. 1228/2003 and Commission Regulation (EU) No. 774/2010 established that transit fees be replaced by a postage stamp tariff granting access to the entire European network, TSOs be compensated for the costs incurred for hosting cross-border energy flows on their networks, and network charges paid by generators in each member state be kept within a certain range. But despite these harmonized rules, lower-level actors such as NRAs continued to enjoy discretion on a number of aspects concerning network tarification regulation, as evidenced, for example, by the fact that network charges levied on generators were not harmonized fully (European Parliament and Council 2003; European Commission 2010a).

Second, reviews continued to assess the performance of local implementation experiences. Regulation No. 1228/2003 provided for the Commission to monitor implementation and submit to the European Parliament and Council, no more than three years later, a report on the experience gained accompanied by proposals for revision, if appropriate (European Parliament and Council 2003: art. 14). Commission Regulation No. 838/2010 nothing but reinforced these provisions, tasking the ERGEG's successor with overseeing the implementation of the common tarification rules and reporting on them every year as well as carrying out a technical and economic assessment and providing an opinion to the Commission after two years (European Commission 2010a: Annex Part A, 1.4, 5). In 2012, moreover, the Florence Forum asked the ACER to determine whether the existing ITC mechanism needed improvement (Florence Forum 2012).

Following the provisions on rule revisability and the invitation of the Forum, and based on the review of implementation experiences, finally, the ACER did recommend revisions to the existing rules. Assessing the appropriateness of the existing range of transmission charges, including the provision of efficient locational signals and the results of monitoring for the years 2011–2012 as well as building upon an economic assessment of such charges at the national and transnational levels, the ACER recommended setting the network charges levied on generators directly to zero. In short, it recommended eliminating the hitherto allowed range (ACER 2014c).[6]

In addition, building on a consultancy study, a public consultation, and the support of the NRAs composing its board, the ACER recommended to

---

[6] The European Commission, however, has not yet followed up such a recommendation (EUI 3f).

the Commission that a new regulatory framework be set up to 'better reflect all the on-going developments' (ACER 2013a: 2). Besides technical changes concerning the methodology for calculating costs, the ACER advised that the ICT mechanism should focus only on existing infrastructures, whereas two major recent developments should be addressed outside of the ITC mechanism. One is the need to compensate TSOs not only for the losses incurred in hosting energy flows on their networks, as done by the ITC mechanism, but also for the unscheduled energy flows that have been increasing as a result of the growing shares of renewables. The other is the need to promote additional investments by TSOs in cross-border networks actively, as distinct from compensating TSOs for making their already existing networks available (ACER 2013a, b). As a result, regulatory efforts are currently ongoing with regard to both cost allocation agreements for new cross-border investments and *ex post* compensation for the costs and losses associated with the loop flows caused by renewables (Rangoni and Zeitlin 2021: 829–830). Thus, the review of implementation experiences once again stimulated revisions of the existing rules in a typical experimentalist fashion.

It is too early to assess whether a third cycle of experimentalist governance is on the rise. Yet, it is worth noting that lower-level actors such as NRAs still retain considerable discretion in network tarification regulation. This applies, for example, to types of transmission charges levied on generators other than those now fully harmonized (e.g. connection charges), cross-border cost-allocation agreements for new network investments, compensation for losses induced by unscheduled loop flows of electricity, and distribution network tariffs, which, by incentivizing households to alter their consumption patterns, are bound to play an increasingly important role in decarbonization efforts.

Having discussed how the regulation of both network access and network tarification were addressed by making abundant use of the experimentalist structures available and how the resulting experimentalist governance processes travelled across two decades, the chapter now proceeds to explain such a striking similarity and continuity in governance processes.

Conditions: Uncertainty, Polyarchy, Opposition

How can the striking similarity in experimentalist governance across subcases and its continuity over time be explained? The chapter accounts for this remarkable general finding by drawing attention to re-emergent cognitive uncertainty, firmly multipolar or polyarchic distributions of legal power, and recurrently weak political support, while showing that these three factors were the same in the regulation of network access and network tarification.

Re-emerging uncertainty

In the regulation of both network access and network tarification, the degree of cognitive uncertainty recognized by key actors has been high, and it has remained so even after specific rules on given issues had been developed because the rapid emergence of new issues called for the identification of new solutions.

In the late 1990s, when experimentalism was first pursued, there was little experience with market liberalization and almost none with market integration since the European energy industry was historically organized based on monopolies in closed national contexts (McGowan 1996; Midttun 1997). Since very few jurisdictions had experimented with liberalization, with Britain providing the only example of comprehensive reforms in Europe, this was a very new policy area with little experience to draw on. Further, the integration of national systems into a common market was virgin territory, which raised a host of poorly understood technical issues (Eberlein 2008: 77, 2010: 65). One such issue was how to manage requests for interconnection capacity among national systems, which were growing because of gradual market liberalization and integration. At that time, there was no regulatory framework for allocating transport capacity and managing congestions in the network. Instead, neighbouring vertically integrated companies, in the context of technical cooperation to ensure system security (BUS 7a), negotiated cross-border transport capacity informally. By contrast, the accommodation of growing commercial requests from emerging market players represented, in the Commission's own words, a novel challenge requiring a 'new level of coordination' (European Commission 1999: 6). Although lack of direct experience and significant technical complexity do not necessarily imply cognitive uncertainty,[7] the main publicly available documents of the period all indicate that both public authorities and regulated companies had only general preferences for non-discriminatory network access (European Commission 1992a; European Parliament and Council 1996; Florence Forum 1998a, b, 1999a).

---

[7] Some particularly knowledgeable actor could still have very specific preferences on how to address a given issue despite its remarkable complexity.

By 2000, as seen, actors had developed clearer views on the appropriate rules on network access. This is evidenced by the Guidelines voluntarily agreed in 2000, which recommended the use of auctions to promote the broader goal of non-discriminatory network access (Florence Forum 2000b: 4–8), and which the 2003 Regulation then codified (European Parliament and Council 2003). These more specific preferences thus indicate that, by the 2000s, actors had become confident that auctions were more desirable than the previously dominant administered methods.

Yet, new questions rapidly emerged about what specific type of auction to use. Both interviewees and annual reports on the implementation of the internal market suggest that, in the early 2000s, the Commission did not have precise answers to this question (BUS 2a; European Commission 2004, 2005). Neither did other public- or private-sector actors. Indeed, a number of proposals and reports by such actors show that, while implicit auctions were soon identified as theoretically superior, no one knew whether and how such an ideal solution could really be implemented in continental Europe (ETSO 2001, 2002a, b, c; Europex 2003; ETSO and Europex 2004; Frontier Economics and Consentec 2004; Eurelectric 2005). The key problem was that back then, the Scandinavian market offered the only existing experience. Yet, that market was managed by a single electricity exchange as opposed to the several, national ones present in the rest of European markets. Until 2006, actors had not implemented implicit auctions in Europe except for the fundamentally differently organized Nordic market. Thus, many doubted that they could really apply this option to continental Europe despite the absence of a central electricity exchange (EUI 1a; BUS 7a).

By the late 2000s, uncertainty also about this question had declined, as evidenced by converging declarations of the Commission, the ERGEG, and generators and suppliers in favour of implicit rather than explicit auctions (European Commission 2007a, b: 5; ERGEG 2007b; Eurelectric 2005: 7). Actors had thus also become confident about what specific type of auction to employ.

However, once clarity had emerged in favour of implicit rather than explicit auctions, actors became unsure about the detailed arrangements to use, namely, price coupling or else volume coupling. As suggested by the ACER's Director Alberto Pototschnig, many actors believed that both alternatives could work (EUI 3a).

As seen, it was through comparisons of subtypes of auctions implemented in macro-regional initiatives that, in 2009, actors voluntarily reached agreement in the PCG and the Florence Forum on a Target Model (Florence Forum

2009), then codified in 2015 (European Commission 2015). As suggested by Dr Matti Supponen, a long serving official at the Directorate-General for Energy (DG ENER) who was closely involved in the regulatory process, the reform of network access regulation essentially entailed the adaptation of the Nordic model to the continental Europe context, including the application of such a model despite the absence of a central European electricity exchange. However, in practice, this proved to be so complicated that neither the Commission nor any other actor could have conceived it on its own and imposed it unilaterally. Instead, as seen, this required experimentalist processes, in which the TMC project came to represent 'the' experiment, and the Commission acted as the main convener (EUI 1a).

The experimentalist arrangements set up in the mid-2010s and used since then to regularly review the efficiency of existing bidding zone configurations over which lower-level actors retain discretion and to revise them as appropriate suggest that, even in the most recent years, actors have not come to perceive having reached any definitive rule.

Turning attention to network tarification, one finds similarly high and re-emerging uncertainty. Among the poorly understood issues raised by the creation of the internal market, there was how to facilitate trade and, at the same time, compensate transit countries for the extra costs incurred due to the hosting of cross-border transactions (Eberlein 2008: 77–78). As suggested by the Chairman of the Electricity Committee of the European Federation of Energy Traders (EFET), Peter Styles, initially, no common system for cross-border tarification was in place (BUS 7a). This is confirmed by Florence Forum minutes, according to which 'at present, such mechanisms and systems do not exist. As a matter of fact, up to now, cross-border transactions were limited to technical exchanges (stand-by and emergency exchanges over short distances) among the owners of the high-voltage grid [. . .] The old rules [. . .] do not cover commercial electricity exchanges through liberalised markets' (Florence Forum 1998b). Instead, tariffs were negotiated among neighbouring, vertically integrated companies, which were both generators and TSOs at the same time (BUS 7a). Countries charged transit fees or export charges to compensate for the extra costs of hosting cross-border flows. As summarized by the Commission, then:

> For most eligible customers it is in fact organisationally and economically difficult to choose a supplier situated in another Member State, in particular if a third or fourth Member State has to be transited. The reason for this is simple: there is no tariff framework for cross-border transactions. Each transaction has to be negotiated, and each concerned transmission system

operator will require a transmission fee, which is not necessarily coordinated with the transmission fees already payable to other transmission system operators. Thus, the sum of all required transmission fees will in most cases add up to a prohibitive amount, making it cheaper for the customer to stick to the local supplier.

(European Commission 1999: 14–15)

While the lack of experience with cross-border tarification does not necessarily ensure that actors only had generic preferences on how to regulate this issue, the lack of references to specific rules in the available primary sources does. The main documents of the time offer no reference to non-transaction-based tariffs or ITC mechanisms (European Commission 1992a, 1998a, b; European Parliament and Council 1996; Florence Forum 1998a, b). As confirmed by Fernando Lasheras Garcia, Director of Iberdrola's representative office in Brussels, in the late 1990s, the broad goal of non-discriminatory tarification was known, but the detailed methods to achieve such a framework goal were not (BUS 6).

By the early 2000s, uncertainty had temporarily declined as evidenced by the voluntary agreements brokered in the Florence Forum, namely, on postage-stamp tariffs not based on transactions, a provisional ITC mechanism, and harmonized transmission charges levied on generators (Florence Forum 1999c: 1, 2002: 1, 2003: 4); all subsequently codified and made binding (European Parliament and Council 2003; European Commission 2010a).

Nevertheless, actors remained wary that problems could subsequently resurface, as they did. This helps to explain why both Regulation (EC) No. 1228/2003 and Commission Regulation (EU) No. 774/2010 provided for the Commission, the ERGEG, and the ACER to monitor the performance of the existing rules and suggest possible revisions on that basis (European Parliament and Council 2003: art. 14; European Commission 2010a: Annex Part A, 1.4, 5). During the 2010s, as seen, it became evident that there was a need to incentivize TSOs to build new interconnection capacity, a pro-active aspect not anticipated by the ITC mechanism, which concentrates instead on existing networks. Equally, it became visible that new rules are needed to cope with increasingly important unscheduled flows of electricity that derive from the growing penetration of intermittent renewables and which cause additional costs to TSOs, a problem which, again, was not anticipated during the late 1990s—late 2000s, when renewables were less salient than they are today.

In short, in both sub-cases, uncertainty—as perceived by key actors—has been a driving force behind those actors' choice to engage in experimentalist processes. Further, it has remained high throughout several policy cycles.

This functional pressure has thus been favourable rather than inimical to non-hierarchical governance. But it has not operated alone.

Firmly multipolar distributions of power

Polyarchy, understood as the constraints on hierarchical authority associated with formal rulemaking procedures, has been strong across the two sub-cases. It thus helps to explain why actors chose to employ experimentalist processes in both. Since, in the energy sector, delegation of powers from member states to the supranational level was traditionally very limited (Padgett 1992; Matlary 1997), in the regulation of both network access and tarification, the Commission could initially only count on the ordinary legislative procedure, which obliges it to secure the approval of the Parliament and Council. Since, from the late 1990s to the early 2000s, the distribution of legal powers was strongly multipolar, the Commission could not impose rules hierarchically. Instead, it had to cooperate with parties to develop them through experimentalist processes.

Further, the distribution of legal powers remained polyarchic also after the mid-2000s, hence contributing to accounting for the longevity of experimentalist governance. In the mid-2000s, the Commission was entrusted with the additional power to adopt binding rules subject to the approval of committees, confined to member states representatives, and operating according to comitology procedures (European Parliament and Council 2003: arts. 8, 13). However, even though the Commission could now bypass the approval of both Parliament and Council as required in the ordinary legislative procedure, it remained subject to the green light from member states in comitology.

Thus, even if key actors such as the Commission had had the cognitive ability to know the best rules in advance, they would have faced another constraint against hierarchical governance, namely, multipolar distributions of legal power, which remained firm. Nonetheless, the chapter reveals that one gets an even fuller picture by going beyond functional uncertainty and legal powers, extending attention to politics.

Persistent opposition

In addition to conditions of cognitive uncertainty and multipolar distributions of legal power, in the late 1990s, the Commission approached network access regulation in the absence of a clearly aligned coalition that would have enabled it to impose its view on others. European energy markets were historically managed on a national basis by state-owned, vertically integrated monopolists that undertook all aspects of the service in question (McGowan 1996; Midttun 1997; Baldwin et al. 2011: 444), and the rules governing the actions of TSOs and how access was given to network users such as producers and suppliers were drawn up nationally. In that context, the publicly owned, vertically integrated incumbents typically controlled underdeveloped interconnectors and were often able to distort competition (Eberlein 2010: 62). From the 1990s onwards, the Commission began to extend EU regulation with the aim of ending long-standing national monopolies and allowing effective competition in an internal market, a key objective of the Commission since it had begun to bring energy into the single market agenda in the mid-1980s (Jabko 2006). However, the Commission's efforts met resistance from many member states that, often in alliance with historically state owned incumbents, were keen to retain tight control over a sector they considered of strategic geopolitical and economic importance (Padgett 1992; Matlary 1997). At that time, not every member state had even created a sector-specific NRA, an important example being Germany, which continued to rely exclusively on the general competition authority until the mid-2000s. Besides the conflict between national and EU authorities, energy liberalization and re-regulation had to confront a second, often related conflict. This saw, on the one hand, incumbent producers and suppliers, which historically also owned transmission networks, and, on the other, new entrants, which needed access to those networks in order to compete on the market (Eberlein 2008: 80; Supponen 2011). Since, in the early 2000s, the ownership of competitive and network activities was separated in three member states only, the preferences of incumbents and new entrants clashed (European Commission 2001b: 3, 5, 32). Indeed, with the support of their member states, some companies strongly resisted the opening up of markets stimulated by Brussels (Stern 1998: 173).

Although the voluntary agreement brokered in the Florence Forum in the early 2000s demonstrates a convergence of preferences in favour of market-based auctions (Florence Forum 2000b: 4–8), actors kept pulling in different directions with regard to the subsequent question, namely, the type of auctions to be used. Implicit auctions demanded more cross-national uniformity than explicit ones, which can work despite differences across national systems (Knops et al. 2001: 21), and represented the most used option in the early 2000s (Knops et al. 2001: 18; Florence Forum 2005; ERGEG 2007a; Eurelectric 2005; EUI 3a; BUS 1). Furthermore, while the Commission and the ACER were promoting market integration through further harmonization, NRAs were often less active and supportive, even in comparison to electricity generators and suppliers, suggests the ACER's Director (EUI 3a). Traders supported the development of network access rules as long as these left some regulatory differences across borders, given that arbitrage is key to their business. Since implicit auctions do not allow such arbitrage, traders resisted the transition from explicit to implicit auctions, suggest Dr Martin Povh and Mr Pototschnig, respectively Officer and Director of the ACER (EUI 4; EUI 3a). National electricity exchanges, finally, strenuously resisted the creation of a single European exchange as this would have fundamentally threatened their very existence, suggest both the former Head of Market Development at the Italian electricity exchange, Dr Guido Cervigni, and the Chairman of Eurelectric Markets Committee and Vice-President of Regulatory Affairs at Endesa, Dr Juan Jose Alba Rios (BUS 1; BUS 2a).

Once consensus had emerged amongst most actors for implicit rather than explicit auctions (Eurelectric 2005: 7; ERGEG 2007b; European Commission 2007a, b: 5), however, different views arose about how to implement such auctions. Germany was the strongest supporter of the less harmonized volume-coupling arrangements, which leave the calculation of prices in the hands of national exchanges. The Nordics, by contrast, were the chief advocates of the more tightly harmonized price coupling, which calculates simultaneously both volumes and prices and coincided with the arrangements that those countries were employing already (EUI 3a; BUS 7a; EUI 1b). As seen, by 2009, most actors agreed in favour of price-coupling arrangements (Florence Forum 2009), with such position being codified in 2015 (European Commission 2015).

Yet, even after key actors' preferences became similar with respect to price-coupling arrangements, today, these actors' preferences continue to differ on other major network access aspects, the most notable example probably being the possible revision of existing bidding zones. Such experimentalist reviews, which, as seen, were introduced in 2015 and have been reinforced and carried out ever since (European Commission 2015: arts. 32–34; European Parliament and Council 2019: arts. 14–15; ACER 2020), have proven exceptionally controversial (EFET 2019; BUS 8). One key reason is that they can directly affect national prices, including by splitting a single country—like Germany—into different zones with different prices (Egerer et al. 2016). Besides the cognitive recognition that existing configurations might not be the most efficient, then, also their politically controversial nature helps to explain why, also in this latest phase, actors refrained from unilateral, top-down governance.

Turning to network tarification regulation, here too, actors had conflicting preferences. Professor Ranci, co-founder and Vice-President of the CEER and President of the Italian NRA, suggests that the Commission wanted to maximize the circulation of energy. National governments favoured the interests of their TSOs but also those of their main generators and suppliers. These latter companies sometimes favoured liberalization and sometimes not, depending upon the market power they could exercise in an only partially integrated European market. Conversely, large consumers had precisely opposite preferences (REG 1a). In effect, the Forum meetings show that, in alliance with network users (Eurelectric), traders (EFET), large consumers (International Federation of Industrial Energy Consumers, IFIEC; European Chemical Industry Council, CEFIC) and electricity exchanges (Europex), the Commission, NRAs, and member states raised issues and requested amendments to the overall level of compensation and the collection mechanism initially proposed by TSOs, represented by the ETSO (Florence Forum 2000a: 2–3). In addition, two distinct categories of member states existed: those that intended to charge exporters with costs and those that favoured a system of repartition of costs and revenues for all users of the network. As clarified by Fernando Lasheras Garcia, Head of Iberdrola's representation in Brussels, there was a tension between transit countries interested in maximizing payments and external countries interested in minimizing such payments (BUS 6). Indeed, the Commission, large industrial consumers, traders, local distributors, and a number of member states and NRAs favoured the elimination of export charges (Florence Forum 2000b: 2–3), whereas transit countries wished to maintain such charges, with Germany being the last one to remove them (BUS 7a).

Even after the development of initial agreements on network tarification rules in the early 2000s, key actors kept navigating through very sensitive issues. Documents such as the Commission's impact assessment and the draft guidelines produced by the ERGEG in the late 2000s show that NRAs debated extensively the appropriate form of a revised ITC mechanism without reaching consensus, hence proposing not to go beyond the status quo. The same evidence also tells that TSOs faced increasing difficulty in agreeing on such a mechanism amongst themselves (ERGEG 2006, 2007c: slide 5; European Commission 2010b: 26). Indeed, interviewees like Mr Styles from EFET suggest that conflicts 'did not explode but were clearly there'. One of the reasons why the Commission decided not to pursue more ambitious harmonization of network tarification was precisely because it was politically too difficult. TSOs were at ease with the basic existing ITC mechanism. 'That was a hard compromise nobody wanted to disturb', starting from German generators and government, which would be among the main losers from more harmonized network tarification rules.[8] A complementary reason however, Mr Styles continues, is that it was hard to see clear competition and discrimination effects that would have allowed making a case for further harmonization (BUS 7a). This is also confirmed by Tom Maes, Chairman of the ACER Task Force on Tariffs, Vice-Chairman of the ACER and CEER Working Group on Gas, and Principal Advisor at the Belgian NRA; as well as by Mark Copley, Vice-Chair of the Electricity Working Group of the ACER and Associate Partner on Wholesale Markets at the British NRA. Both interviewees share the opinion that it was hard to argue that further harmonization of tariffs would have been beneficial to the internal market. In addition, neither member states nor the Commission wanted more harmonization as this would have brought on the agenda controversial issues, notably the harmonization of subsidies to renewables (REG 2; REG 4). As anticipated, the Commission has not yet followed up the ACER's recommendation of setting all generator charges to zero (EUI 3f). To be sure, this does not suggest that experimentalist processes have failed. What the chapter does suggest is that, also in network tarification, a persistent diversity of preferences has contributed to keeping actors away from top-down development and enforcement of fixed rules.

Having argued that actors engaged in experimentalism across sub-cases and time not only due to functional pressures from uncertainty and legal pressures from multipolar distributions of power but also because of political pressures associated with strong opposition, the chapter now turns to the last question addressed in the book: how were otherwise reluctant parties induced to participate and overcome gridlock?

Mechanisms: Both Shadow of Hierarchy and Penalty Defaults

As just discussed, the regulation of both network access and network tarification was replete with redistributive conflicts and diverse preferences, which increased pressure to engage in experimentalist processes. But how were experimentalist processes, then, able to deal with reluctant actors and avoid stalemate?

---

[8] The agreed inter-TSO compensation mechanism is a basic system because it simply compensates for costs rather than also providing price signals for guiding investments. To provide locational signals, the charges paid by generators would have to have a positive value. However, in many cases, they are now equal to zero. German generators, in particular, would be among the main losers, given that the charges levied on generators in Germany are currently equal to zero.

A first mechanism underpinning experimentalist governance was the threats of positive legislation that the Commission cast on actors participating in the Florence Forum, thus the shadow of hierarchy. In network tarification regulation, in 2001, the Commission put forward a legislative proposal, which was accompanied by explicit calls upon Forum participants to reach agreement on a provisional ITC mechanism rapidly (Eberlein 2008: 81–82), which they did shortly after.[9]

Analogously, in the regulation of network access in the late 2000s, actors operated against the background of a legislative proposal, put forward by the Commission in 2007, for stricter unbundling of naturally monopolistic networks from the potentially competitive generation and supply (Eberlein 2010: 71).

However, the strongest evidence of mechanisms supporting experimentalist processes concerns the use and threat of competition law as opposed to that of sectoral legislation. Using its antitrust powers, the Commission initiated actions that helped dealing with network congestions caused by pre-liberalization-era, long-term reservations of transport capacity. In this way, it brought those contracts to an end and thus fostered network access by new entrants—for example, on the Skagerrak cable concerning the Norwegian–Danish and Danish–German borders, and on the UK–French interconnector (Albers 2002: 937–938; Cameron 2002: 321–322; Eberlein 2008: 83). In its battle against legacy long-term priority access rights, the Commission was broadly supported the by European Court of Justice (ECJ), as evidenced, for instance, in the 2005 decision on the Dutch–German interconnector (Cameron 2007: 343–354; de Hauteclocque 2013: 117–123). In the late 2000s, after an extensive two-year inquiry into the energy sector during the period 2005–2007 (European Commission 2007c), the Commission launched a series of investigations for alleged abuses of dominance by way of restriction of access to monopolistic networks. In the process, it obtained the strongest form of network separation (i.e. 'ownership unbundling') through the back door, thanks to commitments offered directly by major firms such as the German E.On, whereas legislation had eventually failed to impose such a strict rule (Eberlein 2010: 71; von Rosenberg 2009; Talus 2016: 73–74). Equally, the Commission extracted commitments helping cross-border network access from TSOs such as the Swedish Svenska Kraftnat (de Hauteclocque 2016: 350–351).

---

[9] One cannot say the same for network access regulation since there, Forum participants had agreed on Guidelines already in 2000 (Florence Forum 2000b: 4–8).

Similarly, in network tarification, to avoid a prohibition of their notified merger (which eventually resulted in the German champion E.On, currently the second largest European electricity firm, right after the French EdF), the German companies VEBA and VIAG offered to the Commission major commitments. Among other things, they amended the German agreement on network tarification, bringing it in line with what was agreed in the Florence Forum (Albers 2002: 921–922, 933–935; Cameron 2002: 325–326; Eberlein 2008: 84). Furthermore, the Commission signalled that it was ready to use, and at times did use, its state aid powers. This ensured that the methods chosen by member states to compensate for the costs of pre-liberalization-era investments that had become 'stranded' as a result of market liberalization were not recouped through levies on cross-border networks, which would have gone against what was agreed in the Forum and hurt cross-border trade (Albers 2002: 925).

Building on the discussions and operationalizations introduced in Chapter 1, the chapter suggests that such a pervasive use—and threatened use—of competition law should not be interpreted, as is often the case, as the shadow of hierarchy (Eberlein 2005, 2008, 2010), but instead as penalty defaults (Sabel and Zeitlin 2008: 306–307). The key reason is that a careful examination reveals that in virtually no case did the Commission impose, or threaten to impose, a specific positive rule, that is, what is at the heart of the shadow of hierarchy. By contrast, the Commission's competition decisions involved negative prohibitions to continue certain behaviours and the application of corresponding fines. At most, they featured specific positive remedies that, however, were offered directly by lower-level regulated firms rather than being imposed by hierarchical fiat by the Commission itself.

Overall, then, experimentalist governance processes were able to lead to policy outcomes neither exclusively through the shadow of hierarchy nor only via penalty defaults. Instead, a combination of both mechanisms underpinned the effectiveness of experimentalist governance and helped it to avoid impasse.

Conclusion

This first empirical chapter allows initial development of four general arguments. First, analysis of the electricity domain, specifically network access and tarification regulation, shows that experimentalist architectures may indeed lead to experimentalist processes. In both sub-cases, actors effectively used experimentalist structures, offering the potential for discretion of lower-level actors, review of their implementation experiences, and common revisions on that basis. Thus, key rules on access to electricity networks and their tarification were far from stable and developed and enforced from the top by higher-level actors such as the European Commission. Instead, they were built on experiments undertaken by member states, NRAs, and TSOs, with their comparison and debate—especially in the Florence Forum and thanks to regulatory networks (the CEER and the ERGEG) and networked agencies (the ACER)—regularly leading to rule revision. Tables 2.1 and 2.2 summarize the governance processes dominant in EU electricity regulation over the past two decades. While the case of finance (Chapter 5) will confirm the finding that experimentalist structures lead to experimentalist processes, the cases of natural gas, communications, and pharmaceuticals (Chapters 3, 4, and 6) will warn that this is far from inevitable.

Second, the chapter's findings lend support to claims that experimentalist governance is sustainable, and indeed self-reinforcing, rather than

Table 2.1 Governance of EU electricity network access regulation, 1996–2021

	Late 1990s–early 2000s	Early 2000s–late 2000s	Late 2000s–mid-2010s
Rule-making	1996 Directive left discretion on administered vs market-based methods	2003 Regulation left discretion on explicit vs implicit auctions	Discretion on price vs volume-coupling arrangements
Monitoring	Examples from most experienced markets (e.g. UK, US, Spain, Nordics) reviewed in Florence Forum	Regional Initiatives (e.g. TMC project between France, Belgium, and the Netherlands; Italy–Slovenia interconnection) reviewed in mini fora and Florence Forum	Regional Initiatives (notably TMC, and Denmark–Germany interconnection) comparatively reviewed in dedicated multi-stakeholder group, the PCG, and Florence Forum
Revision	Spanish–French experience mentioned in 2000 Guidelines for market-based methods; then codified by 2003 Regulation	Late 2000s converging declarations for implicit auctions built on Regional Initiatives	2009 Target Model for price coupling inspired by TMC; then codified by 2015 Commission Regulation
	Experimentalist governance	Experimentalist governance	Experimentalist governance

Source: author.

Table 2.2 Governance of EU electricity network tarification regulation, 1996–2021

	Late 1990s–late 2000s	Early 2010s onwards
Rule-making	1996 Directive left discretion on tarification methods (e.g. nodal, distance-related, postage stamp)	2003 Regulation and 2010 Commission Regulation left discretion (e.g. range of charges on generators)
Monitoring	National, cross-border, and cross-sectoral examples (e.g. Germany, Sweden, US, Scandinavia, postal services, telecommunications) reviewed in Florence Forum	Implementation of rules reviewed by the ACER and in Florence Forum
Revision	1999, 2002, and 2003 agreements on postage stamp, inter-TSO compensation (the ITC mechanism), and charges on generators, all built on reviews; then codified by 2003 Regulation and 2010 Commission Regulation	2013 and 2014 ACER Recommendations for charges on generators to zero, ITC mechanism limited to existing networks, and new rules to expand networks and compensate for unscheduled flows, all informed by inclusive reviews of implementation experiences
	Experimentalist	Experimentalist

Source: author.

self-limiting and hence bound to eventually wither away. In network access, experimentalism helped to make and revise rules throughout three distinct policy cycles: first, in favour of market-based auctions rather than administered methods such as pro-rata and first come, first served; then, for auctions implicitly allocating transport capacity together with energy rather than explicit auctions treating each component separately; and more recently, in support of tighter price-coupling arrangements simultaneously calculating both volumes and prices across borders rather than looser volume-coupling arrangements leaving the calculation of prices in the hands of national actors. Equally in network tarification, experimentalist processes first facilitated the development of a common tarification system breaking away from transit fees, the harmonization of network charges levied on generators located in different countries, and the creation of a mechanism for compensating TSOs for the costs incurred in hosting cross-border electricity flows on their networks. Not long ago, experimentalist processes have helped to refine these rules, for example, network charges levied on generators and the ITC mechanism. Further, they have stimulated the development of new rules to

Table 2.3 Trajectory of experimentalist governance in EU electricity regulation, 1996–2021

Issue	Sequence			Trajectory
Network access	Experimentalist governance, late 1990s–early 2000s	Experimentalist governance, early 2000s–late 2000s	Experimentalist governance, late 2000s–mid-2010s	Self-reinforcing
Network tarification	Experimentalist governance, late 1990s–late 2000s	Experimentalist governance, early 2010s onwards		Self-reinforcing

Source: author.

address novel issues that have emerged in the meantime, notably the need to actively stimulate the expansion of cross-border networks and compensate for the increasingly significant costs caused by unanticipated flows of electricity, in turn driven by a growing share of intermittent renewable energy. Table 2.3 highlights the long-term evolution of experimentalist governance in EU electricity regulation from 1996 to 2021. Although sub-cases from natural gas and pharmaceuticals will show that experimentalist governance might be followed by hierarchical governance and thus be self-limiting (Chapters 3 and 6), others from the same domains and still another from the communications sector will strengthen confidence in the self-reinforcing trajectory (Chapters 3, 4, and 6).

Third, electricity permits development of preliminary arguments about scope conditions for experimentalist governance. In both network access and tarification, actors at first had to navigate a completely uncharted territory, given the novelty of market integration. But even after they had developed initial reforms and become more familiar with the policy environment, new problems whose resolution was not immediately clear emerged. These included what type of auctions to use and, thereafter, which detailed arrangements to favour. In addition, questions arose about how appropriate the ITC mechanism really was to compensate for costs deriving from a higher penetration of renewables and positively stimulate stronger cross-border interconnections. Besides cognitive uncertainty, multipolar distributions of legal power also put pressure on higher-level actors like the Commission to engage in experimentalist rather than hierarchical processes, given the need to get approval of the Parliament and Council or at least of member states within comitology. However, a fuller understanding of why actors chose to engage in experimentalist processes is gained by looking at the lack of readily available political support, which would have allowed the Commission and its allies to hierarchically impose rules on others. In both sub-cases, the Commission initially faced strong opposition from member states and incumbent firms. But even after initial rules had been agreed upon, actors continued to have diverse preferences on alternative options at subsequent regulatory cross-roads, which thus kept favouring experimentalist processes. In summary, functional, legal, and political factors all positively affected actors' engagement with experimentalist rather than hierarchical governance. The longevity of experimentalism, furthermore, was aided by firmly multipolar distributions of legal power as well as re-emerging cognitive uncertainty and political opposition. The finding that, together with political opposition, functional factors like cognitive uncertainty are not inimical but, on the contrary, favourable to experimentalist governance will be corroborated in all the following chapters. Conversely, all the next chapters will challenge the importance of multipolar distributions of legal power, suggesting that, in itself, this is neither a sufficient condition for experimentalist governance (Chapters 3, 4, and 6) nor a necessary condition for it (Chapters 4 and 5).

Finally, the chapter allows initial exploration of the mechanisms inducing participation and avoiding gridlock within experimentalist governance, thus helping it to deliver policy outcomes effectively. In both network access and tarification, the Commission at times unblocked impasse by threatening to initiate legislation or actually doing so. Yet, the chapter found that the use—or threatened use—of competition law played an even more important role. Because the former involved specific positive rules, whereas the latter featured negative prohibitions and fines—or at most positive commitments offered directly by lower-level actors, the chapter suggests that a combination of shadow of hierarchy and penalty defaults underpinned experimentalism. Table 2.4 shows that neither of the two mechanisms dominated the scene entirely. While the communication and pharmaceutical cases will demonstrate that penalty defaults may operate on their own (Chapters 4 and 6), evidence from natural gas and finance (Chapters 3 and 5) will buttress this chapter's finding that, most often, shadow of hierarchy and penalty defaults work jointly.

Overall, the case of electricity regulation in the EU between 1996 and 2021 shows how recurring cognitive uncertainty, firmly multipolar distributions of power, and persistent political opposition all prompted actors to use the experimentalist architectures available actively and consistently. A combination of shadows of positive hierarchy and negative penalty defaults, thereafter, helped such experimentalist processes to overcome stalemate and deliver policy outcomes effectively.

Table 2.4 Mechanisms underpinning experimentalist governance in EU electricity regulation, 1996–2021

Issue	Shadow of positive hierarchy	Negative penalty defaults
Network access	2009 Target Model for price coupling agreed against background of 2007 legislative proposal for stronger network unbundling	Rules favouring network access agreed first against backdrop of late 1990s–early 2000 prohibitions and fines against long-term interconnection reservations (e.g. Skagerrak cable); then, of late 2000s–2010 commitments to remedy abuses of dominance (e.g. E.On, Svenska Kraftnat)
Network tarification	2002 Florence Forum agreement on inter-TSO compensation, the ITC mechanism, prompted by 2001 legislative proposal for first cross-border regulation	1999 Forum agreement on postage stamp implemented in Germany as commitment to get 2000 (VEBA, VIAG) merger approved; then, agreement shielded through late 1990s–early 2000s prohibitions and fines against state aid via levies on cross-border networks

Source: author.

3

Common Architectures, Diverse Processes, and Trajectories

European gas markets 1998–2021

No matter whether one looks at cooking, heating, or the generation of electricity, natural gas is vital to our daily lives. Today, natural gas accounts for nearly one-quarter of both global primary energy demand and electricity generation. What is more, in the future, its importance is set to grow. Being the cleanest-burning fossil fuel, gas provides a number of environmental benefits compared to other fuels such as oil and coal, especially in terms of air quality and greenhouse gas emissions. In contrast to nuclear energy, moreover, it does not present catastrophic risks either. Finally, the possibility of storing natural gas and the flexibility of gas-fired power plants allow gas to respond not only to seasonal demand fluctuations but also to short-term fluctuations caused by an ever-growing share of variable renewable energy, at once enhancing security of supply and environmental sustainability.[1] In short, natural gas is important, and this fact of life will not change any time soon.

Yet, natural gas also poses considerable risks and challenges. This could not be clearer than at the time of writing, when the 2022 Russian invasion of Ukraine is urging Europe to 'end its Russian energy habit'.[2] Indeed, gas market dynamics are responsible for worldwide rises in energy bills that seem comparable to the 1973 oil crisis.[3] In the past decade or so, recurrent gas crises had already made Europeans painfully aware of their dependence on very few—typically state-owned—gas producers such as Gazprom, which, prior to the invasion, provided around 40% of the gas imported in the European Union (EU). But problems are not limited to external relations. Within Europe, too, natural gas was traditionally organized based on disconnected national markets, each managed by a publicly owned, vertically integrated monopolist undertaking all aspects of the industry management, from the production

---

[1] See https://www.iea.org/fuels-and-technologies/gas (las accessed 15 February 2023).
[2] See *Financial Times*, 25 February 2022, 3 March 2022.
[3] See *Financial Times*, 20 December 2021.

Experimentalist Governance. Bernardo Rangoni, Oxford University Press. © Bernardo Rangoni (2023).
DOI: 10.1093/oso/9780198849919.003.0004

and/or import of gas, through its transport, to its supply to final consumers. As a result, incumbent companies like Royal Dutch Shell, BP, Total, and ENI, often supported by national governments, were generally able to foreclose market entry by controlling underdeveloped pipelines of their own property. Today, the boundaries between these oil and gas giants and their national governments remain, at best, opaque.

Like electricity examined in Chapter 2 and all the other domains analysed in the book, gas is not only important in itself but also because it hosts experimentalist architectures offering the potential for experimentalist processes, marked by discretion of lower-level actors, review of their implementation experiences, and revision of common solutions in their light. In gas, the key experimentalist structure is, in particular, the European Gas Regulatory Forum, also known as the Madrid Forum. Mirroring the Florence Forum for electricity, the Madrid Forum for gas was created by the European Commission in 1999, right after the first round of EU legislation on market liberalization and integration. Since then, its key task has been to provide, twice a year, a neutral and informal framework for discussion and exchange of experiences with the implementation of EU legislation and the creation of the internal gas market, starting from the two sub-cases examined in this chapter, namely, network access and network tarification. Participants include national regulatory authorities (NRAs), their European networks (the Council of European Energy Regulators, CEER; the European Regulators' Group for Electricity and Gas, ERGEG), and then the EU networked agency (Agency for the Cooperation of Energy Regulators, ACER), national governments, the European Commission, transmission system operators (TSOs) and their EU-level networks (Gas Transmission Europe, GTE; then the European Network of Transmission System Operators for Gas, ENTSO-G), suppliers and traders, end consumers, network users, and gas exchanges as well as climate and energy non-governmental organizations representing civil society. The networks of regulators and TSOs may themselves be considered experimentalist arrangements, given their multi-level nature, which might facilitate learning from reflection on lower-level implementation experiences (Sabel and Zeitlin 2008: 282–283; Eberlein 2010: 64, 66; Rangoni 2019: 69–71).

As the electricity domain, moreover, gas has hosted experimentalist architectures for a significantly long period, thus providing an opportunity to test polar opposite claims about the long-term sustainability of experimentalist governance and the initial optimistic findings in this respect emerged from the electricity case.

Compared to electricity, however, natural gas offers some useful similarities and variations in potential scope conditions for experimentalist processes. To begin with similarities, the distribution of legal powers in gas is identical to electricity as well as across the two sub-cases, namely, extremely multipolar until the mid-2000s and strongly multipolar thereafter. This is because, even though in the mid-2000s the Commission became empowered to adopt rules without the approval of the European Parliament, as required in the ordinary legislative procedure, it still must obtain approval of the member states sitting in comitology committees. The expectation here would thus be that actors engage in experimentalism in both network access and tarification and continue doing so for the whole period analysed. When it comes to functional and political factors, however, the gas domain presents some variations. While, in the case of electricity and in the sub-case of gas network tarification, key actors never perceived to have reached a definitive rule, as the chapter will illustrate, in the sub-case of gas network access, the Commission considered to know the best rules from the mid-2000s onwards. The experimentalist literature would thus expect actors to engage in experimentalist processes to a different extent, depending on the degree of perceived cognitive uncertainty. Regulatory networks studies, on the contrary, would expect just the opposite, that is, that the greater the uncertainty, which is a specimen of functional demands, the more actors will favour hierarchy, not experimentalism. In contrast to the electricity case and the gas tarification sub-case, finally, the sub-case of access to gas networks also features a strong coalition between the Commission and some key NRAs. The expectation drawn from EU and global governance studies, hence, is that actors will engage in experimentalist processes to a different extent, inversely proportional to the political support they can count on.

Finally, the mechanisms potentially available in natural gas to unblock impasse mirror those present in electricity. These include the Commission's powers to initiate—or threaten to initiate—legislative proposals and/or competition decisions. But, as the chapter will show, they also include mechanisms directly embedded in the sectoral rule-making framework, namely, the Commission's power of elaborating rules directly should the EU networked agency (the ACER) prove unable to do so. The chapter thus provides an opportunity to test, against the background of the very same toolbox, the argument developed from the electricity case that the shadow of positive hierarchy and negative penalty defaults tend to operate together rather than in isolation from each other.

Overall, natural gas thus offers an excellent opportunity to subject to a first test the arguments about the relationship between experimentalist structures, processes, and outcomes developed from the study of the electricity domain. First, it allows studying whether, and to what extent, experimentalist architectures mirroring those present in electricity were actively used in natural gas. Second, it permits further testing of the opposite polar views that experimentalist governance is bound to be self-limiting and wither away or that, on the contrary, it is self-reinforcing and thus sustainable, with electricity having provided initial support to the latter claim. Third, it allows analysis of the scope conditions favouring or hindering the use of experimentalist processes, offering a distribution of legal powers identically multipolar to electricity as well as across sub-cases, but degrees of cognitive uncertainty and political support that are partially different. Finally, since gas hosts the very same set of mechanisms present in electricity that actors can use to stimulate participation and avoid impasse, it allows probing the findings from electricity to show that, rather than being in conflict, the shadow of hierarchy and penalty defaults may be complementary.

The chapter allows refinement of three general arguments and corroboration of a fourth one. First, it cautions against a finding from electricity (Chapter 2), showing that experimentalist architectures do not always and necessarily lead to experimentalist behaviour. In natural gas, actors employed experimentalist structures such as the Madrid Forum much more to regulate network tarification than to regulate network access. The value of a perspective rejecting determinism in favour of agency will find further support in the communication and pharmaceutical cases (Chapters 4 and 6).

Second, by finding evidence of both a self-reinforcing and a self-limiting trajectory in the long-term evolution of experimentalism, the chapter at once corroborates and curbs findings from electricity exclusively supporting the former trajectory. In a first period running from the late 1990s to the mid-2000s, actors employed the Madrid Forum and the CEER to compare and debate the approaches used by NRAs and TSOs on network access and tarification and to develop common rules on both issues on that basis. Yet, after the mid-2000s, the two sub-cases took sharply different trajectories. While, thanks to experimentalist structures, network tarification continued to see much debate and review of lower-level implementation and agreement on reforms in this light, network access saw the Commission developing stable rules in a more top-down manner and then relying on the ERGEG and the ACER to monitor compliance. This finding is important because it demonstrates empirically that in the end, experimentalist governance can indeed lead to a return of hierarchical governance. Pharmaceuticals (Chapter 6) will illustrate this further. However, this finding will be out-balanced by sub-cases from the communication and pharmaceutical domains (Chapters 4 and 6), reinvigorating confidence—first originated in electricity (Chapter 2)—that experimentalist governance tends to be durable.

As for the conditions for experimentalist processes, third, the chapter casts doubts about the influence of multipolar distributions of legal power, while confirming that of cognitive uncertainty as well as political opposition. From a viewpoint emphasizing the importance of multipolar distributions of legal power, it is hard to explain why the extent of experimentalist governance is different between network access and tarification despite the same legal powers, and why, after the mid-2000s, experimentalism declined in network access regulation despite the distribution of powers remaining strongly multipolar. These findings suggest that polyarchy is not a sufficient condition for experimentalist governance. Subsequent Chapters (4 and 6) will not only corroborate this but also, thanks to evidence from the communication and financial domains (Chapters 4 and 5), will suggest that polyarchy is not a necessary condition either.

By contrast, analysis of the gas domain confirms that functional factors, and specifically uncertainty, are a positive rather than negative scope condition for experimentalist governance, right as political opposition is. During a first phase from the late 1990s to the initial reforms developed in the mid-2000s, in both network access and tarification, key actors faced both great uncertainty—due to the virgin territory they were exploring—and the need to form consensus among actors—which had very diverse preferences. Yet, after the mid-2000s, uncertainty and opposition took different values in the two sub-cases. In network tarification, uncertainty about the best rules remained high, and the highly redistributive nature of the issue implied a continuous need to mould coalitions. In network access, by contrast, the Commission had become convinced that the way forward was simply a stricter version of the existing rules and found the support of major NRAs such as the German and Austrian authorities, which shared the same conviction. The finding about the positive influence of both cognitive uncertainty and political opposition on experimentalist processes will be confirmed in all subsequent chapters.

Finally, the chapter lends support to the argument, developed in Chapter 2, that the shadow-of-hierarchy and the penalty-defaults mechanisms are far from mutually incompatible. In natural gas, the Commission facilitated access to networks by fighting against long-term contracts through its competition law powers. However, since this involved negative prohibitions and fines as well as settlements offered directly by lower-level firms, as opposed to specific positive rules imposed from the top by the Commission, it must be understood as penalty defaults. The Commission employed the shadow of hierarchy too, however. When the NRAs sitting within the ACER's Board of Regulators failed to reach agreement on network tarification, the Commission (unsuccessfully) attempted to overcome impasse not through negative penalties but by repeatedly threatening to impose rules directly itself, as the network codes procedure empowers it to do in these circumstances. Although the communication and pharmaceutical cases will find penalty defaults operating alone (Chapters 4 and 6), the electricity and gas cases, together with finance (Chapter 5), on the whole provide more abundant evidence that shadow of hierarchy and penalty defaults are most commonly married.

The remainder of the chapter is structured as follows. First, the key experimentalist structures identified in the gas domain are introduced; underlining their potential for experimentalist discretion of lower-level actors, review of performance with their implementation experiences, and revision of common rules on that basis. Then, the chapter looks at the governance processes employed in practice in the two sub-cases as well as their evolution over time, stressing that, while in both instances governance processes were largely experimentalist during the late 1990s to mid-2000s, in network access, they subsequently became more hierarchical, that is, dominated by stable rules developed and enforced by higher-level actors. Thereafter, the chapter explains this puzzling variation in processes and trajectories. It underlines the limited explanatory value of polyarchy, given that distributions of legal power were the same in the two sub-cases and remained polyarchic after the mid-2000s. It argues that focusing attention on uncertainty and opposition is more useful since, after the mid-2000s, these varied across the two issues. The chapter then analyses the mechanisms employed in the attempt to overcome gridlock, stressing how experimentalist governance was underpinned both by the shadow of positive hierarchy and by negative penalty defaults. It concludes by offering wider implications for experimentalist governance.

Experimentalist Structures

As in every other policy domain studied in the book, structures creating the possibility for experimentalist processes have also become institutionalized in natural gas, mirroring in particular those established in electricity (Sabel and Zeitlin 2008: 282–283; Eberlein 2010: 64, 66; Rangoni 2019: 69–71). The major illustration is the Madrid Forum for Gas Regulation, the twin institution of the Florence Forum for electricity created one year after it. As with the Florence Forum, the Madrid Forum did not stem from EU legislation but was

organized by the European Commission right after the first round of EU legislation on market liberalization and integration. Since 1999, its main objective
has been to offer a neutral and informal institutional setting for the debate
and exchange of experiences on the implementation of EU legislation and the
creation of the internal gas market. From the very start, it concentrated on
the two sub-cases analysed in the chapter, identified as crucial to the opening
and connection of national gas markets. The Forum has been performing this
function by bringing together, twice a year, a variety of actors, ranging from
public authorities at both EU and national level, through private-sector companies and their EU-level associations, to additional stakeholders. These actors
include in particular the European Commission, national ministries, NRAs
and their European networks (the CEER and the ERGEG) and then the EU
networked agency (the ACER), national TSOs and their European networks
(GTE and then the ENTSO-G) as well as trade associations representing producers and importers (Eurogas) and traders (European Federation of Energy
Traders, EFET).[4] Just like the Florence Forum, therefore, the Madrid Forum
is an experimentalist architecture because, by design, it aims to convey implementation experiences of a multitude of actors at different levels of governance
in order to inform the formulation and regular revision of EU rules.

For the very same reasons, furthermore, one can interpret the various networks participating in the Madrid Forum as experimentalist arrangements
themselves. Created informally in 2000, following the initiative of a few NRAs
seeking to exchange views and experiences on the novel challenges of market liberalization and integration, in 2003, the CEER saw the creation of a
more formalized regulatory network (the ERGEG), established directly by the
Commission as its official advisory body on internal market issues (European
Commission 2003a). The ERGEG has performed this role especially by producing non-binding guidelines of good practice. In 2011, the ERGEG evolved
into the ACER, an EU regulatory agency.[5] The ACER's key task is to contribute to the development of detailed binding rules known as network codes.
It does so by proposing non-binding framework guidelines, on which basis the
ENTSO-G then elaborates more detailed network codes, which are eventually
made binding after the Commission successfully proposes them to comitology
committees composed of member state representatives (European Parliament

---

[4] See https://energy.ec.europa.eu/topics/markets-and-consumers/wholesale-energy-market/gas-network-codes/madrid-forum_en (last accessed 15 February 2023).

[5] While the ERGEG ceased to exist when the ACER became operational in 2011, the CEER continues to exist alongside the ACER.

and Council 2009a, c: art. 6). But despite its different legal nature and outputs relative to the CEER and the ERGEG, in fact, the ACER remains a multi-level networked body since its board consists of the heads of NRAs—just as the boards of the CEER and the ERGEG (and of the ENTSO-G, when it comes to regulated TSOs). In addition, again mirroring electricity, also in natural gas the Commission, the ACER, and the ENTSO-G have recently established informal groups to evaluate how the network codes already produced are being implemented, identify issues that might arise from their application, and consider possible revisions accordingly (European Commission et al. 2017). Thus, thanks to their multi-level and networked nature, not only the Madrid Forum but also the networks of regulators (and of TSOs) participating in it can be considered experimentalist arrangements which, in principle, offer the possibility of debating and reviewing local implementation experiences and elaborating and revising common rules on that basis as distinctive of experimentalism.

Having introduced the key experimentalist architectures that the natural gas domain has now hosted for a significant time, and having explained why they offer the potential for experimentalist governance processes, the chapter now proceeds to analyse to what extent such potential has been realized in practice.

Common Structures, Diverse Processes, and Trajectories

Comparison of the processes to regulate network access and tarification in natural gas reveals a surprising variation. In a first period running from the late 1990s to the mid-2000s, governance processes in both issues were predominantly experimentalist because lower-level actors such as NRAs and TSOs had much discretion to experiment with various approaches and their implementation experiences were extensively reviewed, especially in the Madrid Forum, which inspired the elaboration of common rules. Yet, from the mid-2000s onwards, processes across the two issues took sharply different routes. Whereas network tarification regulation continued to be largely experimentalist, network access saw the development and imposition of stable rules directly by the European Commission, which then used the ERGEG and the ACER to enforce compliance.

Thus, experimentalist governance experienced polar opposite long-term trajectories. While in tarification, experimentalist processes proved sustainable throughout two decades, in network access, they eventually led to traditional hierarchical governance.

Regulating both network access and tarification
with experimentalism, initially

Experimentalist governance for network access, late 1990s–mid-2000s

The first indication that during the late 1990s–mid-2000s actors engaged in experimentalist processes to regulate network access is that lower-level actors such as member states and companies enjoyed leeway to experiment with diverse approaches. The first 1998 Gas Directive, which marked the beginning of the liberalization and re-regulation of European gas markets, set out the general framework and principles for the introduction of competition in the industry but, in line with the principle of subsidiarity, left much of the technical and practical details of implementation open to national interpretation. In particular, it granted member states a wide margin of discretion regarding key regulatory issues, including the regime of access to the natural monopoly of transmission pipelines (European Parliament and Council 1998).

Second, from its very first meeting, the Madrid Forum was actively employed to compare the different approaches to network access regulation being pursued around Europe. The goal was 'identifying the different methodologies and approaches concerning access conditions that were under development in the Member States', considering that 'only a limited number of Member States [had] already adopted a framework governing the conditions for third party access to the gas system'. Callum McCarthy from the British NRA, Lopex Silanes from the Spanish producer and importer Gas Natural, and George Verberg from the Dutch TSO Gasunie outlined the approaches in their countries (Madrid Forum 1999: 2). In the Madrid Forum, the European Commission, member states, and the CEER then invited the industry to establish a new body, bringing together all TSOs in Europe. This body, GTE, was tasked 'to provide technical data regarding the transmission systems within Europe', ensuring 'an appropriate exchange of experience and information in this respect and the development of best practice in the internal gas market'. Specifically, GTE was invited to submit a report outlining, on a state-by-state basis: the measures needed to avoid discrimination in network access, the range of services offered on third-party access and the terms at which they were offered, and the mechanisms needed to ensure that the administrative arrangements relevant to third-party access fostered competition and market entry. To resolve possible issues of congestion, GTE was also asked to provide a matrix outlining relevant points in the internal European gas market and identifying the available transmission capacity between these points as well as details of any existing or envisaged mechanisms for allocating transport capacity in the event of scarcity, including any measure that needed to be taken to ensure that gas capacity was allocated in a non-discriminatory manner between new entrants and incumbent players that were part of a vertically integrated company (Madrid Forum 2000a: 1–2).

These reviews, finally, informed the development of common rules. As a result of the comparative exercises prepared by GTE, Forum participants noted differences in the services offered and terms and conditions imposed, which underscored the need to ensure that such differences did not hinder the single market (Madrid Forum 2000a: 2). They also stressed the importance of published information on available transmission capacities because 'such information will serve to identify as early as possible potential bottlenecks in the trans-European network and possible measures to overcome such bottlenecks as well as considerations with regard to allocation of scarce capacity in case of congestion' (Madrid Forum 2000b: 3). Building on that information, Forum participants then found 'with concern that capacity constraints appear to become an increasingly important matter in the European gas market'. Hence, they pointed to the need to develop appropriate principles for transparent and non-discriminatory allocation of scarce capacity in the event of congestion. Actors established a joint working group of representatives of the Commission, the CEER, and interested member states, with GTE subsequently becoming involved too (Madrid Forum 2001: 2). This group was asked to draw up Guidelines for Good Practice on third-party access services, a first version of which was endorsed in 2002 (Madrid Forum 2002a: 9). Forum participants nevertheless found it 'appropriate and necessary to clarify the Guidelines for Good Practice and to reinforce these in certain respects'. The CEER, the Commission, consumers, and traders stressed, in particular, the positive role that 'non-firm' (i.e. interruptible) transport capacity services could play. A specific working group chaired by the Commission and with participants from NRAs, interested member states, and GTE, plus additional stakeholders such as representatives of consumers and traders, prepared a revised version of the Guidelines (Madrid Forum 2002b: 4–5), which Forum participants agreed upon (Madrid Forum 2003: 1–2). The revised Guidelines paved the way for market-based approaches, namely, interruptible use-it-or-lose-it provisions and secondary markets, understood as non-discriminatory means to ensure that transport capacity be awarded to parties that intended to actually use them (Madrid Forum 2003: 18).

Just three months after agreement on the 2003 revised Guidelines, the Commission used the legislative procedure to table a proposal for a regulation on access conditions to the transmission gas network. The substantive content of the Commission's proposal reflected the revised Guidelines, which were annexed to it. It provided for the allocation of transport capacity compatible with market-based mechanisms, for example, spot markets and trading hubs. Further, it fostered TSOs to facilitate secondary trade of transport capacity by developing standardized contracts, procedures, and services as well as to discourage 'capacity hoarding' and aid reutilization of unused capacity by allowing unused network capacity to be traded, at least on an interruptible basis (European Commission 2003b). Without adding any major changes to the Commission's proposal, in September 2005, the European Parliament and Council adopted Regulation (EC) No. 1775/2005 on conditions for accessing the natural gas transmission networks.

As explained in Chapter 1, one should not necessarily interpret the binding nature of these rules as evidence of hierarchical processes. As explicitly acknowledged, voluntary agreement brokered within the Madrid Forum informed the 2005 Regulation:

> A second set of common rules entitled 'the Second Guidelines for Good Practice' was adopted at the meeting of the Forum on 24–25 September 2003 and the purpose of this Regulation is to lay down, on the basis of those Guidelines, basic principles and rules regarding network access and third party access services, congestion management, transparency, [. . .] and the trading of capacity rights.
>
> (European Parliament and Council 2005: preamble, paras 1–3; see also preamble, paras 11, 13, 15–16, 18)

This is not to say, of course, that the governance processes were completely experimentalist. After the first version of Guidelines had been developed in 2002, Forum participants noted not only a significant degree of uncertainty about the interpretation of the Guidelines but also a widespread lack of compliance with a number of its requirements and considerable differences in their implementation between different TSOs. This stimulated the production of a revised version in order to 'avoid ambiguity in the interpretation of the Guidelines for Good Practice and to ensure a level playing field and raise standards' (Madrid Forum 2002b: 5). Thereafter, in 2004, the CEER prepared, in cooperation with GTE, a monitoring report on compliance with the 2003 revised Guidelines, which albeit noticing an important improvement, still indicated a certain lack of compliance with some key elements (CEER 2004). These monitoring reports were thus important in stimulating first a revision of the Guidelines and then their codification. Because they focused more on compliance enforcement than on performance review of lower-level experiences, moreover, they clearly constitute evidence of hierarchical governance. Yet, such hierarchical traits do not offset the finding that, as seen, rules on network access emerged from four years of experimentalist debates and comparisons of different approaches within the Madrid Forum and ad hoc working groups.

Experimentalist governance for network tarification, too, late 1990s–mid-2000s

Turning our attention to network tarification, similarly experimentalist processes emerge. The first indicator that actors engaged in experimentalist processes is that member states and regulated companies were granted discretion to pursue different approaches to regulate tarification. As mentioned earlier, the first 1998 Gas Directive set out the general framework for the introduction of competition in the industry but left much of the technical and practical details of implementation open to national interpretation. This general consideration applied also to tarification regulation whereby the Directive allowed any combination of tariff principles and structures. In the absence of any common EU regulatory framework, differences in tariff regulation inevitably occurred across member states (Klop 2009: 7–8).

Second, the Madrid Forum was used to compare different approaches to tarification regulation adopted by member states and regulated companies with the objective of 'identifying the different methodologies and approaches concerning access conditions, in particular tarification, that are developing in the Member States'. For this purpose, at the first Forum meeting, Callum McCarthy from the British NRA, Lopex Silanes from the Spanish company Gas Natural, and George Verberg from the Dutch TSO Gasunie outlined the approach to tarification regulation in their respective countries. On this basis, three different methodologies were identified: the 'entry–exit' approach applied in the United Kingdom (UK), the distance-related, 'point-to-point' approach applied in Spain, and a hybrid system adopted in the Netherlands (Madrid Forum 1999: 2–3). GTE was then invited to provide a detailed examination of the tarification mechanisms and levels, for a representative sample of services and types of customers, on a country-by-country basis as well as to offer an overview of specific measures regarding cross-border transit arrangements (if any) (Madrid Forum 2000a: 2).

Third, based on these reviews, actors reached agreements on reforms. As a result of the information provided by GTE, Madrid Forum participants recognized 'very significant differences among tariff structures for transmission in the EU' (Madrid Forum 2000b: 3). They considered that, 'where not based on common principles, [these differences] could have hampered gas trade and market liquidity'. In February 2002, Forum participants thus agreed upon a set of common principles that the CEER had proposed. These principles recommended that all tariffs for the use of gas transmission networks be cost-reflective so that any differences in tariffs applied to different customers for similar services would reflect the underlying costs, thereby avoiding cross-subsidies (Madrid Forum 2002a: 1–2).

Based on the same reviews and by building on the first agreement, actors achieved consensus also on a second reform. The Commission, regulators, most member states, traders, and local distributors expressed serious doubts that distance-related, point-to-point systems would effectively promote trade and market liquidity (Madrid Forum 2001: 3). Instead, they considered that entry–exit systems would best meet the set of principles agreed upon, particularly cost reflectivity, thus facilitating the development of competition in the European gas market (GTE 2002). The CEER, in close consultation with GTE, was invited to examine the concrete consequences of different tarification systems and to present the results of its analysis for discussion (Madrid Forum 2002a: 3). By making explicit references to some implementation experiences with entry–exit systems such as those of the UK and Italy, the paper prepared by the CEER clarified that a key feature of such a system was that entry capacity could be sold without any restriction on its final destination. This, in turn, stimulated the development of hubs where network users that had booked entry or exit capacity could sell or buy gas, ultimately fostering trade and competition. The paper contrasted this system with the point-to-point one, where there was an incentive for network users to swap gas scheduled to flow in opposite directions in order to save the associated transport costs, thus giving a commercial advantage to incumbents over new entrants because of their large portfolios of gas supply contracts (CEER 2002). A study prepared for the Commission by a consultancy equally recommended entry–exit systems, based on their advantages in terms of cost reflectivity and wider promotion of competition. At the October 2002 Forum meeting, the Commission, the CEER, most member states, consumers, traders, and local distributors thus 'confirmed their view that an entry–exit tariff structure would in principle best facilitate the development of competition in the European gas market' (Madrid Forum 2000b: 1–3).

Just as in network access regulation, also in network tarification regulation the Commission tabled a legislative proposal shortly after the Forum had reached agreement (Madrid Forum 2003b). In 2005, the European Parliament and Council adopted such a proposal without making any major changes to it. By mandating that the tariffs applied by TSOs and approved by NRAs reflect actual costs and avoid cross-subsidies between network users, the 2005 Regulation effectively codified and gave binding power to the first agreement brokered in the Forum, namely, the principle of cost reflectiveness (European Parliament and Council 2005: Art. 3.1–2). As this chapter will show, the second agreement on entry–exit systems was to have the same fate.

As discussed for the previous sub-case, binding law-making should not be confused with hierarchical governance. Rather than the binding or non-binding nature of rules, what matters here is that, as seen by using the experimentalist arrangements of the Madrid Forum and the CEER, the European Commission stimulated the comparison of different approaches to network tarification that national authorities and TSOs had discretion to pursue and facilitated the development of reform agreements on that basis.

At the same time, nonetheless, this does not imply that governance was completely experimentalist. In 2003, the CEER provided a checklist of necessary elements for entry–exit systems, which the Commission used for monitoring their implementation. This revealed that an increasing number of member states had implemented entry–exit tariff systems (Madrid Forum 2003: 3–4), to the point that by 2004, GTE's Vice-President Jacques Laurelut argued that 'for many transmission system operators such move from point-to-point to entry/exit is now behind in the past [and] the move toward entry/exit tariff systems is now widely pursued' (GTE 2004: slide 5). Since this exercise was geared more towards compliance monitoring than performance reviewing, it represents a hierarchical element. Yet, this hierarchical element stood in a frame that, as shown, was overall experimentalist.

Having shown that, in a first phase between the late 1990s and the mid-2000s, actors employed predominantly experimentalist processes to regulate both network access and network tarification, the chapter now highlights a puzzling variation in the ensuing period.

Diverging processes to regulate network access and tarification, afterwards

Continuing experimentalist governance for network tarification, mid-2000s onwards

The first indicator that to regulate network tarification actors continued engaging with experimentalist processes is that lower-level actors kept enjoying discretion. In 2007, the Commission proposed another Regulation to the European Parliament and Council, which was adopted in 2009 and made entry–exit systems—the second reform agreed in the Madrid Forum in the early 2000s—binding. Regulation (EC) No. 715/2009, however, left discretion to member states and regulated companies to implement entry–exit systems through a variety of arrangements (European Parliament and Council 2009b: esp. rec. 19). Indeed, since member states had been implementing entry–exit systems through distinct detailed arrangements, it was noted that despite the common transition from the previously dominant point-to-point systems to entry–exit ones, network users continued to face considerable variation in tarification approaches throughout Europe (see, e.g. ACER 2012a). A new question thus emerged about whether those differences could lead to barriers to entry for new players and distortions of cross-border trade and, if so, how these could be addressed.

Second, the Commission extensively employed experimentalist structures over several years to stimulate comparison of different approaches pursued by states and companies. It began by commissioning, in the context of the Madrid Forum, a comparison of the tarification models applied. The aim was to identify possible barriers to cross-border trade resulting from heterogeneity and offer recommendations for harmonization (Madrid Forum 2008). During 2008–2009, consultants were supported by the ERGEG, GTE, a research centre, a user survey, and a virtual test conducted in one macro-regional initiative, which led to a lengthy report of several hundred pages, comparative figures and tables, and country fact sheets (KEMA and REKK 2009). After its debate in the Forum (2011), the Commission funded another study, during 2010–2011, which built on twenty-three experts from fourteen countries, an expert hearing, a discussion meeting with academics, a public consultation, evidence from previous studies, and new comparisons, for example, of Italy, the UK, Portugal, Belgium, and the Czech Republic. This study eventually reached similar conclusions to the previous one: differences in tariff levels were justifiable because of national factors (e.g. policy priorities, historical evolutions), whereas heterogeneities in tariff structures risked creating distortions to competition and cross-border trade (Ruester et al. 2012). As suggested by the ACER's Gas Officer Thomas Querrioux, consultants and academics were employed to 'get a picture' of the methods used across member states as well as for conceptual clarification (EUI 5). This is also confirmed by Tom Maes, Chairman of the ACER Task Force on Tariffs, Vice-Chairman of the ACER and CEER Working Group on Gas, and Principal Advisor at the Belgian NRA, who suggests that these studies definitely gave an overview of the approaches used throughout

Europe, and helped the Commission to make a case for harmonization (REG 2). Stephen Rose, Chairman of the Union of the European Electricity Industry (Eurelectric) Working Group Gas to Power and Head of Gas Market Design at RWE, equally agrees that 'there was a lot of discussion and comparison of tarification methodologies' (BUS 5).

These comparisons and debates, finally, led to rule revision. By building upon these studies, in 2012, the Commission asked the ACER to develop framework guidelines on harmonized transmission tariff structures (European Commission 2012a). Thus, rather than using its comitology powers to deal directly and exclusively with member state representatives (cf. with network access regulation, discussed below), the Commission favoured the lengthier and more inclusive procedure for developing network codes, which involves the ACER, the ENTSO-G, and several consultations with additional stakeholders (European Parliament and Council 2009c: art. 6). Further, the Commission supported the creation of an ad hoc informal group composed of representatives from the industry and observers from the ENTSO-G and a research centre to provide the ACER with expert advice.[6] The ACER itself went beyond its formal requirements, undertaking several public consultations and industry events throughout 2012 and 2013.[7] In parallel, the Commission asked consultants to elaborate yet another study, which, by defining a list of best practices and assessing entry–exit implementation in several member states against them, identified typical deviations including with regard to cost allocation methodologies (KEMA and COWI 2013). By making explicit reference to this as well as previous studies and the comparisons therein provided, and prompted by the Commission to be more ambitious on the level of harmonization of cost allocation methodologies (European Commission 2013a), the ACER's Framework Guidelines identified four methodologies to be allowed. It also introduced the obligation to justify national choices against certain criteria, publish the results of a cost allocation test, and carry out a counterfactual exercise ensuring that the methodology chosen is the most adequate (ACER 2013c). The Commission then requested the ENTSO-G to elaborate a draft network code on that basis, which the ENTSO-G did by going beyond

---

[6] See https://extranet.acer.europa.eu/en/The_agency/Organisation/Expert_Groups/EG_on_Har monised_Gas_Tariff_Structures/Pages/default.aspx (last accessed 15 February 2023).
[7] These included a consultation on the scope of the Framework Guidelines, a consultation on an initial draft, a workshop, an 'open house' event in which it shared with stakeholders proposed changes to the initial draft, a consultation on a revised chapter, and a related 'Q&A' session and workshop (see https://extranet.acer.europa.eu/es/Gas/Framework%20guidelines_and_network%20codes/Paginas/Harmonised-transmission-tariff-structures.aspx, last accessed on 15 February 2023).

its formal consultation requirements,[8] revising the draft code after the ACER had found it partially inconsistent with the Framework Guidelines (ACER 2015b). It is worth noting that at this stage, when initially unsatisfied, neither the Commission nor the ACER took over the process from the lower-level actor (respectively, the ACER and the ENTSO-G), but rather, they sent these subordinate actors back to the drawing board.

In the very last step, however, the overall experimentalist process exhibited a hierarchical trait. In 2015, the ENTSO-G submitted to the ACER a revised draft network code, which narrowed down the methodologies from the four identified in the Framework Guidelines to two only (i.e. postage stamp and capacity-weighted distance methodology) while, at the same time, watering down their prescriptiveness, transforming them into mere references (ENTSO-G 2015). At that point, the ACER's Board of Regulators, composed of the heads of the NRAs, did not reach agreement on a favourable opinion recommending to the Commission the draft network code elaborated by the ENTSO-G (ACER 2015e: 2, 7–8). In response, the Commission took over the rule-making process from the ACER's hands, putting forward the draft code for approval of the comitology committee directly itself despite the absence of an ACER recommendation (Madrid Forum 2015: 2). This led to the 2017 Commission Regulation establishing a Network Code on Harmonised Transmission Tariff Structures for Gas, which defines a set of common parameters for tariff setting and sets requirements on the publication of tariff-setting data (European Commission 2017a). By identifying a reference tariff methodology from which deviation must be explained and justified (against the common benchmark reference), the reform thus struck a compromise between complete lower-level discretion and a single, EU-wide approach, ultimately offering more transparency on how TSOs and/or NRAs exercise their discretion on network tariff setting.

In summary, although the governance process was not fully experimentalist, the dominant type of governance was as the revision of the existing network tarification rules built on and made explicit reference to the reviews that, thanks to experimentalist arrangements, for several years appraised the variety of approaches that lower-level actors like NRAs and TSOs had discretion to pursue. When one turns attention to the regulation of network access, by contrast, the pattern is starkly different.

---

[8] During 2014 and 2015, the ENTSO-G held stakeholder joint working sessions, workshops, meetings, and a number of consultations (see https://www.entsog.eu/tariff-nc#tar-nc-meetings-sjws-workshops, https://www.entsog.eu/tariff-nc#tar-nc-consultation-documentation, and https://www.entsog.eu/tariff-nc#tar-nc-stakeholder-support-process-ssp, last accessed 15 February 2023).

Discontinuing experimentalist governance for network access, mid-2000s onwards

As early as around the adoption of the 2005 Regulation, concerns of consumers and new entrants[9] prompted the Commission to launch an in-depth sectoral inquiry[10] which, in a typically experimentalist fashion, reviewed the performance of the existing rules in light of their implementation. During the following year-and-a-half, the Commission sent 3,000 questionnaires to regulated firms, reviewed the state of congestion in about 40 pipelines and important points connected to key routes, and undertook an in-depth analysis of pipelines that appeared especially congested (European Commission 2007a: 70–89). The study, which was one of the most thorough in the Commission's history, assessed *inter alia* the (in-)effectiveness of the network access rules mandated by the 2005 Regulation, namely, interruptible use-it-or-lose-it provisions and secondary markets. In 2007, the sector inquiry concluded that long-term transport capacity bookings filled up cross-border networks, leaving market players that did not have such legacy contracts without access to networks and thus markets. The problem was expected to persist given that the duration of the pre-liberalization legacy contracts between incumbent network operators and their supply affiliates was typically fifteen to twenty years and could have been extended. Worse still, incumbent companies often used less transport capacity than they had reserved, again precluding new market players from accessing networks and consequently entering markets (European Commission 2007a: 89, c). The key issue emerging from the sector enquiry, therefore, was that although there was enough physical infrastructure capacity, the existing rules were ineffective in promoting its efficient use; on the contrary, they allowed incumbents to hinder entry and competition. The inquiry thus revealed that the current rules were functioning poorly (European Commission 2007a: 217). Indeed, as confirmed by the Chairman of Eurelectric Working Group Gas to Power and Head of Gas Market Design at RWE, Mr Rose, the sector inquiry was the driving force behind regulatory reform (BUS 5).

However, once the need to reform the existing rules emerged, actors did not decide to inform the development of such reforms by employing experimentalist architectures such as the Madrid Forum to compare and debate approaches

---

[9] See http://europa.eu/rapid/press-release_IP-05-716_en.htm?locale=en (last accessed 15 February 2023).

[10] See http://europa.eu/rapid/press-release_MEMO-05-203_en.htm?locale=en (last accessed 15 February 2023).

experimented by lower-level actors, even though such institutional structures remained available.

Far from drawing inspiration from reviews of local implementation experience, reforms originated in a largely top-down manner. In contrast to what originally envisaged (European Parliament and Council 2009c: art. 8), the Commission took advantage of its power of bypassing the network codes procedure. This 'may be called for when the full process to develop EU-wide binding codes is likely to take longer or where the ENTSO-G might be ill-suited to be entrusted with drafting, for example because of potential conflicts of interest'. Indeed, the Commission considered itself 'better placed to come up more rapidly with a more neutral proposal, taking the diverging views of the different member states and different stakeholders into account' (European Commission 2012b: 6–7). It thus asked directly its formal advisory body, the ERGEG, for input to revise the existing rules with the aim to 'rapidly adopt new provisions' and reducing congestion (ERGEG 2009a: 2). Without conducting any review exercise, the ERGEG suggested that use-it-or-lose-it provisions on a firm basis would have improved the situation by bringing unused transport capacity back to the market on a non-interruptible basis (ERGEG 2009a: 6–7, 20) and thus recommended strengthening the current interruptible provisions simply by making them firm (ERGEG 2009b, 2010a). The Commission agreed with the ERGEG,[11] and building on its advice, put forward a proposal directly to the comitology committee. This resulted in Commission Decision 2012/490/EU, which, rather than granting discretion, mandated from 2016 onwards the consistent application of firm use-it-or-lose-it at all European pipelines facing congestion above certain thresholds. Below those thresholds, the default solution is instead an oversubscription and buy-back scheme lobbied for by most of the industry, whereby TSOs oversell firm capacity and then buy it back as appropriate from the market (European Commission 2012d). Nevertheless, firm use-it-or-lose-it provisions did become compulsory for a number of major pipelines (BUS 4). Furthermore, some important NRAs,

---

[11] In line with the ERGEG, the Commission considered that the existing regime, in which new entrants could obtain only interruptible capacity while established players had long-term firm capacity reservations, provided a very asymmetrical risk profile among competitors to the detriment of new entrants. This made it very hard, the argument proceeded, for new entrants to enter the gas market on equal terms with incumbent players because the use of interruptible capacity was subject to the possibility that the original capacity holder would change its mind and claim back that capacity. Given that interruptible capacity was only a 'second-class' right, it made it very difficult to compete with 'first-class' rights' holders (European Commission 2012c: 19–20, 24–25). By contrast the firm use-it-or-lose-it solution, which basically restricts the possibility for original capacity holders to change their minds, was considered very effective as it immediately allows unused capacity to be freed and remarketed to other network users (European Commission 2012b: 5, see also 2012c: 36).

most notably the German and Austrian ones, have been implementing it even where not obliged to do so (see, e.g. ACER 2014b, 2015a, 2016b).

Similarly, though more subtly, another set of reforms on network access regulation was also developed through largely hierarchical processes. Although rules on capacity allocation were developed through the network codes procedure and thus in a less overtly hierarchical manner than for the rules on congestion management just discussed, a closer look reveals that here, too, the process was more top-down than it might appear at first. For a start, the ACER requested amendments to the draft network code elaborated by the ENTSO-G in no less than eleven areas (ACER 2012b). Thereafter, when the ENTSO-G revised the draft code by taking on board only seven of the amendments requested by the ACER (ENTSO-G 2012), the Commission recommended to the Agency to submit the draft code via a different legal basis. The ACER did so, recommending on its own initiative to the Commission the adoption of the network code subject to specific amendments in controversial areas concerning transport capacity breakdown, its application to new capacity, the sale of unbundled capacity, and tariff provisions (ACER 2012c). This culminated in Commission Regulation (EU) No. 984/2013, establishing a network code on capacity allocation mechanisms in gas transmission systems, which the comitology committee adopted by positive vote. At their heart, the rules defined by the Commission (2013b)—that is, harmonized capacity allocation mechanisms based on auctions and a small set of standardized bundled capacity products at interconnection points—are exactly what had been advocated by the ERGEG, the Commission's formal advisory group (see, e.g. ERGEG 2009e, 2010b). Thus, in fact, also the rules on capacity allocation— in addition to those on congestion management—were largely elaborated by hierarchical fiat.

Once adopted, moreover, these rules fostered compliance enforcement rather than performance appraisal. The 2012 Commission Decision, for example, set in place provisions to verify compliance with the revised congestion management rules, tasking the ACER to produce annual monitoring reports (European Commission 2012d: Annex: para. 2.2.1.2). Accordingly, since 2014, the EU agency has regularly assessed the levels of congestion at European cross-border networks, verifying that the mandatory oversubscription and buy-back scheme is actually applied and identifying cross-border networks at which congestion levels meet the thresholds triggering the compulsory application of firm use-it-or-lose-it (ACER 2014b, 2015a, 2016b, 2017b, 2018). The networked agency, in other words, has been working more to ensure compliance by NRAs and TSOs with hierarchically defined rules than to review the performance of implementation experiences of these lower-level actors.

Finally, although in the mid-to-late 2010s some revisions were made to the network code on capacity allocation, these are minor technical changes such as auction timing (European Commission 2017b). Rules are therefore largely stable, as typical of hierarchical governance. Equally, the ACER has been recommending revisions to the Commission regarding congestion management procedures. But according to the ACER's former Director Alberto Pototschnig (EUI 3d) and as confirmed by the Agency's publicly available reports (ACER 2021: 13–14), these recommended revisions do not concern the regulatory remedy per se but rather the criteria or metrics set in the 2012 Commission Decision to trigger its application. Thus, for capacity allocation as for congestion management, rules have thus far remained largely stable, in sharp contrast to the revisability distinctive of experimentalist governance.

In summary, in network access regulation, from the mid-2000s onwards, the European Commission refrained from using experimentalist structures to facilitate debate and comparison of lower-level experiences and development of reforms on that basis. Instead, by ignoring and even converting such experimentalist arrangements to hierarchical purposes, it opted for the elaboration of stable rules in a more top-down fashion, followed by compliance monitoring.

Why have actors initially engaged in similarly experimentalist processes and then pursued sharply different forms of governance in the two issue areas? Why was experimentalist governance so durable in network tarification and so tenuous in network access? The chapter now turns to explore these questions.

Conditions: Not Polyarchy but Uncertainty and Opposition

The chapter shows that the puzzling governance processes and trajectories observed in network access and tarification from the late 1990s to the present date cannot be explained by distributions of legal power, which were identical in the two sub-cases and remained strongly multipolar. Instead, the chapter underlines the explanatory value of cognitive uncertainty and political opposition. Initially, both factors were strong in the two sub-cases, thus fuelling experimentalism in network access as well as tarification. But afterwards, they weakened in the former while remaining powerful in the latter, which explains the variation in governance processes from the mid-2000s onwards as well as the different resilience of experimentalist governance in the two sub-cases. Functional and political factors, therefore, were more influential than legal ones and bolstered one another.

Identical, firmly multipolar distributions of power

In seeking to explain the variation found, polyarchy does not go very far. Throughout, in the regulation of network access and of network tarification, the European Commission was subject to exactly the same constraints on the unilateral development of rules.

Until the mid-2000s, it could only adopt rules by proposing them to the Parliament and Council via the ordinary legislative procedure. While this very strongly multipolar distribution of powers is consistent with the experimentalist processes initially employed to regulate both issues, the same cannot be said for the following period, when such processes diverged in the face of equally multipolar constraints.

Although, in the mid-2000s, the Commission was entrusted to adopt rules without the approval of both the Parliament and Council as required in the ordinary legislative procedure, the distribution of powers remained strongly polyarchic because the Commission still needed to get its proposal accepted by member state representatives sitting in comitology committees (European Parliament and Council 2005: arts. 9, 14). It is worth noting that this also applies to the most recent rules (namely, the network codes), which are ultimately adopted via comitology, too (European Parliament and Council 2009c: art. 28). Yet, as seen, such a polyarchic or multipolar distribution of legal powers did not prevent the Commission from pursuing network access regulation through more hierarchical processes from the mid-2000s onwards, while it remained committed to experimentalism in network tarification.

Distributions of legal power that have been identical across sub-cases and have remained strongly multipolar over time, therefore, are at odds with governance processes that, at some point, have taken a hierarchical path in just one of the two instances.

Initially similar uncertainty and opposition

Drawing attention to cognitive uncertainty and political opposition instead yields more explanatory value. In the first phase, from the late 1990s to the mid-2000s, actors faced uncertainty in both sub-cases since market liberalization and integration posed remarkable cognitive challenges. Market liberalization featured the separation of production from transmission and the confinement of regulation to networks so that third parties could access such networks and thereby compete in production and supply (see, e.g. Newbery 1997). Nevertheless, this meant a break with the past, when the same company used to own the gas fields, transported gas to homes and businesses, and eventually retailed it to customers (Baldwin et al. 2011: 444). To make things more complex, historically limited interconnection capacity had to be reconciled with requests that were gradually increasing because of progressive market integration. Yet, historically, European energy networks had not been designed with cross-border trade in mind. The existing regulatory frameworks did not cover commercial exchanges between liberalized markets. Instead, long-term contracts dominated trade over cross-border pipelines. After the entry into force of the first Directive, however, reservation of capacity for long-term contracts had to begin competing with the short-term transactions of eligible customers and traders. Indeed, the main documents indicate that in the late 1990s, the Commission and other key actors only had generic preferences for non-discriminatory network access (European Commission 1992b, 2000; European Parliament and Council 1998; Madrid Forum 1999, 2000a).

The same documents show that the Commission and other key actors did not have specific preferences on how to regulate network tarification either. Thus, they do not refer to particular tarification methods like the cost reflectivity principle or entry–exit systems (European Commission 1992b, 1998a, 2000; European Parliament and Council 1998; Madrid Forum 1999, 2000a).

In short, at the beginning of market liberalization and integration, key actors such as the Commission did not have precise preferences for specific rules on network access or network tarification. They faced high levels of uncertainty, which helps to explain why, in both sub-cases, actors initially engaged in experimentalist processes especially by employing the experimentalist architecture of the Madrid Forum.

Nonetheless, one gains a fuller understanding by turning attention to political considerations, as distinct from functional ones. From the 1990s onwards, the Commission began to extend EU regulation, notably through a series of liberalizing and re-regulatory directives. The legal and political rationale for EU action has been to end long-standing national legal monopolies and allow effective competition to create a single energy market, a key aim of the Commission since it started bringing energy into the broader, single-market agenda in the mid-1980s (Jabko 2006). However, many member states resisted the Commission's ambitions, seeking to protect their control over this strategic sector (Padgett 1992; Matlary 1997). Importantly, the Commission could not form alliances with NRAs, which, at that time, were not even present in every member state. A chief example is Germany, which continued to resist the creation of a sector-specific NRA until 2005. The conflict between EU and national public authorities was aggravated by the one between potential new entrants and incumbent firms, the latter traditionally being vertically integrated and hence in control of the transmission networks essential to market access. Indeed, 'certain companies mounted a ferocious defence of the *status quo* in their own countries and in Brussels in response to the process of liberalisation, and some found much support from their member states' (Stern 1998: 173; Klop 2009).

In network tarification, the preferences of key actors were equally diverse. Right after the establishment of GTE, the Commission, the CEER, and member states requested Eurogas—the association representing the European gas industry—and GTE to re-examine the division of capabilities and independence between the new body's constituent parts. The aim was to ensure that GTE was fully capable of taking into account the interests of all network users without discriminating between new entrants and vertically integrated incumbents (Madrid Forum 2000b: 1). In addition, the Commission, regulators (the CEER), consumer organizations, traders (EFET), and local distributors (the Voice of Local Energy Distributors across Europe, GEODE) considered entry–exit systems to best meet the principle of cost reflectivity and facilitate competition. GTE, on the contrary, suggested that an appropriate balance between distinct objectives (e.g. cost reflectivity, simplicity) had to be established and that each system (i.e. entry–exit, point-to-point) had its own comparative advantages (Madrid Forum 2002a: 3). Hence, while the CEER, the Commission, member states, consumers, and traders considered that tarification systems had to become more harmonized and, in particular, based on entry–exit systems, GTE resisted such harmonization, arguing instead that considerable differences existed across domestic markets and that, accordingly, tarification systems had to be chosen on a case-by-case basis at the national level (CEER 2002; GTE 2002; Madrid Forum 2002b: 2).

Thus, besides pressures from cognitive uncertainty, an additional reason explaining the initial engagement in experimentalist processes in both network access and tarification has to do with the rather diverse preferences of key actors, which favoured the perceived need of creating consensus around common rules, not least to facilitate their smooth implementation afterwards. Put another way, during the initial period, key actors such as the European Commission had neither the cognitive ability nor the political support to develop, impose, and enforce stable rules hierarchically. Instead, pressures from high uncertainty and strong opposition commended engaging in experimentalist discretion, debates, and revisions.

Subsequently different uncertainty and opposition

In the second period running from the mid-2000s onwards, uncertainty and support varied across the two sub-cases. In network tarification, there was a surge of uncertainty, suggests the Assistant to the Director General for Energy of the Commission, Dr Edith Hofer (EUI 2). Indeed, the Commission did not have a clear idea of how to proceed, argues the Chairman of Eurelectric Working Group Gas to Power and Head of Gas Market Design at RWE, Mr Rose. It was frustrated by different detailed arrangements adopted by member states to implement entry–exit systems, which clearly risked threatening the internal market. It knew that something had to be done but did not know exactly what (BUS 5). That the Commission—and other key actors—did not have precise preferences on how to regulate tarification is also shown by the main contemporary policy documents (European Parliament and Council 2005, 2009c; KEMA and REKK 2009; ACER 2012a; Ruester et al. 2012). In none of them did key actors express preferences for specific tarification methodologies. Instead, documents show that actors began developing more precise preferences only around 2013 (ACER 2013c; KEMA and COWI 2013).

The situation could not have been more different in network access, on which the Commission had a very precise idea of what rules to impose. Even in the conclusions of the sector inquiry published in 2007 that triggered the reform of the existing rules, the Commission had already 'highlighted the importance of enhancing the scope for entry through [. . .] strict application of use-it-or-lose-it provisions' (European Commission 2007a: 327, c: 13). A specific preference for firm use-it-or-lose-it was then reaffirmed throughout all the policy documents key to the revision of the existing rules (ERGEG 2009a, b, c, 2010a,b; European Commission 2012c, 2012d). The Commission, indeed, had a clear idea of what it wanted to do, namely, to release transport capacity in the short term. It effectively sought a 'quick cure', choosing a faster and less inclusive procedure suggests Mr Rose (BUS 5). To achieve its objective, the Commission had a clear preference for firm use-it-or-lose-it also confirms Dr Margot Loudon, Deputy Secretary General of Eurogas (BUS 4). The Commission had very specific preferences about both its goals and how to achieve them confirms still another interviewee, namely, Dr Annegret Groebel, Vice-President of the CEER and Head of the International Relations Department of the German NRA (REG 3a). Analogously, also for the bundling of transport capacity and the auctioning of bundled products, according to the ACER's Director Mr Pototschnig, 'it is clear that (i) there is no use for capacity unless you can get it on both sides of an interconnector and its bundling is the easiest way of ensuring this, and (ii) auctioning is the obvious way of allocating a scarce resource in the most efficient way' (EUI 3d). Thus, to some key public authorities, the best rules on both congestion management and capacity allocation were clear.

In this second phase, between the mid-2000s and the present date, moreover, the conditions surrounding the regulation of network access and network tarification were also quite different from a political perspective. In network tarification, the Commission would have favoured full harmonization, that is, a single tarification approach throughout the EU. However, as suggested by Dr Loudon of Eurogas, the Commission met the resistance of the industry (BUS 4). The industry was itself partially divided, as shown by stakeholders 'concern about ENTSO-G internal decision-making process, which was perceived to have put too much focus on TSOs interests (the protection of TSO revenues) over the needs of market participants' (ACER 2015b: 2). Importantly, in stark contrast to network access, the Commission also met the resistance of member states and NRAs, which were interested in accommodating national sensitivities suggest both Mr Rose and Mr Maes, respectively from Eurelectric and RWE, and from the CEER, the ACER, and the Belgian NRA (BUS 5; REG 2). This is also reflected in the first version of the Framework Guidelines adopted by the ACER's Board of Regulators—composed of the heads of NRAs, which the Commission deemed not ambitious enough and formally asked to revise (European Commission 2013a; EUI 5). Mark Copley, Vice-Chair of the Electricity Working Group of the ACER and Associate Partner for Wholesale Markets at the British NRA, suggests that the compromise initially found in the revised ACER Framework Guidelines, which, as seen, had identified four tarification models, was then lost in the ENTSO-E Network Code, whereby two methodologies became mere references (REG 4). Indeed, the final text of the Regulation was significantly watered down, so that it imposes more transparency than harmonization, conclude Mr Pototschnig and Mrs Bartok, both from the ACER (EUI 3a; EUI 6). The perceived need to mould consensus, finally, is well illustrated by the Head of the Austrian NRA, Mr Boltz, who was pivotal in the process. He 'reminded the BoR [Board of Regulators] members that the purpose of the high-level cooperation between the EC, ENTSO-G and ACER was to arrive at an unqualified recommendation that would facilitate discussions in Comitology' (ACER 2015c: 12).

For regulating network access, by contrast, besides being confident about its own preferred rules, the Commission was not alone. The Commission could count on the support of the ERGEG, which, as discussed, as did the Commission, saw firm use-it-or-lose-it as a superior alternative to interruptible use-it-or-lose-it. More precisely, the Commission was especially supported by the German NRA, which was among the key promoters of firm use-it-or-lose-it, even in the absence of any practical implementation experience suggest Mrs Bartok and Thomas Holzer, respectively Team Leader and Officer at the ACER (EUI 6; EUI 7). The German NRA believed that stricter rules were needed and favoured a stricter application of the existing provisions rather than 'changing fundamentals', which, it suspected, would have created even stronger resistance from the industry. In effect, enforcing the existing solutions more strictly rather than changing them completely is the approach that the German NRA generally follows, suggests the Head of its International Relations Department and Vice-President of the CEER, Dr Groebel (REG 3a). In this specific instance, this coincided with the Commission's preferences as well as those of the Austrian NRA, which also had a similar position (EUI 3a). To be sure, this is not to say that conflicts had completely disappeared. Incumbent importers and suppliers as well as TSOs strongly resisted the proposal for firm use-it-or-lose-it put forward by the Commission in alliance with key NRAs and new entrants (ERGEG 2009d: 19–22; ENTSO-G 2011; see also ERGEG 2011: 45–46; European Commission 2012c: 15, 36). As seen, the substantive outcome was a compromise that, to some extent, accommodated incumbents' preferences. This is because it allowed adopting a less aggressive solution—an oversubscription and buy-back scheme—at less severely congested pipelines unless the relevant NRA decided to voluntarily adopt firm use-it-or-lose-it anyway, as done *inter alia* by the Austrian and German NRAs (European Commission 2012d; see also BUS 5; BUS 4). What is argued here, however, is that a strong coalition, formed notably by the European Commission and important NRAs, reduced the political pressure to engage in experimentalist processes from the mid-2000s onwards.

In summary, the chapter has argued that cognitive uncertainty and political opposition can explain the patterns of governance observed across sub-cases and time, rather than polyarchic distributions of legal power. Both factors were initially high in network access as well as tarification, thus helping to account for experimentalist processes that, at first, were pervasive across the board. Yet, from the mid-2000s onwards, while in the regulation of network tarification persistently strong cognitive and political pressures kept pushing actors towards experimentalism, in the regulation of network access, confidence and support of key NRAs allowed the Commission to hierarchically develop and impose its own preferred rules on recalcitrant incumbents.

But if the regulation of European gas markets has, by and large, been replete with the redistributive conflicts just discussed, how have experimentalist processes managed the associated risk of impasse? The chapter now turns to this last question.

Mechanisms: Both Penalty Defaults and (Ineffective) Shadow of Hierarchy

Network access regulation does not provide much evidence that experimentalist processes were underpinned by the shadow of hierarchy, characterized by the threat of specific positive rules, as opposed to the negative sanctions distinctive of penalty defaults. The European Commission put forward a legislative proposal for a common regulation on cross-border trade only in December 2003 (European Commission 2003b), that is, after Forum participants had already agreed on Guidelines in September (Madrid Forum 2003). Thus, the Commission did not incentivize parties to cooperate by casting the shadow of legislation simply because those parties had reached agreement on network access rules already. At most, one might concede that actors were discussing in the Madrid Forum against the background of the Commission's 2001 legislative proposal for a second Gas Directive, which, in 2003, pushed the separation of monopolistic network and competitive activities (e.g. import, supply) a step forward, namely, from accounting or management to legal unbundling (Talus 2011: 265–266).

Instead, evidence of mechanisms involving negative prohibitions and sanctions and/or proposal of solutions directly from lower-level regulated firms is more abundant. During the period in which experimentalist governance was still dominating network access regulation, the Commission used its competition powers extensively. It did so to fight not only long-term supply contracts between external producers and European importers and between European importers and domestic customers but also long-term transport capacity contracts. An example is the Marathon case, where, thanks to its antitrust powers, the Commission obtained settlements from Ruhrgas, BEB, Thyssengas, Gasunie, and Gaz de France, all of which favoured network access by new entrants (Fernández Salas et al. 2004). But since these competition cases involved fines, obligations to end certain contracts, and settlements offered from lower-level firms rather than being imposed by higher-level authorities, they should not be understood as shadow of hierarchy (cf. Eberlein 2008: 83) but rather as penalty defaults.[12]

---

[12] Although not strictly within the analytical scope of this book (which is confined to the mechanisms supporting non-hierarchical governance, not also hierarchical governance), it is worth noting

When one shifts attention to network tarification, the findings are reversed. On this issue, the chapter did not find evidence of negative penalty defaults. Instead, it reveals that the shadow of positive hierarchy was cast multiple times in a nested institutional setting even though, ultimately, this proved unsuccessful to overcome stalemate.

To aid the regulation of network tarification via experimentalist processes in the early 2010s, higher-level actors used the powers embedded in the network codes procedure to cast their shadow on lower-level actors in no less than three distinct but nested instances. As seen, the Commission considered the original version of Framework Guidelines prepared by the ACER not ambitious enough. It therefore asked the Agency to revise it, under the implicit threat of taking control of the process (European Commission 2013a). Thereafter, the ACER did not find the first draft of the Network Code developed by the ENTSO-G to be fully in line with its own Framework Guidelines. It thus asked the ENTSO-G for amendments, accompanied by an implicit threat analogous to the one cast upon itself a couple of years earlier (ACER 2015b). Finally, an explicit discussion within the ACER's Board of Regulators reminded NRAs that 'The risk is that failure to find agreement would leave the Commission to pursue in comitology its own approach without an ACER Recommendation' (ACER 2015d: 12). Yet, despite the explicit threat, and notwithstanding all the additional time, hearings, stakeholder joint working sessions, and high-level groups formed by the Commission, the ACER and the ENTSO-G, the ACER's Board of Regulators proved unable to deliver a favourable opinion on the Code (ACER 2015e: 2, 7–8) so that, as seen, the Commission eventually did take over. In the shadow-of-hierarchy language, the threat turned out not to be credible.

Taken together, the evidence thus suggests that actors attempted to aid participation in experimentalist processes through a combination of negative penalty defaults and shadows of positive hierarchy, even though, in this particular instance, the latter proved ineffective.

---

that the Commission continued to use legislation, and even more so competition decisions, also after governance processes had become less experimentalist and more hierarchical. Thus, after the sector inquiry, the Commission not only proposed legislation introducing the strongest form of network unbundling (i.e. ownership unbundling), which, due to resistance, especially from France and Germany, became eventually accompanied by other less strict options (Talus 2011: 266), but also pursued several network-access-related cases with its competition law powers, notably obtaining commitments to reduce long-term capacity reservations by GDF Suez and E.On, as well as network divestiture from major firms such as ENI, E.On, and RWE (Talus 2011: 278–279), that is to say, achieving precisely the network unbundling that positive legislation had failed to secure.

Conclusion

By offering institutional architectures and distributions of legal power identical to electricity (Chapter 2), this chapter on natural gas has provided an
excellent opportunity to refine three of the general arguments previously
developed and to corroborate a fourth one. First, the chapter issues an important warning that experimentalist governance architectures do not inevitably
result in corresponding governance processes. Analysis of European gas markets shows that the regulation of network tarification has made extensive use
of experimentalist arrangements such as the Madrid Forum to review the
implementation experiences that lower-level actors had discretion to pursue,
and to elaborate and revise common rules on that basis. By contrast, the regulation of network access has, from the mid-2000s onwards, taken a more
hierarchical turn, whereby the European Commission developed stable rules
bypassing the Madrid Forum and then used the experimentalist structure
of the ACER to monitor lower-level actors' compliance. Tables 3.1 and 3.2
summarize the governance processes that have prevailed in the regulation of
European gas markets over the past two decades. The case of natural gas and,
specifically, the sub-case of network access from the mid-2000s to the present

Table 3.1 Governance of EU gas network access regulation, 1998–2021

	Late 1990s–mid-2000s	Mid-2000s onwards
Rule-making	1998 Directive left discretion on third-party access	2012 Commission Decision for firm use-it-or-lose-it and 2013 Commission Regulation for auctioned bundled capacity imposed by Commission, in line with Commission's advisory body (the ERGEG)
Monitoring	Examples from most experienced markets (e.g. UK, Spain, the Netherlands) and comparative European overview by TSOs' network (GTE) reviewed in Madrid Forum	The ACER used to monitor compliance
Revision	2003 Guidelines for interruptible use-it-or-lose-it built on GTE's review; then codified by 2005 Regulation	Firm use-it-or-lose-it and auctioned bundled capacity largely stable
	Experimentalist governance	Hierarchical governance

Source: author.

Table 3.2 Governance of EU gas network tarification regulation, 1998–2021

	Late 1990s–mid-2000s	Mid-2000s onwards
Rule-making	1998 Directive left discretion on tarification methods (e.g. entry–exit, point-to-point)	2009 Regulation left discretion on arrangements to implement entry–exit systems
Monitoring	Examples from most experienced markets (e.g. UK, Spain, the Netherlands) and comparative European overview by TSOs' network (GTE) reviewed in Madrid Forum	Several studies of tarification (e.g. levels, structures) used in member states reviewed in Madrid Forum during early 2010s
Revision	Implementation experiences (e.g. UK, Italy) mentioned in 2002 agreements on cost-reflective tariffs and entry-exit systems; then codified by 2005 and 2009 Regulations	The ACER 2013 Framework Guidelines and the ENTSO-G 2015 Network Code for two cost-allocation methods (i.e. postage stamp, capacity-weighted distance methodology) informed by comparative studies; then codified by 2017 Commission Regulation
	Experimentalist governance	Experimentalist governance

Source: author.

date thus reveal that actors can disregard, or even convert to hierarchical purposes, experimentalist structures like the Madrid Forum and the ACER. The finding that the potential for experimentalist processes offered by experimentalist architectures is not always unleashed will be further corroborated in the communication and pharmaceutical cases (Chapters 4 and 6).

Second, the chapter at once corroborates the finding from electricity that experimentalist governance can be durable and challenges it by showing that experimentalism can also lead to hierarchical governance. In natural gas, initially, key actors approached the regulation of both issue areas by using the Madrid Forum to compare and review initiatives undertaken by NRAs and TSOs and to agree on major common rules on that basis, namely, interruptible use-it-or-lose-it and secondary markets, on the one hand, and cost-reflective tariffs and entry–exit systems on the other. Yet, from the mid-2000s onwards, the two sub-cases took sharply different paths. While in network tarification, governance processes continued to be largely marked by reviews of lower-level discretion and development on reforms in this light, in network access, the Commission favoured the imposition of rigid rules from the top, ignoring the Madrid Forum and actually employing the ACER to monitor compliance.

Table 3.3 Trajectory of experimentalist governance in EU natural gas regulation, 1998–2021

Issue	Sequence		Trajectory
Network access	Experimentalist governance, late 1990s–mid-2000s	Hierarchical governance, mid-2000s onwards	Self-limiting
Network tarification	Experimentalist governance, late 1990s–mid-2000s	Experimentalist governance, mid-2000s onwards	Self-reinforcing

Source: author.

Experimentalist governance, in other words, proved resilient in one instance but fragile in the other. Table 3.3 illustrates the two polar opposite trajectories. The chapter thus provides an important caution against overly optimistic assumptions that experimentalist governance is always durable. Pharmaceuticals (Chapter 6) will re-issue such a warning. Sub-cases from communication and pharmaceutical markets (Chapters 4 and 6), however, will restore confidence that, as first suggested in electricity (Chapter 2), experimentalism is most often sustainable.

Third, the chapter permits revision of the preliminary arguments developed about the factors favouring or hindering experimentalist governance. On the one hand, its findings are inconsistent with claims identifying polyarchic or multipolar distributions of power as a scope condition for experimentalism. Although the distribution of legal powers was exactly the same across the two sub-cases and remained strongly multipolar also after the Commission became equipped with comitology (which still requires the approval of member states), as seen, from the mid-2000s, network access and tarification experienced sharply different forms of governance, with the latter turning to hierarchical governance. This finding thus suggests that polyarchy is not a sufficient condition for experimentalist processes. The importance of this legal factor will be further challenged, with some of the following chapters questioning once again the capacity of polyarchy to act as a bulwark against hierarchical governance (Chapters 4 and 6) and others showing that experimentalism may be employed even in the face of centralized powers (Chapters 4 and 5).

On the other hand, the chapter lends support to the argument that both cognitive uncertainty and political opposition are positive conditions for experimentalism. During the first period from the late 1990s to the mid-2000s, in both network access and tarification, actors faced uncertainty due to the novelty of the issues they had to regulate; after all, market liberalization and integration were uncharted territories. Nevertheless, an additional reason pushing towards experimentalism was the perceived need to create consensus on highly redistributive issues on which actors had very diverse preferences, no matter whether one looks at the tension between the Commission and member states or at the battle between incumbents and new entrants. Thus, in this initial phase, actors engaged in experimentalism in both sub-cases because of pressure from both cognitive challenges and political opposition. Yet, after the mid-2000s, while in network tarification key actors like the Commission continued to have only generic preferences and faced resistance not only from most of the industry but also from NRAs that were keen to retain discretion over tariffs, in network access, the situation was different. There, the Commission was convinced that it knew the best rule already, and NRAs such as the German and Austrian shared its preference for a stricter version of the existing use-it-or-lose-it, allowing trumping of the multipolar distribution of legal power and imposing the preferred rules on incumbents. The persistence of uncertainty and opposition in network tarification and its decline in network access, therefore, help to explain the variation observed more recently. The finding that not only political factors such as opposition but also functional factors like cognitive uncertainty make it more—not less—likely for actors to engage in experimentalism will be corroborated in all the following chapters.

Finally, the chapter confirms the finding, which emerged from the previous case, that experimentalist governance tends to rely on several, rather than a single, mechanism in order to avoid stalemate. The regulation of network access through experimentalist processes during the late 1990s–mid-2000s was mostly supported by the use—threatened or actual—of competition law. Yet, this involved fines, prohibitions, and commitments offered directly by regulated companies rather than specific positive solutions imposed by higher-level authorities. Thus, it constitutes evidence of penalty defaults. Conversely, the regulation of network tarification through experimentalist processes witnessed, in the early 2010s, several threats by higher-level actors to take over the rule-making process and impose positive rules directly themselves, as distinctive of the shadow of hierarchy. Interestingly, these threats were nested—that is, first cast by the Commission vis-à-vis the ACER, then by the ACER vis-à-vis the ENTSO-G, and then again by the Commission vis-à-vis the ACER. They were embedded directly within the sectoral rule-making procedure (for network codes) rather than the general legislative one. Ultimately, though, they were ineffective in overcoming impasse within the ACER's Board of

Table 3.4 Mechanisms underpinning experimentalist governance in EU natural gas regulation, 1998–2021

Issue	Shadow of positive hierarchy	Negative penalty defaults
Network access	2003 Guidelines for interruptible use-it-or-lose-it agreed against background of 2001 legislative proposal for stronger network unbundling[a]	Rules favouring network access agreed against backdrop of prohibitions, fines, and settlements concerning long-term contracts in late 1990s–mid-2000s (e.g. Marathon case)
Network tarification	During early–mid-2010s, the ACER Framework Guidelines revised after Commission's request, the ENTSO-G Network Code revised after the ACER's request, and the ACER Recommendation prompted by the Commission[b]	None

Notes: [a] At best, one might acknowledge this as evidence of shadow of hierarchy in the network access sub-case. But see the discussion in the 'Mechanisms: Both Penalty Defaults and (Ineffective) Shadow of Hierarchy' section of this chapter arguing that for this issue, evidence of penalty defaults is more robust;
[b] albeit ineffectively.
Source: author.

Regulators so that the Commission eventually did take over. Regardless of the ineffectiveness of the shadow of hierarchy, however, which is perfectly in line with the literature,[13] what matters here is that neither the shadow of hierarchy nor penalty defaults entirely dominated the scene. Instead, as illustrated in Table 3.4, actors used the two mechanisms in combination with one another. Although evidence will be found that these mechanisms, and specifically penalty defaults, can occasionally operate on their own (Chapters 4 and 6), the case of finance (Chapter 5), when considered together with those of electricity (Chapter 2) and natural gas, will provide more robust evidence that shadow of hierarchy and penalty defaults are most often combined.

Taken as a whole, the case of EU natural gas regulation from 1998 to 2021 shows that experimentalist structures do not determine experimentalist processes. The latter are more likely when actors are under pressure from both cognitive uncertainty and political opposition. When actors are confident

[13] Which would explain it in terms of (poor) credibility.

and supported, by contrast, they are more likely to favour hierarchical governance, even overcoming constraints posed by multipolar distributions of legal power. As for long-term evolutions, experimentalist governance may either endure or fade, with both trajectories indeed being possible. Finally, to surpass gridlock, experimentalist governance tends to rely on both the shadow of hierarchy and penalty defaults and thus on a combination of positive and negative mechanisms.

4

Similar Structures, Diverse Processes

European Communication Markets 2009–2021

The texts and calls we send and receive from our loved ones,[1] the emails we exchange with our colleagues, the searches we make on the internet: these are only some of the many possible illustrations of how pervasive the communication domain currently is to our daily lives. A cursory look at major initiatives of organizations such as the European Union (EU), the Organisation for Economic Co-operation and Development, and the World Bank, furthermore, tells us that the digitalization of business and social practices will do nothing but grow in the years to come.

Yet, the communications domain also presents considerable risks. Increasingly large electronic (or more simply, tele-)communication companies such as Deutsche Telekom and Telefónica enjoy natural monopolies over fixed and mobile networks that is not efficient to duplicate, making non-discriminatory access to those networks vital to market entry by competitors, absent which consumers will not reap the benefits of market liberalization. More recently, growing concerns have been emerging that the tech giants dominating digital markets, such as Amazon, Apple, Facebook, Google, and Microsoft, may have become too powerful.[2] This has prompted the EU to provide the Commissioner for Competition with responsibilities over the digital domain, to adopt a new regulatory framework aimed at preventing large companies from abusing their market power, and to take unprecedented competition decisions imposing record fines.[3]

As with the electricity and gas domains examined in Chapters 2 and 3 and all the other domains studied in the book, communications is not only intrinsically important but also hosts institutional structures that offer the potential

---

[1] This chapter builds on but develops collaborative works with Emmanuelle Mathieu (Mathieu and Rangoni 2019) and Giorgio Monti (Monti and Rangoni 2022), respectively on telecoms and tech markets.

[2] For instance, the market capitalization of the five big techs has surpassed that of oil and gas giants such as ExxonMobil, BP, Chevron, and Shell. Already in 2017, they had a combined valuation of $3.3 trillion, representing more than 40% of the value of the Nasdaq 100 (see *Bloomberg*, 15 November 2017).

[3] See *Financial Times*, 20 September 2020.

Experimentalist Governance. Bernardo Rangoni, Oxford University Press. © Bernardo Rangoni (2023).
DOI: 10.1093/oso/9780198849919.003.0005

for experimentalist processes, marked by rule-making centred on lower-level actors' discretion, review of their implementation experiences, and revision of rules in its light. In the sector-specific regulation of telecommunications, the chief experimentalist arrangement is the Body of European Regulators for Electronic Communications (BEREC). Since 2010, its key task has been to assist national regulatory authorities (NRAs) and the European Commission, notably playing a central role in the consultation and notification procedure at the very heart of the sectoral regulatory framework for electronic communications (Sabel and Zeitlin 2008: 281–282; Mathieu and Rangoni 2019: 583–585). In competition policy, including when applied to digital markets and its tech giants, the major experimentalist structures are the European Competition Network (ECN) and the modernized competition arrangements associated with it. In the mid-2000s, they are said to have brought a revolution in the traditionally hierarchical relationship between the European Commission and national competition authorities (NCAs) (Sabel and Zeitlin 2008: 298–299; Svetiev 2010, 2020: 26–53). Both sets of arrangements are experimentalist because, by design, they intend to facilitate regular, EU-level learning from debate and review of implementation experiences at the national level.

Compared to electricity and gas, however, this chapter focuses on a shorter period of around a decade, thus making it less likely to observe multiple policy cycles, which would, in turn, allow testing diametrically opposed claims about the long-term durability of experimentalist governance and overall encouraging findings in this respect from Chapters 2 and 3.

Relative to electricity and gas, moreover, the domain offers useful variation and similarity in possible conditions affecting experimentalist processes. While the distribution of legal powers in telecommunications regulation is multipolar, as is typically the case in the EU, in competition policy, such a distribution is exceptionally centralized. The latter sub-case thus provides a nearly unique opportunity to study the governance choices of higher-level actors and specifically the European Commission in the virtually complete absence of legal constraints on the exercise of hierarchical authority. The experimentalist literature expectation would be that the multipolar distribution of legal powers in telecommunications favours experimentalist governance, whereas their centralization in competition policy hinders it. As the chapter will show, the two sub-cases also differed in cognitive uncertainty and political opposition. In telecommunications, the Commission has been confident that it knew the best rules and has been supported by the European network of NRAs (the BEREC) and the Court of Justice of the EU (CJEU).

In the regulation of Google with competition law,[4] by contrast, the Commission was both unsure about the best rules and feared the potential opposition of the CJEU, which could have allied with complainant firms. The experimentalist literature would thus expect varying degrees of experimentalism, positively in line with perceived cognitive uncertainty. Analyses of regulatory networks, on the contrary, would expect just the opposite—namely, cognitive uncertainty, which is a specimen of functional factors—to be positively associated with hierarchical governance. The same analyses, finally, would expect political opposition to favour non-hierarchical governance and thus experimentalism to thrive more in the regulation of Google than in the regulation of electronic communications.

Finally, just as in electricity and gas, both of the two possible mechanisms supporting experimentalism analysed in the book—the shadow of hierarchy and penalty defaults—were available. This offers helpful ground for further exploration of their actual use and, in particular, of findings emerging from Chapters 2 and 3 that the two mechanisms generally work together rather than being mutually exclusive. To aid overcoming impasse, the Commission can, for example, threaten to use its legislative and/or competition powers, casting a shadow of specific positive rules and of negative prohibitions and fines, respectively.

Overall, communications thus offer a case that is both important in itself and that helps testing and refining the arguments about the relationship between experimentalist architectures, processes, and outcomes developed from electricity and gas (Chapters 2 and 3). First, it provides another case to study whether, and to what extent, experimentalist architectures actually translate into corresponding behaviour; in this respect, while electricity aroused enthusiasm (Chapter 2), natural gas curbed it (Chapter 3). Second, despite its shorter temporal span, the case enables further testing of the opposite polar views that experimentalist governance is doomed to be self-limiting and wither away or else that it is self-reinforcing and hence resilient, with electricity and gas having provided, overall, more support to the latter view. Third, it permits additional analysis of the conditions favouring or hindering experimentalist governance by offering variation across sub-cases in legal, functional, and political factors. Findings from the previous cases have hitherto suggested that both uncertainty and opposition positively affect experimentalism (Chapters 2

---

[4] It is beyond the scope of the chapter to examine all competition cases conducted in the digital domain. The chapter thus focuses on one major one (namely, Google Search (Shopping)), which was the first European case against Google, saw the imposition of a then record fine, and led to two additional cases (AdSense and Android).

and 3), while findings from gas have warned that multipolar distributions of legal power might not be sufficient to ensure experimentalism (Chapter 3). Finally, the case permits deeper investigation of the mechanisms incentivizing participation within experimentalist processes—namely, of the previous findings that, contrary to what is implied by the shadow-of-hierarchy literature and claimed by the experimentalist literature, shadow of hierarchy and penalty defaults are far from antithetical.

Utilizing the case characteristics, the chapter bolsters three general arguments and challenges a fourth one. First, it reinvigorates the finding from natural gas that experimentalist architectures do not always and automatically translate into corresponding behaviour (Chapter 3). In both the sub-cases analysed in the chapter, experimentalist architectures were available. Yet, while the Commission built on the modernized competition arrangements to request Google to develop rules itself, appraise the performance of such rules once implemented, and request revisions accordingly, in telecommunications, the Commission did not employ the BEREC to review the implementation experiences of NRAs and change its initial regulatory position in their light; quite the opposite. It leveraged the experimentalist network to align NRAs' rules with its own. This finding, which suggests rejecting determinism in favour of agency and demonstrates that experimentalist structures may not only be ignored but also even converted to hierarchical uses, will find further support in the pharmaceutical case (Chapter 6).

Second, the chapter finds that even within the relatively short period of a decade, experimentalist processes spanned more than one policy cycle. Thus, in the regulation of Google, the Commission engaged in experimentalist governance twice. In spite of the shorter timeframe compared to those examined in electricity and gas, the chapter thus reinforces previous findings which, although not ruling out the possibility that experimentalism may lead to a return to hierarchical governance (Chapter 3), on balance, provide more robust support to the opposite, self-reinforcing trajectory (Chapters 2 and 3).

Third, the chapter aids further clarification of the scope conditions for experimentalist governance. It does not just confirm that functional pressures are, as political ones, positive rather than negative conditions for non-hierarchical governance; it also strengthens the critique against the importance of distributions of legal power by showing that multipolar distributions of power are not only insufficient (as already suggested in Chapter 3) but also unnecessary to experimentalist governance. In telecommunications, the Commission favoured a more hierarchical route despite the generally multipolar

distribution of legal powers. It did so by building on both its cognitive confidence and on the political alliance with the BEREC and the CJEU vis-à-vis
recalcitrant NRAs. In the competition case against Google, by contrast, the
Commission engaged in experimentalist governance, continuously, regardless
of its extremely centralized powers. It did so because it was under a double
pressure: on the one hand, from the complexity of the case; on the other, from
a potential rival coalition between the CJEU and complaint firms. The positive
influence on experimentalism of both uncertainty and opposition will be further corroborated in all the following chapters. So will be the lack of influence
of distributions of legal power, with the financial case, in particular, providing
an additional demonstration that experimentalism is possible even in the face
of centralized powers (Chapter 5).

Finally, running counter to the previous chapters, this chapter finds that
rather than the threatened imposition of specific positive rules distinctive
of the shadow of hierarchy, the menace of negative prohibitions and fines
typical of penalty defaults underpinned experimentalism. Thus, while the
Commission has been threatening Google with adopting a prohibition decision and imposing associated fines, and it has, at some stage, carried out such
threats (notably fining Google €2.42 billion for having abused its position of
dominance on internet search engines), the Commission has, nevertheless,
consistently refrained from imposing—or threatening to impose—any precise
positive rule directly itself. The possibility that penalty defaults may operate as a stand-alone mechanism will be illustrated again in pharmaceuticals
(Chapter 6). Finance, however (Chapter 5), when considered together with
electricity and gas (Chapters 2 and 3), will offer greater evidence that, most
commonly, shadow of hierarchy and penalty defaults operate together.

The remainder of the chapter is organized as follows. First, a brief overview
of the chief experimentalist structures is offered, underlining why such structures provide the opportunity for experimentalist rule-making and revision
based on review of lower-level implementation experiences. Then, the chapter
looks at the governance processes actually employed to regulate telecommunications and Google, underlining their variation despite similarly experimentalist arrangements. Thereafter, the chapter accounts for this puzzling
variation, highlighting that, while inconsistent with distributions of legal
power, it can be explained by focusing attention on cognitive uncertainty
and political opposition. Finally, the chapter analyses the mechanisms used to
stimulate participation in experimentalist processes of otherwise recalcitrant
actors, stressing the importance of negative penalty defaults. It concludes by
drawing out wider implications for experimentalist governance.

Experimentalist Arrangements

As every policy domain studied in the book, communications hosts experimentalist architectures offering the potential for experimentalist processes
marked by review of implementation experience with lower-level discretion
and rule revision in its light. In electronic communications, the 'Framework
Directive' that in 2002 introduced the competition-inspired framework that
has been governing the sectoral regulation ever since (European Parliament
and Council 2002; Cave et al. 2019; REG 5b) has, on the one hand, given
NRAs discretion. Specifically, NRAs are entrusted with key tasks on market definition, identification of players with significant market power, and
imposition—or removal—of remedies to address the identified competition
problems. On the other hand, however, the framework requires NRAs to con-
sult other NRAs as well as the European Commission prior to the adoption
of their draft measures (European Parliament and Council 2002: art. 7). By
design, it thus favours exchanges and deliberation across multiple levels of
governance. Such reviews are further stimulated by the European network of
NRAs, which was formalized into the BEREC in 2009 (European Parliament
and Council 2009d; Mathieu and Rangoni 2019: 583–585), whose main purpose is to provide an interface between NRAs and the Commission (Sabel and
Zeitlin 2008: 281–282).

Equally, in general competition regulation (which applies transversally to
every sector), experimentalist structures were institutionalized by the reforms
that modernized the framework in 2003 (Council of the European Union
2003). Traditionally, competition policy has been one of the most centralized EU domains, over which, for decades, the European Commission enjoyed
exclusive and largely unconstrained powers. Yet, in 2003, reforms broke with
such a tradition, empowering NCAs to apply EU competition policy con-
currently with the Commission. This decentralization was accompanied by
the formal introduction of the commitments procedure, which allows the
Commission to consider and accept commitments offered directly by firms
to address the identified competition issues rather than reverting to more
conventional prohibition decisions imposed directly on firms by the Commission (Svetiev 2014). As in telecommunications, the space for lower-level
discretion is complemented by mechanisms 'for disseminating learning about
regulatory interventions by national authorities and the Commission, reviewing such interventions, and using the information gathered to regularly revise
policies', thus opening the possibility 'for all participants to contribute towards
the development of the new European competition law' (Svetiev 2010: 84, 97,

2020: 26–53). The ECN, the European regulatory network bringing together NCAs and the Commission and providing a forum for discussion and cooperation, further stimulates such mutual consultation and information exchange. Thus, the modernized competition arrangements and the associated network constitute a novel experimentalist architecture, intended to facilitate EU-level learning from review of experiences with national-level discretion (Sabel and Zeitlin 2008: 298–299, 2010: 298–300; Svetiev 2010, 2020: 26–53).

Having introduced the experimentalist architectures present in both sub-cases and outlined their experimentalist potential, the chapter now proceeds to analyse how they have really worked in practice.

Similar Arrangements, Different Processes

Comparison of the governance processes actually used to regulate European communication markets during the period 2009–2021 reveals surprising variation in the face of similar experimentalist arrangements. In telecommunications, the Commission did not just abstain from leveraging the BEREC to learn from the experiences of NRAs. Quite the opposite; it built on the BEREC to ensure that the rules adopted by NRAs were in line with its own preferences. In the regulation of Google through competition policy, by contrast, after having employed the modernized arrangements to re-allocate to itself all the cases pending before NCAs against the tech giant, the Commission did not impose stable rules by hierarchical fiat. Instead, it required Google to propose remedies directly itself, reviewed their performance, and requested revisions accordingly.

What is more, despite the relatively brief period analysed, to regulate the United States (US) big tech, the European Commission engaged in two cycles of experimentalism, thus providing evidence in support of experimentalist governance long-term sustainability.

Regulating telecommunications with hierarchy

Had actors employed experimentalist processes to regulate electronic communications, one would observe NRAs enjoying discretion in proposing and experimenting with regulatory measures, the BEREC facilitating the comparison and debate of such lower-level experiences, and the Commission building on these benchmarking exercises and reflections to identify the most successful experiments and revise its own initial rules and approaches accordingly. Yet, this is not what happened in practice.

To be sure, processes were not completely hierarchical. NRAs, not the Commission, have been putting forward draft measures. Indeed, from the entry into operation of the BEREC in 2010 to 2021, NRAs have notified the Commission of 1,316 draft regulatory measures they intended to adopt.[5] Yet, this apparent lower-level discretion has been mitigated by the Commission, which sought to align NRAs along its own lines, geared monitoring towards compliance enforcement rather than performance review, and almost never revised its own regulatory positions, which have therefore remained largely stable, as distinctive of hierarchical governance.

A first indicator that governance was largely hierarchical is that rule-making saw NRAs' discretion being curbed by the Commission's effort to impose its own view from the top. Although the Commission accepted the great majority of the draft measures notified by NRAs through relatively brief, one-month investigations (1,230), in more than half of the cases (699), the Commission issued comments that NRAs should consider before adopting the measure. Moreover, it is likely that the Commission accepted other draft measures without comments (484) only after having verified their consistency with its own rules. In addition, in a non-negligible number of cases (forty-seven), NRAs voluntarily withdrew their draft measures, at times explaining such a choice by explicitly referring to the Commission's intention of opening a more extended, Phase II investigation. In the (eighty-six) cases where the Commission did open more extended investigations because it considered that the measures proposed by NRAs would have created barriers to the single market and be incompatible with EU law, the Commission vetoed NRAs' draft measures on eight occasions. This prompted voluntary withdrawals in a greater number of instances (thirty-seven), which were often accompanied by explanations referring to the concerns expressed by the Commission and acknowledged by the NRA at hand. In an equal number of cases, moreover, the Commission recommended specific positive modifications, though their influence on how NRAs eventually adopt their draft measures is contested.[6] These hard figures

---

[5] Unless otherwise specified, the figures and analysis in this section are based on the Overview of notifications database of the European Commission, https://circabc.europa.eu/faces/jsp/extension/wai/navigation/container.jsp?FormPrincipal:_idcl=FormPrincipal:_id1&FormPrincipal_SUBMIT=1&id=c5db898d-6d79-4d1e-808b-4abe9067d635&javax.faces.ViewState=6rXzC47tteB%2FlWDtJmbD3lc%2FpMYvtQWg07fnkJWpJo8US9V%2FxUjTVHjKo8wLtFdKY3%2FOqx6mgI%2FX29JKgmZBoricpnslnhpOfZcpIce4C8Qhj4ZfSlFLaXvBdundoo0EvDOpR5GfPu8tes9khUqap%2FTTRdc%3D (last accessed 16 February 2023).

[6] On the one hand, while acknowledging that 'taking into utmost account doesn't mean "follow"' and that these recommendations are not binding, senior European Commission officials suggest that

aside, it is insightful that, according to a senior official of an NRA, conflicts emerge when 'NRAs are doing things that are not normal' (REG 13), a perspective which is clearly at odds with the systematic self-doubting supposed to be characteristic of experimentalism.

Second, monitoring focused more on compliance enforcement than on performance evaluation of lower-level experiences. During the Phase II extended reviews, the Commission explains its serious doubts, the BEREC issues an opinion, and the relevant NRA provides additional information; third parties, too, may submit additional comments. Thus, in principle, the 'close cooperation to identify the most appropriate and effective measure' between the NCA, the BEREC, and the Commission, which may be extended to additional stakeholders, could be used to review the performance of NRAs' experiences, in a distinctively experimentalist fashion. Yet, in practice, rather than pooling NRAs' experiences in order to facilitate their evaluation by the Commission, most often, the BEREC shared the Commission's serious doubts on NRAs' draft measures. Indeed, since it became operational, the BEREC did not share the Commission's doubts in only five cases, all of which, moreover, happened to take place at the beginning of the network's life (REG 10). Besides economic and technical analyses, the Commission typically supported its serious doubts by explicitly referring to the Framework Directive's 'Procedure for the consistent application of remedies' (European Parliament and Council 2002: art. 7a), its own guidelines (e.g. on significant market power) and recommendations (e.g. on relevant markets, termination rates), its previous decisions vis-à-vis other NRAs, competition law principles and cases by itself and the CJEU, the BEREC's opinion and reports, and possibly even measures that the NRA in question had previously adopted insofar as these contradicted the ones at hand. In short, the Commission employed the BEREC and the

---

the success rate of the Commission's recommendations is nonetheless relatively high. They support this claim notably by pointing at termination markets, which, by nature, are prone to dominance and hence constitute most of the Phase II cases. There, the significant resistance to follow the Commission's recommendations ultimately saw almost all NRAs following such recommendations. To explain why, often, the recommendations were either immediately followed or led to follow-up reviews, the interviewees underlined their influence in subsequent judicial appeals (see the discussion in the next section). They also suggested that it might be easier and faster for NRAs to amend a measure in the absence of a formal recommendation and that 'NRAs are usually well informed and can expect a certain outcome, either in view of extensive pre-notification meetings or more formal requests for additional information'. Finally, the same interviewees argued that NRAs might wish to control reputational damage, in particular 'if at some point a certain agreement or understanding is reached and the NRA is prepared to adjust the measure' (EUI 20; EUI 21; EUI 22).

On the other hand, however, a senior official of the BEREC points out the 'general smiles about the "utmost account" requirement' associated with the Commission's recommendations (REG 10), with a senior official of an NRA confirming that 'with utmost account [...] there are adaptations but not major adaptations. NRAs have invested a lot, with public consultations etc. to develop a draft measure [...] so [they are] not really willing to change it much' (REG 13).

consultation and notification procedure to favour the consistent implementation, at the national level, of the set of rules shaped by itself and its EU-level
allies. Such a predominant focus on compliance is also corroborated by interviewees, who suggest that 'there is also a lot of communication at informal
level' too, which, however, aims 'to ask other NRAs "what problem did you
have with the Commission and how did you address it?"' (REG 13), again
resonating with top-down dynamics.

Finally, the Commission virtually never changed its initial approach in the
light of reviews of lower-level implementation experiences. Indeed, in sharp
contrast to the relatively frequent changes applied by NRAs to their initial draft
measures, over the past decade, the Commission lifted its initial reservations
in no more than six cases. Further, it did so only after the relevant NRA had
revised the original version of its proposed measure to address the Commission's serious doubts (EUI 20; EUI 21; EUI 22)! Hence, it might only be a slight
exaggeration to conclude that the Commission more or less never learnt from
NRAs.

In summary, far from using the BEREC and the consultation and notification procedure at the very heart of European telecommunications regulation for reviewing NRAs' performance and learning from it at EU level,
the Commission employed these experimentalist architectures to discipline
NRAs along the lines preferred by itself and other EU actors such as
the CJEU.

Regulating tech giants (Google) with experimentalism, twice

When one turns attention to the regulation of tech giants, specifically Google,
the story could have not been more different. During 2009–2010, the European Commission received formal complaints by firms, and re-allocated to
itself cases pending before NCAs that Google could have abused its dominant
position in the general web searches market by displaying its own specialized search services (e.g. Google News, Google Flights) more prominently
than those of its competitors. Yet, after having centralized the case in its own
hands, the Commission did not impose stable rules on Google and monitor
compliance with them. Instead, it engaged with experimentalist governance,
extensively and repeatedly.

First, the Commission entered into negotiations with the tech giant using
the modernized commitments procedure (Council of the European Union
2003: art. 9), thus inviting Google to present proposals that could address

the identified competition problem. During the period 2010–2014, Google presented three sets of proposed commitments. Before it proposed the third set, the Competition Commissioner warned the company that this would have been the last attempt; if unsuccessful, the Commission would have reverted to a more traditional prohibition decision, which includes fines (EUI 12a). Lower-level actors—in this case, Google—thus enjoyed discretion in the elaboration of rules.

Second, reviews focused on assessing the (anticipated) performance of the measures proposed by Google rather than verifying compliance with rules imposed upon it hierarchically. Thus, the expected ability of the rules proposed by Google to resolve the identified competition issues effectively was 'market tested'; that is to say, the Commission, with the involvement of complainant firms that *inter alia* included Microsoft, Expedia, and TripAdvisor, appraised the measures proposed by Google.

Finally, far from being stable as typical of hierarchical governance, rules were explicitly conceived as revisable. As described by the then Competition Commissioner Joaquín Almunia right after receiving the third set of proposed commitments: 'if Google improves the presentation of its services, so must the presentation of rival links [. . .] This means that any new vertical search services developed by Google must also be subject to the commitments [. . .] [T]hese commitments are forward-looking' (European Commission 2014a: 2–3).

After this first round of experimentalism in the late 2000s–early 2010s, complainant firms and specifically 'some US firms that had a very strong network to test the results of the possible implementation of the commitments' also rejected the third set of proposals (EUI 12a). At that point, the Commission carried out the previously cast threat, reverting to a conventional prohibition decision, which featured the imposition on Google of a then record fine of €2.42 billion.

But despite this apparently hierarchical turn, governance processes actually remained experimentalist. First, the Commission kept refraining from directly imposing any specific positive rule. It is telling, in this respect, that the Commission dedicated only 2 out of 700 paragraphs of its 2017 Decision to how the identified abuse had to be addressed. In those couple of paragraphs, moreover, the Commission explicitly stated that 'It is for Google, and not the Commission, to make a choice [. . .] thereby bringing the infringement to an end' (European Commission 2017c: art. 4.5(144)). Hence, lower-level actors (namely, Google) continued to enjoy discretion in rule-making.

Second, in an equally distinctive experimentalist fashion, the Commission set out arrangements for monitoring and assessing the performance of the measures developed and implemented by Google. Albeit used in this context, the term 'compliance' is actually a misnomer since the Commission's Decision did not provide any specific rule with which to comply! Instead, the Decision requested Google to send, at intervals of four months over the next five years, reports on the measures that it had taken to achieve the Decision's objectives. In addition, it outlined arrangements providing for technical experts and complainant firms to contribute to the evaluation of the effectiveness of those measures (European Commission 2017c: art. 12.2(704–705); EUI 12a).

Finally, such experimentalist reviews appear likely to prompt revisions in the near future. Even though, at the time of writing, the Commission has not yet requested Google to revise the measures thus far implemented, growing concerns of complainant firms and their consultants about the ineffectiveness of such measures[7] suggest that experimentalist revisions based on review of lower-level experiences might well be on the horizon.

In summary, in sharp contrast with telecommunications regulation, tech giants regulation over the past decade has been characterized by a consistent use of experimentalist architectures, which has led, throughout two policy cycles, to constant discretion of lower-level actors like Google to make rules directly themselves, regular reviews of their performance, and frequent rule revisions on that basis. But how can the puzzling finding of diverse governance processes despite similar institutional structures be explained? The chapter now turns to this question.

Conditions: Uncertainty and Opposition, Not Polyarchy

The chapter underlines that the governance processes found do not square with the distributions of legal power in place: in telecommunications, the Commission favoured a more hierarchical approach in spite of the multipolar or polyarchic distribution of powers; conversely, for regulating big techs, the Commission engaged in experimentalist governance despite the powers concentrated in its own hands. The chapter explains the variation in governance across the two sub-cases in the light of their different cognitive uncertainty and political opposition. In telecommunications, the Commission could trump multipolar constraints on hierarchical governance because of its cognitive confidence and the political support of other key actors such as the BEREC and the CJEU. By contrast, the complexity of the Google case and the potential

---

[7] See *Financial Times*, 28 September 2020.

contestation by the CJEU and complainant firms pushed the Commission away from hierarchical governance, even though it did have the legal powers to pursue that avenue.

Inconsistent distributions of power

Looking at distributions of legal power does not bring the explanatory analysis very far. In telecommunications, the distribution of powers is polyarchic in that no single actor can impose its own preferred rules on others without taking into account their views. As discussed, the Commission does not have the power to develop regulatory measures unilaterally. On the contrary, NRAs are entrusted with that responsibility. However, as also seen, NRAs must notify their drafts to the Commission, which can issue veto decisions, when the measures concern market definition and identification of players with significant market power, and positive recommendations when these drafts refer instead to remedies (European Parliament and Council 2002: art. 7).[8] More generally, the Commission is subject to the constraints imposed by the ordinary legislative procedure as well as by comitology (European Parliament and Council 2002: art. 22). But despite the sector-specific restraints posed by the consultation and notification procedure and the cross-sectoral ones characteristic of the EU more broadly, as discussed, the Commission has nevertheless pursued governance processes that, overall, were more hierarchical than experimentalist.

Conversely, actors have sought to regulate tech giants, specifically Google, through the application of general competition, one of the most centralized domains in the EU. Relying directly on Treaty provisions, for decades, the Commission enjoyed largely unconstrained and exclusive powers not only to prohibit anti-competitive agreements and abuse of dominance but also to curb state aid, issue directives to end state monopolies bypassing the Council of Ministers and European Parliament, and, since 1989, control mergers. Although the 2003 modernization reform brought a fundamental reorganization that meant a greater involvement of NCAs as well as the formalization of the procedure of commitments proposed directly by firms, the Commission

---

[8] The new regulatory framework adopted at the end of the 2010s has introduced only slight modifications. It has extended the Commission's veto powers to remedies, but, in contrast to the Commission's proposal of extending veto powers to any remedy, insofar as the Commission and the BEREC were in agreement on the case at hand (REG 5b), the new veto powers are circumscribed to very specific instances, that is, co-investments and symmetrical access (European Parliament and Council 2018: arts. 32–33).

remains empowered to take over cases from NCAs whenever it deems it appropriate (Council of the European Union 2003: see esp. art. 11.6). Thus, the distribution of legal powers in this sub-case is, especially by EU standards, exceptionally centralized. Yet, as seen, such an extraordinarily concentrated distribution of legal powers notwithstanding, the Commission walked away from hierarchical governance.

Diverse uncertainty

Unsatisfied with legal explanations, the chapter turns its attention to cognitive uncertainty, arguing that this functional factor has much more explanatory value. In telecommunications regulation, the Commission is generally confident that it knows the right solution. As mentioned, the framework that has governed the sectoral regulation since the early 2000s and that has arrived largely intact to the current day is, essentially, a competition-based regime based on the key steps of market definition, market analysis, and imposition of remedies on players with significant market power. Indeed, from the very start of telecommunications liberalization, the vision has been that sector-specific regulation should have been temporary and gradually abandoned, leaving the sector under the exclusive supervision of general competition regulation (European Parliament and Council 2002: rec. 27, art. 15.1). Such a vision, moreover, has been materializing: the number of markets susceptible to *ex ante* sector-specific regulation has sharply declined, from an initial eighteen in the early 2000s to only two in 2020 (cf. European Commission 2003c with European Commission 2020a). Furthermore, competition is one of the oldest EU policies, and the Directorate-General for Competition (DG COMP) is commonly considered one of the strongest DGs. As a result, the Commission has been able to muster its expertise in competition law and economics to the point that NCAs and ministries, often, have perceived the Commission as having a paternalistic attitude towards them, 'teaching them' how to implement telecommunications regulation (Mathieu and Rangoni 2019: 581, 585–586).

Yet, the Commission is not equally confident in every area of competition policy, the one concerning Google being the most controversial. As explained by the former Chief Competition Economist of DG COMP, Professor Massimo Motta, in the area of abuse of dominance the once influential 'Chicago School', with its faith in markets and scepticism of government intervention, has not yet been replaced by a fully fledged alternative paradigm. In practice, in the US, the trust in markets and the view that courts' lives should not be overly complicated has led to simple rules championing laissez-faire. In Europe, by contrast, greater suspicion about markets and large firms has led to an 'ordo liberal' approach whereby activities that would be lawful if conducted by small firms become illegal when pursued by dominant players (EUI 13a). In effect, interviewees suggest that this area is the frontier of competition because of greater complexity and sophistication as well as a lower number of EU cases and case law (BUS 14; EUI 12a). In the case against Google, in particular, the then Competition Commissioner Almunia explains that the Commission considered that:

> a commitment procedure would have been more efficient, because markets were moving very fast and because it was the first time that DG COMP was investigating these kinds of infringements, of a big platform, with a strong capacity to innovate, develop new services to explore new markets [...] was very very complex [...] we are talking of 2010–11, ten years ago.
>
> (EUI 12a, EUI 12b)

Indeed, the last set of revisable commitments offered by Google explicitly recognized the sectoral turbulence and complexity (European Commission 2014a: 2–3). Equally, such environmental volatility is acknowledged by the Commission Decision continuing to grant discretion to Google to develop remedies itself, while, at the same time, obliging it to submit regular reports to be evaluated with the help of experts (European Commission 2017c: arts. 4.5(144), 12.2(704–705)). In short, as Mr Almunia suggests, the Commission's choice of engaging in experimentalism was influenced by the:

> level of complexity, fast-moving markets that require forward looking approach (i.e., not only analysing the past but also what will happen next), new areas under investigation, new players, maybe the need of new definitions of the relevant market, very intelligent and innovative players, and changes in technologies and consumer preferences.
>
> (EUI 12a)

Diverse opposition

But, however illuminating cognitive explanations are, one gains a fuller understanding by also looking at politics, which had not vanished. In telecommunications regulation, there is consensus in the literature that the relationship between the Commission and NRAs has been conflictual throughout.

Indeed, such a consensus is even more striking when one considers that this scholarship is otherwise divided. From the beginning of market liberalization and integration in the 1990s, the Commission has constantly sought to reduce the degree of discretion of NRAs through progressive centralizations of power, which national actors have strenuously resisted (Kelemen and Tarrant 2011; Simpson 2011; Boeger and Corkin 2012; Blauberger and Rittberger 2015). Paradoxically, while in energy, the Commission sought to overcome the resistance of member states and historically state-owned incumbents by forging alliances with NRAs, in telecommunications, member states were relatively more favourable to liberalization, and privatization advanced faster, thus weakening the pressure for the Commission to seek alliances with NRAs (REG 3c; Mathieu and Rangoni 2019: 587–588). To address such a conflictual relation with NRAs, however, the Commission could count on a powerful coalition. As seen, the BEREC has most often shared the Commission's serious doubts, thus defending the Commission vis-à-vis NRAs rather than vice versa. In addition, the Commission was also buttressed by the courts, as evidenced by a long track record of case law in which the CJEU typically backed up the Commission (see, e.g. Monti 2008). Indeed, interviewees suggest that the first and most important reason why NRAs may voluntarily withdraw their draft measures is the 'persuasive value of [the] Commission's serious doubts and the opinion of BEREC [. . .] Obviously the Commission's view and those of "the entire regulatory community" have some weight in subsequent appeals and judicial review' (EUI 20; EUI 21; EUI 22).

In the regulation of Google, by contrast, the Commission could not rely on an equally strong, readily available coalition. To be sure, at the end of 2021, the CJEU has upheld the €2.42 billion fine imposed by the Commission on the US tech giant.[9] Yet, throughout the case, the Commission was aware of 'the problem that the complainants have always the possibility to go before the European Court of Justice', as Competition Commissioner Almunia suggests (EUI 12b). Moreover, as mentioned, this area offers very little case law, which means that, especially at the time, the Commission acted in a void of EU jurisprudence (BUS 14; EUI 12a; EUI 12b). The Commission thus continuously engaged in experimentalist processes, including by paying much attention to the expert comments of complainant firms, not only for functional

---

[9] Though the ruling was delivered by the European General Court (i.e. the lower tribunal of the CJEU) and thus an appeal before the higher tribunal is still possible (see https://www.euronews.com/2021/11/10/google-loses-appeal-against-2-4-billion-eu-fine-over-its-shopping-service, last accessed 16 February 2023).

reasons but also because of a dormant rival coalition between these firms and the CJEU, which could have awakened at any moment.

In summary, the chapter has argued that, while the variation in governance processes observed in the regulation of telecommunications and tech giants is at odds with distributions of legal power, such a variation can be explained by drawing attention to functional factors—uncertainty—and political ones—opposition, both of which differed across the two sub-cases. Nevertheless, if, when regulating Google, the Commission faced considerable political opposition, how did it manage to stimulate participation and avoid the experimentalist processes it pursued ending up in gridlock?

Mechanisms: Penalty Defaults Only

Narrowing down attention to the regulation of tech giants—the sub-case in which the dominant form of governance was experimentalist—reveals a surprising finding, namely, that experimentalist governance was supported exclusively by penalty defaults.

Had the European Commission relied on the shadow of hierarchy to induce actors, and specifically Google, to cooperate, one would observe threats by the Commission of taking over the process, itself imposing clearly defined positive rules on the tech giant. As seen, during the negotiations about the commitments proposed by Google, the Commission did threaten to revert to a more traditional decision, a threat that it eventually implemented. But, as also underscored, despite this seemingly hierarchical shift, in practice, the Commission kept refraining from developing specific positive measures itself. Instead, it explicitly gave such a task to the lower-level actor (European Commission 2017c: art. 4.5(144)) without ever threatening to reverse such a choice and take the issue in its own hands.

By contrast, the evidence suggests that experimentalist processes to regulate Google resorted to penalty defaults. As seen, the Commission threatened to— and eventually did—impose a then record fine of €2.42 billion, together with a negative prohibition of continuing the identified abuse of dominance (European Commission 2017c). With the help of experts and complainant firms, today, the Commission closely watches the implementation of the remedies elaborated by Google. This might well lead to a revision of the 2017 Commission's Decision, a new fine on Google for having failed to remedy the identified competition problems effectively, and a request to develop novel solutions that are better performing. Nevertheless, insofar as the Commission will continue to rely on negative sanctions and prohibitions rather than specific positive rules, Google's participation in experimentalist processes will keep being stimulated by penalty defaults, not by the shadow of hierarchy.

Conclusion

The communications case has provided an opportunity to scrutinize the general arguments developed through extended analysis of the electricity and natural gas domains (Chapters 2 and 3), reinforcing three such arguments while challenging a fourth one. First, study of the regulation of the communications domain from 2009 to the present date shows that, despite the presence of comparable experimentalist structures in both sub-cases, the regulation of telecommunications and of tech giants embraced distinct governance processes. To regulate tech markets, and specifically Google, the European Commission built on the modernized competition arrangements to request the tech giant to develop solutions itself, review their effectiveness in solving the identified issues, and require their revision accordingly. In electronic communications, by contrast, the Commission did not employ the BEREC and the consultation and notification procedure to review and learn from NRAs' experiences, as it could have done. Instead, it leveraged such experimentalist structures to align NRAs' measures with its own, stable rules. Tables 4.1 and 4.2 summarize the governance processes dominant in the regulation of European communication markets. The finding that experimentalist structures do not determine corresponding processes but actors' agency may disregard, or even convert, such institutional structures to hierarchical uses,

Table 4.1 Governance of EU telecommunications regulation, 2010–2021

	2010 onwards
Rule-making	NRAs' discretion curbed by Commission through consultation and notification procedure (e.g. investigations, comments, vetoes, recommendations)
Monitoring	Consultation and notification procedure (e.g. Commission's serious doubts) and the BEREC therein (e.g. opinions) used to foster NRAs' compliance with EU rules
Revision	Commission's initial reservations on NRAs' draft measures never lifted in light of additional information by NRAs Hierarchical governance

Source: author.

Table 4.2 Governance of EU regulation of tech giants (Google), 2009–2021

	2009–2014	Mid-2010s onwards
Rule-making	Discretion of Google to propose commitments	2017 Commission Decision still requires Google to develop remedies itself
Monitoring	Anticipated performance of proposed commitments market tested	Google's compulsory reports on effectiveness of its remedies regularly being reviewed by Commission, complainant firms, and experts
Revision	Revisability embedded in third set of proposed commitments	Commission Decision requiring Google to revise remedies—considered ineffective—on the horizon[a]
	Experimentalist governance	Experimentalist governance

Note: [a] Now, this is a possibility, which the evidence suggests likely to materialize.
Source: author.

which had first emerged in gas (Chapter 3), will be further corroborated in pharmaceuticals (Chapter 6).

Second, the chapter strengthens confidence that experimentalist processes may endure across several policy cycles rather than gradually wither away. Within a single decade, the regulation of Google featured two iterations of experimentalist governance. First, during the period 2010–2014, the Commission engaged in negotiations with the firm, reviewing the anticipated performance of its proposed commitments and welcoming provisions for rule revisability. Thereafter, despite a hierarchical façade associated with the reversion to a more traditional prohibition decision in 2017, the Commission kept insisting that it was the lower-level actor that had to develop rules, whose effectiveness is being reviewed and may lead to rule revisions in the near future. Table 4.3 illustrates the self-reinforcing trajectory of experimentalist governance in the big tech sub-case. Of course, this finding does not strike out the possibility that experimentalist governance might endogenously lead to its own decline and to a return to hierarchical governance—a possibility that had already manifested empirically in one gas sub-case (Chapter 3) and will do so again in a pharmaceutical sub-case (Chapter 6). However, this chapter's finding builds on and, at the same time, reinforces evidence from the electricity case and from another gas sub-case (Chapters 2 and 3) in favour of the self-reinforcing trajectory. An additional pharmaceutical sub-case (Chapter 6) will tilt overall confidence in favour of such a self-reinforcing dynamic.

Third, the chapter advances understanding of the conditions for experimentalist governance, further challenging the influence of distributions of

Table 4.3 Trajectory of experimentalist governance in EU communications regulation, 2009–2021

Issue	Sequence		Trajectory
Telecommunications	None: only hierarchical governance, 2010 onwards		Not applicable
Tech giants (Google)	Experimentalist governance, 2009–2014	Experimentalist governance, mid-2010s onwards	Self-reinforcing

Source: author.

legal power whilst providing additional support on the positive effect of cognitive uncertainty and political opposition. Insofar as these are understood in legal terms, power distributions in the two sub-cases are at odds with the forms of governance found. In telecommunications, the Commission pursued overall hierarchical processes despite the multipolar constraints posed by the consultation and notification procedure at the heart of sectoral regulation and the ordinary legislative and comitology procedures governing EU rulemaking more widely. Conversely, although in the regulation of Google the Commission was equipped with exceptionally centralized powers, thanks to competition law, it did not use such powers hierarchically. In contrast to experimentalist literature's expectations, a polyarchic or multipolar distribution of power is hence not only insufficient for experimentalism, as was suggested in gas (Chapter 3) and will be argued in pharmaceuticals too (Chapter 6), but also unnecessary, as it will be demonstrated again in finance (Chapter 5). The chapter argues that in telecommunications, the Commission could overcome multipolar constraints on hierarchical governance vis-à-vis undisciplined NRAs because it was both confident that it knew the best rules beforehand and could rely on major allies, namely, the BEREC and the CJEU. To regulate Google with competition policy, instead, the Commission did not make use of its extraordinarily centralized powers because it navigated through particularly complex waters and feared the awakening of a latent yet powerful opposition of the CJEU and complainant firms. Thus, in line with expectations drawn from experimentalist studies and in contrast to those drawn from regulatory networks analyses, functional pressures—specifically uncertainty—aid experimentalist governance and not hierarchical governance. Consistently with the latter studies, moreover, political factors too aid experimentalist governance. The finding about the positive influence on experimentalism of both uncertainty and opposition is consistent across all chapters.

Finally, by finding evidence of penalty defaults only, the chapter challenges the argument developed in previous chapters that this mechanism tends to operate together with the shadow of hierarchy. The experimentalist processes employed to regulate Google were not underpinned by threats of specific positive rules imposed by the Commission, as would have been the case if the shadow of hierarchy was at work. Instead, such processes were aided exclusively by threats of negative fines and prohibitions, which, as seen, were actually carried out in the late 2010s. Equally, at the time of writing, Google is under the menace of additional fines, should the rules it has itself elaborated turn out to be ineffective, as many actors suspect. But there is no sign that the Commission is threatening to develop clearly defined rules itself rather than imposing additional fines and obliging Google to come up with improved rules, whose performance will once again be reviewed. Table 4.4 illustrates the mechanism that has been supporting experimentalist processes in the communications case, concentrating, by definition, only on the sub-case dominated by experimentalist processes. Although this finding demonstrates that—as will be shown again in pharmaceuticals (Chapter 6)—penalty defaults might occasionally operate on their own, electricity, gas, and finance (Chapters 2, 3 and 5) altogether provide more robust evidence that the shadow of hierarchy and penalty defaults generally work in combination with one another.

As a whole, the regulation of European communication markets over the past decade shows that experimentalist arrangements do not automatically determine corresponding governance processes. When employed, experimentalist governance exhibits durability across different policy cycles.

Table 4.4 Mechanisms underpinning experimentalist governance in EU communications regulation, 2010–2021

Issue	Shadow of positive hierarchy	Negative penalty defaults
Tech giants (Google)	None	During 2010–2014, commitments proposed by Google stimulated by Commission's threat of prohibition decision and fines; from 2017 onwards, remedies elaborated by Google prompted by the Commission's threat of revision of the prohibition decision and new fines

Note: Since, in the sub-case of electronic communications regulation, the governance processes employed were not experimentalist but hierarchical, this table looks only at digital markets and specifically the regulation of big techs, namely Google, where processes were experimentalist. *Source*: author.

While distributions of legal power appear irrelevant to either hinder or favour experimentalism, functional and political factors are influential. When actors are confident that they know the best rules in advance and are supported by powerful political coalitions, they may be able to trump multipolar constraints on hierarchical governance. Conversely, when they are unsure about the best rules and cannot rely a strong reform coalition to impose rules on others, they may refrain from using hierarchically the powers, which, nevertheless, might be centralized in their own hands. Finally, to induce participation and avoid impasse, experimentalist governance might be underpinned exclusively by negative penalty defaults.

5

Experimentalist Architectures, Processes, Outcomes

European Financial Markets 2011–2021

How we buy groceries and pay bills, how we acquire our first flat and get kids in the best possible schools, how we plan retirement and prepare for 'rainy days', how we expand our own business and enjoy the products and services offered by others: these are only a few of the many possible illustrations of how pervasive finance is to our daily lives. Indeed, a recent and now thriving line of scholarship has underlined the 'financialization of everyday life' (van der Zwan 2014). A cursory look at human history, moreover, shows that for hundreds, if not thousands, of years, finance has been with humankind (Ranci 2012). This suggests that finance is not likely to vanish in the future either. In short, it does not take long to recognize that, without a doubt, finance was, is, and will remain essential to the broader economy and society.

Yet, as is all too familiar, it is equally clear that finance can also be detrimental to the real economy and society at large. The 2008 global financial crisis is only the last episode of a series of crises that, especially since the 1980s, have regularly erupted around the globe. In the lead-up to what has become infamously known as the 'Great Financial Crisis', credit rating agencies (CRAs) issued excessively accommodating opinions on the creditworthiness of financial institutions and their sub-prime mortgage-related products, which, as the crisis has painfully demonstrated, were far from risk free. A few years later, during the subsequent debt crisis of the euro area, CRAs were further criticized for downgrading some Eurozone countries, which had damaging effects on their public finances. Today, the CRAs market is dominated by the 'Big Three' (Moody's, Standard and Poor's, and Fitch), who are said to lack transparency and suffer from conflicts of interests, given that their fees depend on the institutions they are asked to rate. But the problems with finance are not confined to CRAs; they run much deeper. Indeed, the relationship between finance and other parts of the economy and society have always been ambivalent. While the latter needs the former, the Great Financial Crisis has revealed the extent

Experimentalist Governance. Bernardo Rangoni, Oxford University Press. © Bernardo Rangoni (2023).
DOI: 10.1093/oso/9780198849919.003.0006

to which banks and other financial institutions can leverage moral hazard and information asymmetries to sell to ordinary consumers complex, obscure products containing toxic assets, trigger a crisis of global proportions, and eventually be rescued at taxpayers' expense rather than being held responsible for the consequences of their own actions. These observations thus call particular attention to investment products sold to retail consumers, epitomized by the packaged retail investment and insurance-based products (PRIIPs).

Like all the policy domains studied in this book, finance is not just intrinsically important; it also offers a case featuring experimentalist architectures, which create the potential for rule-making marked by lower-level actors' discretion, review of local implementation experiences, and recursive revision in its light. Throughout the first decade of the 2000s, multi-level architectures governed all areas of finance—banking, securities, and insurance and occupational pensions. Based on their own 'front-line' experience, European committees of national competent authorities (NCAs) were tasked to produce guidelines and standards aiding the implementation of European Union (EU) legislation as well as to advise EU institutions, notably the European Commission, on how to improve such legislation and its implementing rules (Sabel and Zeitlin 2008: 296–298; Posner 2010). In 2010, these committees evolved into EU agencies, collectively known as the European supervisory authorities (ESAs), specifically comprising the European Banking Authority (EBA), the European Securities and Markets Authority (ESMA), and the European Insurance and Occupational Pensions Authority (EIOPA). Although the three ESAs are more formalized and strongly empowered than their predecessors, their boards continue to consist of NCAs. The ESAs thus retain the networked and multi-level character typical of the previous committees as well as of the broader architecture in which they are themselves embedded (Moloney 2015: 556–557; Ferran 2016: 292–293, 312–315; Zeitlin 2016: 1078–1079).

Relative to the domains analysed thus far, however, finance offers useful variation and similarity in the factors that might affect experimentalist governance processes. While the distribution of legal powers in the regulation of PRIIPs is as multipolar or polyarchic as is typically the case in the EU, in the regulation of CRAs, it is more centralized. This is because the ESMA was entrusted with direct and exclusive supervisory powers over CRAs, including licensing—the power of 'life or death' over CRAs.[1] Although the ESMA's board is composed of NCAs and the use of these powers is procedurally constrained,

---

[1] The ESMA has analogous powers also on trade repositories and securitization repositories. In 2022, these powers were extended, for instance, to critical benchmarks and their administrators and data reporting service providers.

this remains, at least by EU standards, a strongly centralized distribution of powers, making the CRAs sub-case similar, in this respect, to that of general competition regulation, whose application against Google was analysed in Chapter 4. The experimentalist literature expectation would thus be that the multipolar distribution of legal powers in the PRIIPs example favours experimentalist governance, whereas their centralization in the CRAs example hinders experimentalism. As the chapter will show, the two sub-cases are, instead, similar in cognitive uncertainty and political opposition. In regulating CRAs as well as PRIIPs, higher-level actors such as the European Commission recognized both their state of uncertainty and the need to build coalitions that were not readily available. The experimentalist literature would, hence, expect experimentalist governance in both sub-cases, in line with the cognitive uncertainty perceived in each of them. Analyses of regulatory networks, on the contrary, would expect just the opposite, namely, cognitive uncertainty—which is a specimen of functional factors—to be positively associated with hierarchical governance. The same analyses, finally, would expect the strong political opposition present in both sub-cases to favour non-hierarchical, experimentalist governance.

Finally, as all the other domains analysed in the study, finance offers a variety of mechanisms that higher-level actors might use to overcome impasse and induce otherwise recalcitrant actors to participate in experimentalist processes. These include generic mechanisms typical of the EU such as threats by the Commission to initiate legislation or competition cases. The mechanisms available also include sector-specific ones such as threats by the Commission to take over the elaboration of binding technical standards from the ESAs or threats by the ESMA to impose sanctions on CRAs. Regardless of their cross-sectoral or sector-specific nature, what matters for this study is whether a given menace involves specific positive rules—thus embodying the shadow of hierarchy—or else negative inducements such as sanctions, hence representing penalty defaults.

Altogether, finance offers a case that is important in its own right and that helps probe the arguments about the relationship between experimentalist structure, behaviour, and outcomes developed in the previous chapters. First, it provides an additional opportunity to examine whether, and how far, experimentalist arrangements actually lead to experimentalist processes. While the electricity case had delivered enthusiastic findings (Chapter 2), the gas and communication cases then mitigated such enthusiasm (Chapters 3 and 4). Second, finance allows further examination of the scope conditions for experimentalist governance. Notably, it offers a test for the argument, developed in competition regulation in digital communications (Chapter 4), that actors may engage in experimentalist processes even when they possess strong hierarchical powers to do otherwise. It also permits further testing of the argument developed so far, according to which the greater the pressure from cognitive uncertainty and political opposition, the more actors engage in experimentalist processes and vice versa. Finally, the case allows us to delve more deeply into the mechanisms supporting participation in experimentalist processes. Findings from electricity and gas suggest that, contrary to what is implied by the shadow-of-hierarchy literature and argued by the experimentalist literature, the shadow of hierarchy and penalty defaults are actually compatible (Chapters 2 and 3). Yet, the digital sub-case somehow questioned these findings, showing that penalty defaults may also operate on their own (Chapter 4).

Leveraging the case characteristics and focusing on the sub-cases of CRAs and PRIIPs, the chapter refines one general argument and strengthens two additional ones. First, it shows that to regulate CRAs, neither the Commission nor the ESMA chose to set ratings directly themselves, leaving this to the discretion of CRAs. Nonetheless, these EU authorities also provided for—and carried out—regular reviews of CRAs' experiences, stimulating revisions of their initial ratings and methodologies. Similarly, to regulate PRIIPs and particularly aid retail consumers' understanding of risks and comparability, actors developed standardized key information documents (KIDs) that financial institutions must provide when selling investment products. Such a solution was largely developed by a multitude of actors, including not only the European Commission and Parliament but also the ESAs and the NCAs composing them, plus additional stakeholders. Provisions were also set up and employed to review the performance of KIDs and consider revisions accordingly; indeed, such reviews and revisions did take place earlier than expected, soon after the beginning of implementation in 2018. Thus, in both sub-cases, experimentalist architectures like the ESAs were used to favour rule-making informed by lower-level actors, reviews of implementation experiences, and revisions on that basis. This finding restores confidence in the ability of experimentalist structures to lead to corresponding processes, first generated in electricity (Chapter 2) and then challenged in gas and communications (Chapters 3 and 4). The pharmaceutical case, however, will once again caution against deterministic assumptions (Chapter 6).

Second, the finance case strengthens previous findings about the scope conditions for experimentalist governance. In both sub-cases, actors, and particularly the European Commission, were aware of the need of building coalitions. They recognized that the unilateral development and enforcement of stable rules was politically inconceivable, no matter whether one considers the possibility of taking over CRAs' key functions or of imposing by hierarchical fiat unprecedented information disclosure requirements over a market worth up to €10 trillion.[2] In both instances, actors were also conscious of the impossibility of identifying completely right credit ratings or KIDs *ex ante*. Yet, in the CRAs sub-case, as mentioned, higher-level actors, notably the ESMA, did have exceptionally centralized powers. These findings therefore confirm that, in contrast to experimentalist literature expectations and in line with what was already suggested in the digital sub-case (Chapter 4), multipolar or polyarchic distributions of power, in fact, are not a necessary condition for experimentalist governance. The pharmaceuticals case will show that, as argued in the gas and communication cases (Chapters 3 and 4), polyarchy is not a sufficient condition either (Chapter 6). By contrast, the chapter's findings corroborate the argument, developed and strengthened in all the previous chapters, that uncertainty and opposition are positive rather than negative conditions for experimentalism. Pharmaceuticals (Chapter 6) will further confirm this finding, which is in line with the experimentalist expectation but partially at odds with those of regulatory networks studies.

Finally, the chapter strengthens confidence that the shadow of hierarchy and penalty defaults tend to operate together and are therefore far from mutually exclusive. CRAs have been under the constant threat of fines and, in a recently growing number of instances, have indeed been fined. Throughout, EU actors have, however, made it clear that they will not interfere with the content of ratings or their methodologies. The first sub-case therefore featured penalty defaults, not the shadow of hierarchy. Conversely, the second sub-case was supported by the shadow of hierarchy rather than penalty defaults. To induce the EIOPA's board to formally adopt the draft amended binding technical standard at the core of the revised delegated regulation on PRIIPs, in December 2020, the Commission successfully threatened to exercise its delegated powers directly. Although the pharmaceuticals case will provide a second demonstration that penalty defaults can operate as a stand-alone mechanism (Chapter 6), findings from this chapter combined with those from energy and communications (Chapters 2, 3, and 4) ultimately result in more robust evidence that the shadow of hierarchy and penalty defaults commonly work jointly.

---

[2] See https://ec.europa.eu/info/business-economy-euro/banking-and-finance/consumer-finance-and-payments/retail-financial-services/key-information-documents-packaged-retail-and-insurance-based-investment-products-priips_en (last accessed 16 February 2023).

The remainder of this chapter is organized as follows. First, it briefly outlines the chief experimentalist architectures present in European financial markets, highlighting their potential to lead to governance processes whereby rule-making builds on lower-level actors, reviews monitor performance in light of implementation, and revisions regularly follow. The chapter then looks at the processes that actors employed to regulate CRAs and PRIIPs, underlining that experimentalism was dominant in both. Thereafter, the chapter accounts for the similarity in governance processes observed, challenging the influence of distributions of legal power while emphasizing the importance of cognitive uncertainty as well as political opposition. The chapter then analyses the mechanisms underpinning experimentalism, pointing to the menace of both negative sanctions and specific positive rules. It concludes by drawing out broader implications for experimentalist governance.

Experimentalist Structures

In the early 2000s, the EU introduced in the regulation of finance, and specifically banking, securities and insurance and occupational pensions, a novel institutional architecture, which, in a typical experimentalist fashion, was multi-level. First, the highest, 'level 1' rules were jointly developed by the European Commission, Parliament and Council, which agreed on EU legislation setting out the broad framework principles and goals. To implement the higher-level legislation, at the lower 'level 2', the Commission then elaborated under comitology procedures rules that are more detailed. It did so, third, based on the advice of committees of NCAs, which identified best practices and produced standards and guidelines at 'level 3'; these committees were, in particular, the Committee of European Banking Supervisors (CEBS), the Committee of European Securities Regulators (CESR), and the Committee of European Insurance and Occupational Pensions Supervisors (CEIOPS). Finally, the lowest 'level 4', centred on implementation, followed. The strongly multi-level and networked character of such architectures creates the space not only for discretion for lower-level actors such as NCAs but also for the regular review of their implementation experiences and the revision of higher-level rules on that basis. Accordingly, the literature interpreted these architectures as experimentalist (Sabel and Zeitlin 2008: 296–298; Posner 2010).

The literature has also underlined that the evolution at the turn of the last decade of the three committees of NCAs into stronger and more formalized EU agencies has not altered the experimentalist nature of these structures. True, the new ESAs are now empowered to contribute to the creation of a 'single rulebook' by proposing level 2 rules—known as binding technical standards—to the Commission, which may then adopt them in the form of delegated regulations. Yet, the Commission can only do so absent an objection from the European Parliament or Council (see arts. 8–15 of European Parliament and Council 2010a, b, c). Further, the ESAs may occasionally have exceptionally strong powers, such as the ESMA's direct and exclusive supervisory powers. However, a tightly defined set of conditions circumscribe such powers, which the ESMA holds over CRAs and trade and securitization repositories only (European Parliament and Council 2011). Furthermore, although the ESAs are EU agencies rather than European networks of NCAs, their boards continue to consist of NCAs' heads (art. 40 of European Parliament and Council 2010a, b, c). More broadly, the ESAs that have replaced the level 3 committees keep operating in a wider framework organized around the pre-existing four institutional levels. As a result, the EBA, the ESMA, and the EIOPA retain the networked and multi-level features of the CEBS, the CESR, and the CEIOPS, just as does the wider institutional framework in which they operate (Moloney 2015: 556–557; Ferran 2016: 292–293, 312–315; Zeitlin 2016: 1078–1079). Having outlined the experimentalist architectures present in the financial services domain and their potential of leading to experimentalist governance, the chapter now proceeds to analyse to what extent such potential has been realized in practice.

Experimentalist Processes in Both Sub-cases

Analysis of the regulation of CRAs and PRIIPs reveals a striking similarity. In both sub-cases, actors disregarded hierarchical processes whereby higher-level authorities directly develop stable rules and then enforce compliance by lower-level actors. By contrast, key actors, such as the Commission, used the experimentalist structures of the ESAs to elaborate rules by relying on lower-level actors such as NCAs and CRAs, review the performance of their implementation experiences, and revise the originally designed rules on that basis. In short, governance processes were predominantly experimentalist.

Regulating CRAs with experimentalism

In the example of CRAs, one could have expected the dominant form of governance to be hierarchical. Until the late 2000s, CRAs had been left to 'self-regulate': until 2010, CRAs operated a self-certification under a voluntary

Code produced by the International Organization of Securities Commissions (IOSCO). Yet, as mentioned, CRAs were then heavily criticized: first, for having underestimated the risks involved in sub-primes and related structured products at the heart of the 2008 global financial crisis; thereafter, for the higher borrowing costs that their decision to downgrade the credit rating of certain countries caused during the subsequent Eurozone sovereign debt crisis. *Inter alia*, CRAs were accused of having market shares that were too high, of lacking transparency and accountability, and of being contaminated by structural conflicts of interest.[3] More broadly, the self-regulatory approach that was in vogue in financial regulation well beyond the specific example of CRAs came to be seen, in the aftermath of the crisis, as too 'light touch' and prone to 'capture' (Black 2010). Against this background, there would be good reasons to expect a transition towards more prescriptive, rigid, and ultimately hierarchical governance.

Yet, CRA regulation has instead taken an experimentalist shape throughout the 2010s. First, EU authorities, such as the Commission and the ESMA, have not taken control of rating setting, leaving discretion over this key task to CRAs. To be sure, the possibility for public authorities to take over this major task was not pure 'science fiction'. At the outset of the establishment of the new regulatory regime, the European Parliament and Council required the Commission to prepare a report exploring the appropriateness of creating a public Community CRA, an invitation that was reiterated right after the Eurozone debt crisis (European Parliament and Council 2009e: rec. 73, 2013: rec. 43). Although the Commission considered the possibility of establishing a public CRA to assess the creditworthiness of member states' sovereign debt or credit ratings more generally, it did not put forward such a proposal (European Commission 2011: 9, 2013c: 9; Mennillo and Sinclair 2019: 279–280). On the contrary, from the very start, EU actors emphasized the 'non-interference with content of ratings or methodologies'. They explicitly stated that 'In carrying out their duties under this Regulation, ESMA, the Commission or any public authorities of a Member State shall not interfere with the content of credit ratings or methodologies' (European Parliament and Council 2009e: art. 23.1, 2013: rec. 27; European Commission 2012e: rec. 4). What is more, the ESMA has decided to adopt a 'risk-based approach' to CRAs supervision, which offers 'tailored approaches' to 'capture the specificities of the industry and its players'. As explained by the Authority itself, 'in defining its supervisory

---

[3] See   https://ec.europa.eu/info/business-economy-euro/banking-and-finance/financial-super vision-and-risk-management/managing-risks-banks-and-financial-institutions/regulating-credit-rating-agencies_en (last accessed 16 February 2023).

actions to address the risks identified, the ESMA does not use a one-size-fits-all approach but tailors its actions to the type of risk or challenge at stake, taking into account its urgency, size and complexity and the history of the supervised entity' (ESMA 2017a: 13–14). In summary, higher-level actors have constantly refrained from curbing CRAs' discretion over rating setting and methodologies.

Second, in return for such lower-level discretion, CRAs must disclose their own methodologies, models, and key assumptions and regularly review experiences with them under the oversight of the ESMA. Thus:

> A credit rating agency shall monitor credit ratings and review its credit ratings and methodologies on an ongoing basis and at least annually, in particular where material changes occur that could have an impact on a credit rating. A credit rating agency shall establish internal arrangements to monitor the impact of changes in macro-economic or financial market conditions on credit ratings.
>
> (European Parliament and Council 2009e: art. 8.5)

Sovereign ratings shall be reviewed at least every six months (European Parliament and Council 2013: art. 1(10)(b)). Furthermore, CRAs shall pay attention to the historical robustness and predictive power of credit ratings resulting from a given methodology as well as the degree to which the assumptions used in the relevant models deviated from actual rates of default and loss. Thus, CRAs 'shall have processes in place to ensure that systematic credit rating anomalies highlighted by back-testing are identified' (European Parliament and Council 2009e: rec. 23, art. 8.3; European Commission 2012e: art. 7). The ESMA, in turn, supervises the internal reviews conducted by CRAs. Without interfering with the content of the methodologies or the substantive ratings, the ESMA must regularly examine the periodic reports that it receives from CRAs on their internal reviews including information on the implementation of 'back-testing' and any key findings resulting from it (European Parliament and Council 2011: art. 1(10), 2013: art. 1(14)). The ESMA's guidelines and annual reports confirm that, in practice, too, the Authority has issued recommendations on the periodic information to be submitted by CRAs, conducted investigations into the rating processes of several CRAs, and continuously examined the quality and accuracy of credit ratings issued and reported by CRAs (see, e.g. ESMA 2015a, 2017a: 9, b).

Third, and finally, the regulatory framework that actors chose to set out exhibits the rapid revisability distinctive of experimentalism. Thus, CRAs shall use methodologies that are 'rigorous, systematic, continuous, and subject to validation based on historical experience'. This means that 'credit rating methodologies and their associated analytical models, key rating assumptions and criteria promptly incorporate findings or outcomes from an internal review or a monitoring review'. In addition, they are 'capable of promptly incorporating the findings from any review of their appropriateness' and 'any finding from ongoing monitoring or a review, in particular where changes in structural macroeconomic or financial market conditions would be capable of affecting credit ratings produced by that methodology'. Finally, 'the anomalies highlighted by back-testing are identified and are appropriately addressed' (European Commission 2012e: arts. 4.4., 5.2, 6(b), 7.4). When a CRA becomes aware of errors in its rating methodologies or in their application, it must immediately notify the ESMA and all affected rated entities. In doing so, it should explain the impact on its ratings, including the need to revise previously issued ratings; publish those errors on its website; and correct errors in the rating methodologies (European Parliament and Council 2013: art. 1(10)(e); ESMA 2021a: 12–13, 16). To illustrate, over the course of 2016, CRAs reported more than 120 errors to the ESMA and over 80 changes in methodologies, though the majority of errors made by CRAs in the application of their methodologies did not have an effect on the credit ratings already issued (ESMA 2017a: 44).

In summary, running counter to common intuition, over the past decade, CRA regulation has been marked by a surprisingly experimentalist shape. This has combined discretion for CRAs with reviews of the performance of their ratings and methodologies and revisions in the light of such assessments. The chapter now turns to the regulation of PRIIPs, where a similarly overall experimentalist story emerges.

Regulating also PRIIPs with experimentalism

The regulation of PRIIPs represents a novel introduction of information disclosure requirements, whose importance becomes clearer when considering that this is also the first regulation cutting across all the three areas of finance. As the regulation of CRAs, it emerged as a response to the global financial crisis, which had highlighted the problem that financial products are generally overly complex and unintelligible for ordinary consumers, thus calling for cross-sectoral reforms. As with the regulation of CRAs, moreover, overall experimentalist governance processes have also dominated the regulation of PRIIPs.

To be sure, governance processes have not been fully experimentalist. The first indicator to distinguish more experimentalist and hierarchical processes, which concerns the role afforded to lower-level actors in the development of the initial rules, provides a mixed picture. Initially, rule-making was highly inclusive. Building upon an information disclosure regime introduced in the late 2000s for a sub-category of PRIIPs known as UCITS (Undertakings for Collective Investment in Transferable Securities) (European Parliament and Council 2009f), in the mid-2010s, the European Parliament and Council adopted a Commission proposal, which introduced mandatory KIDs, that is, information disclosure requirements helping retail consumers to understand and compare complex financial products that could lead to losses (European Parliament and Council 2014). Thereafter, by building on a draft binding technical standard jointly elaborated by the three ESAs, themselves comprised of NCAs and informed by consultations with additional stakeholders, the Commission prepared a proposal for a delegated regulation (European Commission 2016a). The Commission also employed consultants to carry out consumer tests aiming to identify the most user-friendly formats, to give consumers the information needed to compare and choose the products best suited to their investment needs (London Economics and Ipsos 2015).[4]

However, rule-making then became less inclusive. The European Parliament objected to the delegated act proposed by the Commission, notably due to concerns about the temporary exemption for UCITS and estimations based on historical performances that, according to the Parliament, underrepresented the risk that consumers could lose money in particularly adverse scenarios (European Parliament 2016). In response, the Commission elaborated amendments to address the Parliament's concerns and invited the ESAs to amend their draft technical standards accordingly and resubmit them within six weeks (European Commission 2016b). The EBA and ESMA boards successfully adopted an opinion in that respect, though via qualified majority voting. Yet, the EIOPA's board did not achieve the same result due to contrasting views, notably on the regulatory exemption granted to UCITS. As a result, the three ESAs were unable to provide a joint opinion on the amended draft binding technical standard (EIOPA et al. 2016: 1).[5] At that point, the Commission went ahead without the ESAs, recommending directly itself a revised binding technical standard and delegated regulation (European Commission

---

[4] For example, the study showed that retail investors understand monetary figures more readily than percentages.

[5] Moreover, they all expressed concern about the amendments proposed by the Commission on the performance scenarios, considering them potentially misleading (EIOPA et al. 2016: 2).

2017d), to which the Parliament raised no objection (European Parliament 2017).

Thus, while initially lower-level actors contributed to the elaboration of a standardized, three-page template providing in a clear and comparable format key information such as risk and reward profile of the product, possible maximum losses, and performance scenarios, rule-making then became relatively less inclusive in that lower-level actors had less discretion to propose rules. In short, although rules were not developed completely from the top, they were not marked by complete lower-lever discretion either. The other two criteria used to distinguish between types of governance processes, however, clearly support the claim that processes were predominantly experimentalist.

The second indicator of experimentalist processes is that actors established provisions for, and indeed conducted reviews, assessing the performance of the rules initially adopted. Actors planned a review of the Regulation, notably to 'assess whether the measures introduced have improved the average retail investor understanding of PRIIPs and the comparability of the PRIIPs. It should also consider whether the transitional period applying to UCITS or certain non-UCITS should be extended' as well as the possibility of introducing labels for social and environmental investments (European Parliament and Council 2014: rec. 36, art. 33). Provisions to ensure 'timely and appropriate review', moreover, also apply to the KID. Thus:

> PRIIP manufacturers shall review the information contained in the key information document every time there is a change that significantly affects or is likely to significantly affect the information contained in the key information document and, at least, every 12 months following the date of the initial publication of the key information document.
>
> (European Commission 2017d: art. 15.1)

PRIIP providers, in addition, must also 'establish processes for identifying situations where the information contained in the key information document should be reviewed', and 'maintain adequate processes throughout the life of the PRIIP' (European Commission 2017d: recs. 19–20, art. 15.3). In effect, actors conducted such reviews shortly after the entry into force of the Regulation and Delegated Regulation in 2018. In October of the same year, the ESAs initiated a review of the PRIIPs Delegated Regulation to examine the end of the exemption for UCITS funds to provide a PRIIPs KID as well as an additional issue that had emerged almost immediately after implementation had begun, specifically concerning the calculation methodologies for, and the presentation of, performance scenarios. During the period 2018–2020, they undertook two joint public consultations and solicited the advice of the ESMA's Stakeholder Group (ESMA et al. 2018, 2019; ESMA SMSG 2020). In addition, the Commission commissioned a new consumer testing study (DevStat 2020).

Still in a typical experimentalist fashion, finally, these reviews led to regulatory revisions, just as actors had anticipated. Actors recognized that, 'The information contained in the document should be capable of being relied on by a retail investor when making an investment decision even in the months and years following the initial preparation of the key information document' (European Commission 2017d: rec. 19). Thus, the periodic reviews of the information contained in the KID by PRIIP manufacturers 'should include an assessment of whether changes in the data would necessitate a revision and republication of the document' (European Commission 2017d: rec. 20).[6] More broadly, actors foresaw that reflection on the reviews carried out could be accompanied by a new legislative proposal (European Parliament and Council 2014: art. 33.3). In effect, these experimentalist reviews have recently led to the revision of the Delegated Regulation and the binding technical standard underpinning it. Together with the outcome of their joint review (ESMA et al. 2020), the ESAs informed the Commission that, just as a few years before, while the EBA and the ESMA had adopted a draft amendment, the EIOPA had not since its board had failed to achieve a qualified majority (European Commission 2020b: 2). In contrast to the previous episode, however, this time it took the EIOPA only a few additional months to adopt the revised draft technical standard successfully. On that basis, in late 2021, the Commission could successfully recommend to the Parliament and the Council a revised Delegated Regulation. Importantly, this extends the common regulatory framework to UCITS and amends the hitherto problematic methodologies underpinning the calculation of performance scenarios and their presentation, avoiding that retail investors develop inappropriate expectations about the potential return on their investments (European Commission 2021). What is more, a level 1 revision might be on the horizon too. According to the Commission, a revision of the (level 1) PRIIPs Regulation could take place in the wider context of the new Capital Markets Union action plan. This builds *inter alia* on the retail investment strategy due by

---

[6] Similarly to the CRAs sub-case, when a review does conclude that changes to the KID must be made, PRIIP manufacturers shall make such revisions without undue delay, ensuring that all sections of the KID affected by such changes are updated, and publish the revised KID on their websites (European Commission 2017d: art. 16).

mid-2022, itself being informed by a recent study and additional testing of the combined effect of the regulatory framework from the retail consumers' perspective (European Commission 2020b: 2).

In summary, very much in line with the CRAs example, the regulation of PRIIPs has, over the past decade, exhibited overall experimentalist properties, notably rule-making at least in part centred on lower-level actors, frequent review of their implementation experiences, and revision of the initial rules in their light. Having shown that actual governance processes were largely experimentalist in both sub-cases, the chapter now turns to explaining such a striking similarity.

Conditions: Not Polyarchy But Uncertainty and Opposition

How can one explain that, in both CRAs and PRIIPs regulation, actors largely employed experimentalist processes? The chapter argues that, rather than by multipolar distributions of legal power, which were different and thus cannot account for the remarkable similarity in the two sub-cases, explanations lie in the high degrees of cognitive uncertainty and strong political opposition, which were similar. What is more, key actors like the ESMA favoured experimentalist governance even though, in the example of CRAs, they had centralized powers that, in principle, would have allowed for hierarchical governance. They did so because they were acutely aware of the impossibility of setting ratings completely right in advance but also because of the political resistance against the creation of a public CRA and interference with credit ratings. Equally, in the example of PRIIPs, actors such as the Commission engaged in mostly experimentalist processes because they recognized both the complexity of an information disclosure regime that was novel and the need to mould consensus around such an unprecedented, cross-sectoral regulatory initiative. Functional and political factors were thus more influential than legal ones and positively affected experimentalist governance.

Different, inconsistent distributions of power

Looking at distributions of legal power does not take us very far. True, the experimentalist processes largely observed in the regulation of PRIIPs are compatible with the distribution of power which, as in most EU cases, was polyarchic or multipolar. The argument here would thus be that the polyarchic constraints on the exercise of hierarchical authority pushed actors to favour experimentalism. Yet, this is at odds with the observation that, in 2016–2017, such a multipolar distribution of power—which was unaltered—did not hinder the Commission from revising the binding technical standards bypassing the ESAs after these had failed to deliver an agreement jointly.

More importantly, as seen, governance processes were largely experimentalist also in the sub-case of CRA regulation, even though the ESMA holds extraordinarily centralized powers over CRAs. As explained, the ESMA is the single direct supervisor of CRAs within the EU. This means that financial institutions that wish to perform credit rating activities in the Union have to apply to the ESMA, which may accept such applications and grant registration and certification. If it does, however, the ESMA then monitors and investigates potential breaches of the CRAs' rules and may not only issue public notices and fines but also even withdraw registrations (European Parliament and Council 2011). The empowerment of the ESMA as a single supranational supervisor for CRAs with final authority over granting and withdrawing licenses, therefore, means that the ESMA has the power of life and death over CRAs, just as the European Central Bank has on the most systemically important Eurozone financial institutions (Zeitlin 2021: 11). From a perspective emphasizing the importance for experimentalism of multipolar distributions of power, it is thus puzzling that, despite such a centralized distribution of power, higher-level actors, and particularly the ESMA, engaged in experimentalist rather than hierarchical governance. Unsatisfied with distributions of legal power, the chapter turns its attention to cognitive uncertainty, which yields more explanatory value.

Similar high uncertainty

In regulating CRAs, actors recognized that the assessment of creditworthiness—that is, credit rating—is intrinsically uncertain. Indeed, they required CRAs to clarify that 'the rating is the agency's opinion and should be relied upon to a limited degree' (European Parliament and Council 2013: art. 1(10)). Analogous provisions were strengthened to fight not only the dominance of the Big Three but also automatic over-reliance on credit ratings. Thus, besides facilitating entry of smaller CRAs, EU legislation underlined that:

> Financial institutions should not solely or mechanistically rely on credit ratings. Therefore, those institutions should avoid entering into contracts where they solely or mechanistically rely on credit ratings and should avoid using

them in contracts as the only parameter to assess the creditworthiness of investments or to decide whether to invest or divest. [Instead,] financial institutions shall make their own credit risk assessment.

(European Parliament and Council 2013: rec. 9)

Equally, the ESAs 'shall not refer to credit ratings in their guidelines, recommendations and draft technical standards where such references have the potential to trigger sole or mechanistic reliance on credit ratings'. In the same spirit, the Commission shall 'delete all references to credit ratings in Union law for regulatory purposes by 1 January 2020' (European Parliament and Council 2013: art. 1 (6)). Higher-level actors have thus been aware not only of the 'epistemic authority' of the Big Three (Mennillo and Sinclair 2019) but also of the deeper problem that no actor, not even the Big Three, can identify the 'correct rating' beforehand. This helps to explain why actors like the Commission and the ESMA have constantly refrained from imposing ratings or methodologies directly themselves, let alone setting up a single public European CRA. It aids in understanding why, on the contrary, they have encouraged discretion by as many CRAs as possible, continuous monitoring of their performance, and revisions when experience demonstrates *ex post* that the methodologies and/or ratings set *ex ante* were actually incorrect. In short, besides the goal of reducing market concentration, actors' rejection of mechanistic reliance on CRAs' ratings reflect their embracing of the self-doubting at the very heart of experimentalism.

Similarly, in retail investments regulation, the experimentalist discretion, reviews, and revisions observed were explicitly linked to the recognition of complexity and the anticipation of possible issues and changes in circumstances. According to a senior official of an NCA then seconded at the European Commission, 'the Commission would have never been able to do regulatory technical standards itself' as these are 'too technically complex'. Besides leveraging the ESAs, 'there was much consultation with NCAs and stakeholders, plus an *ad hoc* stakeholder consulting working group' (REG 12). Moreover, although actors could build on the previous UCITS regime, they explained the need for reviewing the new framework four years after its entry into force 'to take account of market developments, such as the emergence of new types of PRIIPs, as well as developments in other areas of Union law and the experiences of Member States' (European Parliament and Council 2014: rec. 36, art. 33). Equally, the reviews and revisions foreseen for the KIDs themselves derive from actors' acknowledgement that:

Data that is used for preparing the information contained in the key information document, such as data on costs, risks and performance scenarios, may change over time. Changing data can lead to changes in the information to be included, such as a change in the risk or costs indicators. For this reason, PRIIP manufacturers should establish periodic processes to review the information contained in the key information document.

(European Commission 2017d: rec. 20)

In effect, the anticipation that KIDs might have needed revision was well placed. Providers of PRIIPs must now outline a range of future returns that an investment may deliver in different market conditions, as opposed to providing merely historical performance data as was previously the case. Paradoxically, however, with the introduction of the new regulatory framework, forward-looking scenarios reflecting the strong markets performance over the mid-2010s meant that providers, 'screaming they would be [otherwise] prosecuted' for mis-selling, had to publish overly optimistic projections such as favourable scenarios suggesting annualized returns of more than 1 million per cent![7]

Similar strong opposition

But, however enlightening cognitive explanations might be, an exclusive focus on them would obscure the politics of financial regulation, which had not vanished. Thus, in the sub-case of CRAs, one gains a fuller understanding of why actors favoured the lower-level discretion distinctive of experimentalism by also considering the strong opposition of the industry against the risk of intrusion into CRAs' core business—credit ratings, not to speak of the possibility of creating a European public CRA, which would have threatened CRAs' very existence. Commenting on the Code of Conduct fundamentals for CRAs that the IOSCO was about to revise in the aftermath of the global financial crisis, for example, Standard and Poor's argued that 'The insistence upon specific methodologies appears to be a potential and meaningful intrusion into a CRA's analytical independence.' It claimed that 'by adding a number of details on controls and extensive definition of methodologies the Code would become unnecessarily prescriptive and intrude into what should be ultimately the business and analytical decisions for individual CRAs' (Standard and Poor's 2014: 3, 8). Equally, in the European context, the Association of Corporate Treasurers (ACT) cried out that 'The new proposals give the impression that it is the Commission's wish to control the expression of views on credit and reduce the status, independence and professionalism of CRAs. It raises the prospect

[7] See *Financial Times*, 11 March 2019.

of an intrusion into the CRAs' independence of methodologies' (ACT 2011: 2). Referring to a previous 2010–2011 consultation in which the Commission had mooted the idea of a European CRA (European Commission 2010c),[8] ACT commented that 'These ideas were eventually dismissed and yet much of the new content and tone seems to be trying to create a similar effect through control by ESMA.' It concluded by reiterating that 'The ACT strongly supports the need for non-interference with the content and methodologies of credit ratings' (ACT 2011: 5). In summary, actors rejected hierarchical processes not only because of cognitive uncertainty but also due to political infeasibility.

Similarly, for PRIIPs regulation, interviewees suggest that besides largely technical issues concerning the methodologies for calculating future performance scenarios, fundamental conflicts concerned the scope of the regulatory framework, that is, which products had to be covered by the new regime and which not (REG 14; REG 12). Interviewees further suggest that the Commission took a very expansive understanding of what should be the scope of these rules. Nevertheless, this cross-sectoral regulation proved problematic because the industry had never been regulated on disclosure requirements as well as because of differences across sectors. Indeed, 'this first cross-sectoral experiment was not accepted, with the most frequent objection being "my products are different"', recalls the NCA's Senior Official then seconded to the Commission. 'At first, it seemed that the Commission had managed to do a coup. But conflicts were not on the need for this regulation, but on what and how' (REG 12). More precisely, as seen, in the late 2010s, the EIOPA's board failed to deliver an agreement on a revised draft binding technical standard. The same interviewee explains that this was the result of a minority blocking led by Germany, which has a large market for corporate bonds and thus wanted UCITS to remain excluded from the scope of PRIIPs rules. The Commission, on the contrary, intended to end the UCITS exemption and bring that class of products under the new regime. While the recalcitrant actors wished to re-open the level 1 Regulation establishing the PRIIPs framework, the Commission aimed to protect it, revising the level 2 Delegated Regulation instead (REG 12). From this perspective, then, it becomes clear that actors engaged in largely experimentalist processes not only because they recognized their state of cognitive uncertainty but also because they were aware of the need

---

[8] Responses to the consultation are not publicly available.

for building coalitions around unprecedented rules with highly redistributive implications.[9]

In summary, the chapter has argued that in both sub-cases, processes have been overall experimentalist not because of the distributions of legal power, which were diverse and especially centralized in the CRAs example. Instead, the similarly experimentalist processes have been due to pressure from both cognitive uncertainty and political opposition, which have been strong in both sub-cases. But if both sub-cases were *inter alia* characterized by strong political resistance, which mechanisms induced reluctant actors to participate in experimentalist processes and avoid gridlock?

Mechanisms: Shadow of Hierarchy as Well as Penalty Defaults

Consistent with the book's overall approach,[10] this chapter distinguishes between two main mechanisms that can stimulate otherwise reluctant actors to participate in experimentalist processes, thereby facilitating the transition from experimentalist processes to policy outcomes. The first mechanism—the shadow of hierarchy—incentivizes actors by threatening to take control of the process and impose specific positive rules upon them. The other—penalty defaults—pursues the same aim through negative incentives, such as threats of fines and sanctions or, at the limit, expulsion.

The shadow of hierarchy did not underpin the regulation of CRAs. As described, during the late 2000s–early 2010s, the Parliament and Council asked the Commission to consider the possibility of setting up a European public CRA, either for sovereign ratings in particular or for credit ratings in general (European Parliament and Council 2009e: rec. 73, 2013: rec. 43). This could be interpreted as a shadow of hierarchy insofar as it casts a menace whereby higher-level actors would take over rating setting. Yet, as seen, the Commission repeatedly concluded that this was not an appropriate option (European Commission 2011: 9, 2013c: 9). Therefore, in the shadow-of-hierarchy language, the threat would not have been credible. This is even more the case when one considers that such an option had already been considered, both in the past and in other polities, without ever being implemented (Mennillo and Sinclair 2019: 279–280).

---

[9] This does not imply that experimentalist processes will always manage to mould such consensus. As seen in the example at hand, the Commission at the very end chose to favour a less inclusive rule-making process, which taints with a hierarchical trait an overall experimentalist picture.

[10] See especially Chapter 1.

By contrast, penalty defaults did assist CRAs regulation. As discussed, the ESMA is empowered to issue and revoke licences. Since its creation, it has been the guardian of registrations, first verifying that CRAs that apply to be registered and thus operate in the EU meet all the relevant requirements and then monitoring that they continue to meet such requirements after they have obtained registered status (European Parliament and Council 2009e: ch. I). Thus, in principle, CRAs are under the constant threat of seeing their licences taken away, though of course, the credibility of such an extreme threat is a different question. What is certainly credible, however, is the threat of fines that the ESMA may impose on CRAs. As the single supervisor for CRAs (as well as securitization and trade repositories), the ESMA's powers to deal with infringements not only include the 'nuclear option' of withdrawing CRAs' registration but also the possibility of imposing fines. According to a senior official of a NCA, initially the ESMA favoured a relatively cautious approach, in part because this area had been unregulated for decades. In the last years, however, there have been cases of fines, also significant ones (REG 11). Publicly available evidence, too, corroborates this interpretation. Based on a 2012 review, in 2015, the ESMA took enforcement action against a CRA due to several infringements of the requirements of the CRA Regulation regarding governance and compliance, issuing a public notice and imposing a fine for the first time (ESMA 2015b: 6). The following year, the ESMA took enforcement action against Fitch, one of the Big Three, imposing fines totalling €1.38 million for infringements related to three points of the CRA Regulation (ESMA 2017a: 10). Then, the ESMA fined five banks €2.48 million for having issued credit ratings without having being authorized by the ESMA to do so (ESMA 2018). Additional fines have followed (e.g. ESMA 2020). Most recently, the ESMA has fined Moody's, another one of the Big Three, €3.7 million for breaches of rules on independence and conflicts of interest (ESMA 2021b).

While it was penalty defaults rather than the shadow of hierarchy that underpinned experimentalist processes in the CRAs sub-case, the same cannot be said for PRIIPs. In that sub-case, the chapter found no evidence of negative sanctions, fines, or revocation of licences. Instead, it found evidence of the shadow of positive hierarchy.

After having been notified by the three ESAs that, as a few years earlier, gridlock had occurred within the EIOPA's board, in December 2020 the Commission sent a letter to the ESAs. There, it told that 'In the event the ESAs do not deliver the draft RTS [regulatory technical standards] within the timeframe indicated above [i.e. six weeks], the Commission reserves the possibility to take all necessary steps to preserve and exercise its institutional prerogatives under Article 290 TFEU' (European Commission 2020b: 3). Thus, the Commission explicitly threatened to take over the rule-making process from the ESAs should the NCAs composing their boards have failed to agree. What is more, in this instance, the Commission's threat was credible, given that it had actually used those powers only a few years earlier (European Commission 2017d). Granted, the Commission complemented such a threat by reassuring actors, and specifically the German NCA and its allies, that the review of the level 1 Regulation was scheduled to take place soon and thus revisions at that level could be on the horizon (European Commission 2020b: 2), right as advocated by those actors (REG 12). It is also true that the Commission threatened using its delegated powers directly only once 'the work is technically finished' (European Commission 2020b: 3). But all these considerations do not cancel the fact that, to incentivize NCAs to 'overcome the difficulties'—notably related to the German interests associated with the UCITS exemption—and adopt the draft amending binding technical standard, the Commission did invoke the shadow of hierarchy.

In summary, while CRAs' regulation has been supported by the constant threat of fines, PRIIPs regulation was recently aided by the threat of hierarchically imposed specific positive rules. Putting this evidence together, then, shows that the mechanisms that have been supporting participation and avoiding stalemate in European financial regulation have included both the shadow of hierarchy and penalty defaults. The chapter now turns to the conclusion, discussing the wider implications of its case findings for experimentalist governance.

Conclusion

Finance allows bolstering and refining three general arguments developed in the previous chapters. First, it restores confidence in the capacity of experimentalist structures to lead to corresponding processes. In finance, actors did not ignore or convert to hierarchical purposes the multi-level, networked ESAs. Instead, experimentalist processes dominated the regulation of both CRAs and PRIIPs, in that CRAs and NCAs had discretion to propose solutions, reviews assessed their performance in the light of implementation experience, and that provided the basis for revisions. Table 5.1 summarizes the governance processes dominant in the regulation of European financial markets. This encouraging finding mirrors that from electricity (Chapter 2). It will, however, be counterbalanced by the pharmaceuticals case (Chapter 6) which,

Table 5.1 Governance of EU financial regulation, 2011–2021

	CRAs	PRIIPs
Rule-making	CRAs left discretion on ratings and methodologies	2017 Delegated Regulation largely built on binding technical standard proposed by the ESAs, composed of NCAs
Monitoring	Robustness of ratings and methodologies regularly reviewed *ex post*	Performance of Delegated Regulation reviewed in 2018–2020; that of 2014 Regulation ongoing[a]
Revision	Errors in methodologies and ratings regularly reported and corrected	Delegated Regulation revised in 2021; revision of Regulation possibly on the horizon[b]
	Experimentalist governance	Experimentalist governance

Notes: [a] As part of the broader retail investment strategy due by mid-2022, itself embedded in the wider new Capital Markets Union action plan; [b] building on the above strategy and action plan. *Source*: author.

just as suggested in gas and communications (Chapters 3 and 4), will caution that experimentalist architectures do not always translate into experimentalist processes.

Second, the chapter reinforces the argument that actors are more likely to engage in experimentalism under conditions of greater cognitive uncertainty as well as stronger political opposition, independently of how centralized or multipolar the distribution of legal powers might be. Like the sub-case of competition regulation against tech giants (Chapter 4), the sub-case of CRAs shows that actors may engage in experimentalist processes even if, *de jure*, they possess exceptionally centralized powers. The ESMA is the single supervisor of CRAs and holds life-or-death licensing powers over them. Yet, it—as well as other higher-level actors—has been careful about not interfering with credit ratings or methodologies, leaving ample discretion on this key task to CRAs; not to mention the option of creating a European public CRA, which was considered but not pursued. This finding thus confirms that multipolar distributions of legal power are not a necessary condition for experimentalism, in contrast to that literature's expectations but as argued in the communications Chapter (4). The pharmaceuticals case will show that such a power distribution is not a sufficient condition for experimentalism either (Chapter 6), as already found in gas and communications (Chapters 3 and 4).

In contrast, both finance sub-cases were marked by high uncertainty as well as strong opposition, which helps to explain their similarly experimentalist processes. Actors recognized that no credit rating or methodology can be perfectly set *ex ante*, not even by the Big Three holding considerable epistemic authority. Equally, they anticipated that changes in market developments or the emergence of new types of PRIIPs were likely and that issues could arise during implementation, as they immediately did. For example, PRIIPs providers found themselves obliged to share with customers return scenarios that were totally unrealistic. Thus, one driver for experimentalist discretion, reviews, and revisions was the open recognition of uncertainty and particularly the impossibility of eliminating it *ex ante*. However, actors engaged in these more inclusive processes, leaving more lower-level discretion for political reasons, too. Thus, in the CRAs sub-case the industry strongly resisted any interference on ratings or methodologies and, obviously, the creation of a public CRA. Similarly, in the PRIIPs sub-case, actors including the Commission were aware of the need for building coalitions to facilitate the smooth implementation of unprecedented, highly redistributive information disclosure requirements that apply across all areas of financial services. The positive influence on experimentalism of functional demands—here, uncertainty—is consistent with the expectations of the literature on experimentalist governance but at odds with those of the literature on regulatory networks. The latter studies, on the other hand, are in harmony with the finding that political factors (namely, opposition) aids non-hierarchical governance, including the experimentalist specimen. These findings, which are consistent across all the previous chapters, will also be corroborated in Chapter 6.

Third, and finally, the finance case provides a further confirmation that experimentalist processes tend to rely both on the shadow of hierarchy and on penalty defaults rather than on either one or the other. Constant surveillance by the ESMA has aided the implementation of CRAs regulation. In a growing number of instances, the ESMA has detected and punished infringements by CRAs—including by the Big Three. Conversely, the regulation of PRIIPs was recently supported by the threat of the Commission of using its delegated implementing power to replace the ESAs in rule formulation, should have they failed to overcome gridlock within their boards. Thus, while the first sub-case relied on the menace of negative fines, the second built on the threat of specific positive rules. Table 5.2 illustrates the mechanisms underpinning experimentalist governance in finance. The chapter thus provides additional evidence, in contrast to the digital sub-case (Chapter 4) but in line with the electricity and gas cases (Chapters 2 and 3), that the two mechanisms are not mutually exclusive. Whilst the pharmaceutical case (Chapter 6) will offer a second demonstration that penalty defaults might operate on their own, this will

Table 5.2 Mechanisms underpinning experimentalist governance in EU financial regulation, 2011–2021

Issue	Shadow of positive hierarchy	Negative penalty defaults
CRAs	None	Rules implemented by CRAs under constant threat of fines by the ESMA, regularly imposed from 2015 onwards
PRIIPs	Agreement on draft binding technical standard achieved within the EIOPA's board after Commission's 2020 threat of exercising its delegated powers directly	None

Source: author.

not outweigh the overall evidence that, most commonly, penalty defaults and shadow of hierarchy work together.

Overall, the regulation of European financial markets over the past decade shows that experimentalist structures such as the ESAs have indeed led to governance processes marked by lower-level discretion, reviews, and revisions, as opposed to the development and enforcement of stable rules by higher-level actors. Key actors refrained from hierarchical governance even where, legally speaking, they were equipped with extraordinarily centralized powers, as in the CRAs example. This is because they have been under great cognitive and political pressures, which favoured rules moulded upon lower-level discretion and corrected in the light of reviews of implementation experience. Finally, to induce otherwise recalcitrant CRAs and NCAs to participate and overcome stalemate, experimentalist processes did not limit themselves to either the shadow of hierarchy or penalty defaults but leveraged both.

6

Same Structure, Different Processes, and Trajectories

European Pharmaceutical Markets 1995–2022

Although public health, and specifically medicines, have, and will always be, crucial, it is hard to think of a time when this has been more apparent. The Coronavirus (COVID-19) first identified in December 2019 in a then unknown Chinese city, Wuhan, has rapidly spread worldwide ever since. As a result, at the time of writing, there have been almost half a billion confirmed cases and seven million deaths.[1] If that was not enough, the pandemic has also resulted in the most severe global recession since the 1929 Great Depression.[2] While the World Health Organisation has just determined that the ongoing pandemic no longer constitutes an emergency, and the world is still wrestling with its effects on public health and the economy, the COVID-19 crisis has painfully demonstrated that the only way out is the provision of vaccines. These have been developed by pharmaceutical companies and authorized by medicine authorities in record times, and then administered by health systems with an equally impressive military organization.

Yet, the COVID-19 pandemic has also brought into public view the risks and challenges of authorizing the use of medicines. While the most common side effects of COVID-19 vaccines are mild (e.g. tiredness, headache, temperature) and do not last longer than a week, in rare cases, there have been much more serious problems, namely, allergic reactions, blood clotting, and heart inflammation.[3] Besides the at times deadly effects on the individual at hand, moreover, these serious side effects and the uncertainty surrounding why and under what conditions they emerge have stimulated distrust in the vaccines, in turn, causing additional deaths because of the lack of vaccination.[4] To be

---

[1] See https://covid19.who.int (last accessed 10 May 2023).
[2] See https://blogs.imf.org/2020/04/14/the-great-lockdown-worst-economic-downturn-since-the-great-depression (last accessed 16 February 2023).
[3] See https://www.nhs.uk/conditions/coronavirus-covid-19/coronavirus-vaccination/safety-and-side-effects (last accessed 16 February 2023).
[4] See, e.g. *The Guardian*, 29 August 2021; *Il Messaggero*, 11 September 2021.

Experimentalist Governance. Bernardo Rangoni, Oxford University Press. © Bernardo Rangoni (2023).
DOI: 10.1093/oso/9780198849919.003.0007

sure, while dramatically epitomized by COVID-19 vaccines, these issues apply much more widely to any medicine, as this chapter will show. What is more, as also emerged during the pandemic, these challenges take place against the backdrop of 'big pharma'—companies that are comparable to the giants dominating digital technologies and energy markets and that possess troubling influence on pharmaceutical knowledge, medical prescriptions, and even the framing of health crises (Hauray et al. 2021).

As with all the domains in the book, pharmaceuticals is not only vital but also hosts experimentalist architectures that offer the potential for experimentalist governance processes. Rather than being marked by top-down development and enforcement of stable rules, such processes feature discretion for lower-level actors to contribute to rule-making, frequent review of their implementation experiences, and regular rule revision in their light. The chief experimentalist structure in pharmaceuticals is the European Medicines Agency (EMA). Since its creation in 1995, the EMA's key task has been to provide scientific advice to the European Commission on applications for centralized marketing authorizations, which, if granted, are directly valid in all member states. Today, this is the most used procedure for new, innovative medicines such as those against cancer and HIV/AIDS. It differs from national authorization procedures, used before the creation of the EMA and still employed for less innovative medicines such as generics. Yet, the centralized procedure is not as centralized as its name suggests. In fact, the EMA is composed of experts from national regulatory authorities (NRAs), themselves relying on broader networks of thousands of regulatory officials and representatives of patients and doctors alike. In addition, regulated firms play a key role too. Member states, moreover, have the final say on the adoption of the Commission's draft implementing decisions as these must be adopted in comitology. Furthermore, the EMA has also set up a European Union (EU)-wide electronic database for monitoring adverse effects of authorized medicines, building on mandatory reporting by NRAs (Sabel and Zeitlin 2008: 283–286; see also Hauray 2006). Such an EU post-authorization regime, which also applies to nationally authorized medicines and is coordinated by the EMA, is so important that the Agency considers the 'pharmacovigilance' legislation that came into effect in 2012 the biggest change to human medicines regulation in the EU since 1995.[5] In short, the EMA and the wider institutional setting within which it is embedded promise to leverage NRAs and

---

[5] This chapter focuses on human medicines though the EMA is also responsible for veterinary medicines.

additional lower-level stakeholders, monitor the performance of medicines once authorized, and revise initial marketing authorizations as appropriate.

Furthermore, since the EMA and the strengthened pharmacovigilance regime it coordinates have been operational since 1995 and 2012, respectively, this case allows analysis over significant periods, in turn permitting assessment of rival claims and previous findings about the long-term durability of experimentalist governance.

At the same time, the pharmaceutical domain offers analytically useful similarity and variation in factors potentially affecting experimentalist processes. The distribution of legal powers has been polyarchic or multipolar in both sub-cases, notably because, as typical of the EU, the Commission is subject to constraints on the exercise of hierarchical authority, given that ultimately it requires member states' approval in comitology. Because of the similar and firm polyarchic distribution of powers, the experimentalist literature would expect similar experimentalist processes across the board. In contrast, as the chapter will show, uncertainty and opposition have varied. For innovative medicines like the COVID-19 vaccine developed by BioNTech and Pfizer,[6] actors have been aware of their cognitive uncertainty and have sought decisions by consensus with the EMA and the NRAs at the heart of it. By contrast, for conventional infusion solutions containing hydroxyethyl-starch (HES) that are used to replace lost blood volume and in associated falls in blood pressure,[7] by the late 2010s, the Commission could rely both on an earlier assessment and decision taken at the beginning of that decade and on a coalition led by Germany, which had grown ever since. The experimentalist literature would thus expect varying degrees of experimentalism, positively associated with perceived uncertainty. Conversely, analyses of regulatory networks would expect different degrees of uncertainty—a specimen of functional factors—to be positively associated with hierarchical governance.

---

[6] This chapter focuses on this specific COVID-19 vaccine as it is the most widely used in the EU: although granted marketing authorization only at the end of 2020, at the time of writing, 570 million doses have been given (see https://www.ema.europa.eu/en/human-regulatory/overview/public-health-threats/coronavirus-disease-covid-19/treatments-vaccines/vaccines-covid-19/safety-covid-19-vaccines, last accessed 16 February 2023).

[7] It is beyond the scope of the chapter to systematically examine all conventional medicines that were authorized through national procedures (as distinct from the centralized one). The chapter thus focuses on one example, infusion solutions containing HES, which are medicines used to replace lost blood volume in hypovolaemia (low blood volume caused by dehydration or blood loss) and hypo-volemic shock (a steep fall in blood pressure caused by drop in blood volume), and hence employed in critically ill patients including patients with sepsis (bacterial infection of the blood), or burn or trauma injuries, or patients who are undergoing surgery (EMA 2013a: 1). As always, one should be cautious about the extent to which a specific example might be representative (here, of all conventional medicines authorized through national procedures). But, as the chapter will show, the example does offer a useful contrast with innovative medicines, including COVID-19 vaccines.

The same analyses, finally, would anticipate political opposition to favour non-hierarchical governance, and thus less experimentalism in the regulation of HES solutions in the late 2010s, once a powerful coalition had become available to the Commission.

Finally, as in all cases examined in this book, several mechanisms are available to induce otherwise recalcitrant actors to overcome gridlock and participate in experimentalist processes, notably both shadows of positive hierarchy and negative penalty defaults. Illustrations of the former are the general capacity of the Commission to propose EU legislation as well as the sector-specific possibility of deviating from the EMA's opinion, both of which can cast a shadow under which the EMA and NRAs in its committees deliberate. Nevertheless, the Commission can also employ negative incentives, threatening to impose penalties upon pharmaceutical firms via general competition or sectoral-specific regulation, should these firms engage in anti-competitive behaviour or ignore the information disclosure requirements embedded in their marketing authorizations.

On the whole, then, pharmaceuticals is both a crucial domain and a final test for the arguments about the relationship between experimentalist structures, processes, and outcomes developed in the previous four empirical chapters. First, it offers an opportunity to examine how far experimentalist arrangements translate into experimentalist behaviour, with the previous chapters having supplied enthusiastic and cautious findings in equal amount (cf. Chapters 2 and 5 with Chapters 3 and 4). Second, the case allows probing of polar opposite claims about the long-term sustainability of experimentalist governance, with foregoing chapters having overall challenged the view that this form of governance is doomed to be temporary (cf. Chapters 2, 3, and 4 with Chapter 3). Third, the case permits a final examination of the conditions for experimentalist governance. Thus far, all chapters have shown that both uncertainty and opposition are positive factors for experimentalism, while some chapters have suggested that multipolar distributions of power are neither necessary (Chapters 4 and 5) nor sufficient (Chapters 3 and 4) to it. Finally, the pharmaceutical case allows further exploration of the mechanisms actually used to overcome stalemate, with previous findings suggesting, overall, that shadow of hierarchy and penalty defaults are not necessarily rival (cf. Chapters 2, 3, and 5 with Chapter 4).

The case of pharmaceuticals contributes to four general arguments. First, it underlines, once again, that experimentalist structures do not lead to experimentalist processes always and inevitably. In the vast majority of cases—including the BioNTech and Pfizer COVID-19 vaccine, the European

Commission builds on the opinion developed by the EMA thanks to NRAs and stakeholders, employs the networked agency to pool all suspected adverse reactions into a single database and then analyse them, and regularly revises initial authorizations accordingly. Yet, the regulation of conventional HES solutions in the late 2010s demonstrates that, exceptionally, actors might pursue hierarchical processes too.[8] There, monitoring focused on compliance enforcement rather than performance review, and the Commission deviated from the opinion developed by the EMA and the NRAs composing it, limiting revisions to new risk minimization measures and compliance-monitoring provisions, as opposed to the outright suspension of the marketing authorization recommended by the experimentalist network. This finding thus reinforces earlier warnings from the gas and communication cases (Chapters 3 and 4) against equating experimentalist architectures and processes.

Second, the chapter highlights that both self-reinforcing and self-limiting trajectories are possible. After granting a conditional marketing authorization of the BioNTech and Pfizer COVID-19 vaccine in December 2020, the Commission, building on the EMA's recommendations, has revised the initial authorization eight times already, notably extending the use of the medicine to progressively younger people and, at the same time, updating the relevant information in the light of 582,074 reports of suspected side effects. By spanning eight cycles in just fourteen months, this example thus demonstrates the durability of experimentalism, bringing the recursive rule-making and revisions central to it at an unprecedented pace. Nevertheless, the example of HES solutions for infusion shows that the opposite trajectory is possible, too. In the early 2010s, the Commission followed the opinion that the EMA had developed jointly with NRAs, regulated firms, and external experts, building on reviews of new data from scientific literature and companies. This led to a major revision of the original marketing authorization, which mandated that HES solutions remained available for restricted patient populations but should no longer be used in patients with sepsis or burn injuries or critically ill patients. Yet, in the late 2010s, reviews revealed a lack of compliance with such a decision, showing that the medicine continued to be supplied also to these vulnerable patients despite the restrictions introduced in 2013. At that point, while the EMA—and most of the NRAs therein—recommended suspending HES solutions from the market, the Commission took a less drastic

---

[8] To be sure, the chapter does not imply that, in the pharmaceutical domain, actors have used experimentalist and hierarchical processes in equal measure. On the contrary, it will suggest that the former have been the rule and the latter the exception. What is put forward here, however, is a causal argument about the conditions favouring the use of experimentalist or hierarchical governance.

162 SAME STRUCTURE, DIFFERENT PROCESSES, AND TRAJECTORIES

decision, limiting revisions to a reinforcement of risk minimization measures intended to aid—together with new compliance enforcement provisions—the already existing (but poorly implemented) restrictions. Without altering the overall balance emerging from the previous chapters, which provides stronger support to the durability of experimentalism, the chapter thus offers a second illustration—in addition to that provided in gas (Chapter 3)—that either route is possible.

Third, the chapter confirms previous findings on the positive influence on experimentalism of both cognitive uncertainty and political opposition as well as on the incapacity of polyarchic distributions of power to act, in themselves, as bulwarks against hierarchical governance. The first sub-case is character-ized by higher uncertainty since the medicines authorized via the centralized procedure are particularly innovative. This is even more true for COVID-19 vaccines, which were developed and authorized with unprecedented rapidity. Strong political opposition, in the sense that coalitions are not readily avail-able but must be formed to facilitate subsequent rule adoption, also marks this sub-case. The other sub-case, by contrast, in the late 2010s, featured low uncer-tainty and opposition. This is because the Commission could build on the pre-vious early 2010s experience whereby it had already addressed the regulation of HES solutions for infusion, itself a conventional medicine. Equally, by the late 2010s, the resistance of some countries—first and foremost, Germany—against the outright suspension of a medicine widely used in their domestic clinical practices had grown from a state of isolation a few years earlier into a large coalition bringing together several member states. It was thanks to this strong coalition (and confidence) that the Commission could deviate from the opinion of most NRAs within the EMA and nevertheless gain approval in comitology. Such a powerful political coalition thus explains how the Com-mission was able to overcome the multipolar constraints posed by comitology, engaging in hierarchical governance in the face of polyarchic distributions of legal power.[9] In contrast to experimentalist expectations, these findings thus

---

[9] One could challenge the interpretation presented here, suggesting that this instance is better under-stood as a case of 'power politics' in that the Commission followed the preferences of a major member state, such as Germany, rather than imposing its own view upon it and all other member states. Put another way, this is not a 'pure' illustration of hierarchical governance. However, as clarified in the Introduction as well as in Chapter 1 (and illustrated empirically in various chapters), the book treats hierarchical and experimentalist governance as ideal-types that empirical developments can only partially approximate. In this case, although the higher-level actor did not impose its view on (all) lower-level ones, by forging an alliance with Germany and some other member states, the Commis-sion did impose a view (which it made its own) on other opposing lower-level actors, most notably most regulatory authorities sitting within the EMA. What is more, these considerations only concern the first indicator to distinguish experimentalist and hierarchical processes. The two additional indi-cators central to the analytical framework further make the case for a hierarchical interpretation since

show that polyarchy is not, in itself, a sufficient condition for experimentalism, as already suggested in natural gas and electronic communications (Chapters 3 and 4). In line with all previous chapters and the experimentalist literature but in contrast to that on regulatory networks, moreover, the findings show that functional factors—specifically, uncertainty—are positive rather than negative conditions for non-hierarchical governance. Finally, consistently with both previous chapters and regulatory networks expectations, political opposition aided non-hierarchical governance, including the experimentalist specimen.

Finally, the chapter shows that in this domain, experimentalist processes avoided breakdown by relying exclusively on negative penalty defaults rather than also shadows of positive hierarchy. Once having acquired the marketing authorization, pharmaceutical firms are under the constant threat of fines that the Commission, thanks to the support of the EMA, can impose upon them. By contrast, the Commission did not cast a credible threat over the EMA of retaking control of the marketing authorization process, not least because the Commission has almost never deviated from the EMA's opinion. This finding, therefore, offers a second demonstration, in addition to that already provided from digital communications (Chapter 4), that penalty defaults may operate on their own. However, it does not offset the overall stronger evidence from electricity, gas, and finance (Chapters 2, 3, and 5) that, most frequently, penalty defaults and shadows of hierarchy work together.

The remainder of the chapter begins by introducing the experimentalist architecture identified in the pharmaceutical domain and its potential of leading to rule-making based on lower-level actors, frequent review of their implementation experiences, and regular revisions in their light. The chapter then compares the processes actually employed under the same architecture, stressing how variation followed an initial similarity. It goes on to explain such a variation, discussing how distributions of legal power cannot account for it, given that they were identical and constantly multipolar. Instead, it emphasizes functional uncertainty and political opposition, which varied consistently with the findings. Finally, the chapter examines the mechanisms employed to induce participation in experimentalist processes of otherwise reluctant actors, highlighting their negative nature and thus that, in this case, penalty defaults were the only mechanism in town. It concludes by offering wider implications for experimentalist governance.

---

reviews focused more on compliance monitoring than on performance assessment, and revisions were curbed.

Experimentalist Structures

The EU pharmaceutical domain is governed by institutional structures with clear experimentalist potential. In Europe, all medicines must have a marketing authorization before patients can use them. Companies have two ways of obtaining such authorization: national marketing authorization procedures and the centralized procedure. In the former, individual member states authorize the medicines for use in their own countries. In the latter, instead, the EMA plays a key role by giving an opinion that may result in a single marketing authorization valid throughout the EU. Companies thus use the centralized procedure to market their medicines throughout the Union, thanks to a single marketing authorization. This procedure is compulsory for the most innovative medicines, such as those for rare diseases (known as 'orphan drugs'), HIV, cancer, neurodegenerative disorders, diabetes, and auto-immune diseases as well as for products such as those derived from biotechnology and gene therapy. It can also apply to other medicinal products that, for example, constitute a significant therapeutic, scientific, or technical innovation. As a result, today, the great majority of new, innovative medicines passes through the centralized authorization procedure to be marketed in the EU. The national authorization procedures, by contrast, apply to medicines that were authorized before the entry into operation of the EMA in 1995 and to less innovative medicines such as generics (European Parliament and Council 2004: recs. 7–9, art. 3).[10]

The literature has underlined the multi-level, networked, and deliberative character of both the EMA and the wider institutional framework in which the Agency is embedded (Sabel and Zeitlin 2008: 283–286; see also Hauray 2006). When the EMA receives a marketing authorization application under the centralized procedure, it carries out a scientific assessment and eventually gives a recommendation on whether the medicine should be marketed and, if so, on the text for the packaging and the risk management strategies for the post-authorization phase (see below). The assessment of a new medicine, which usually lasts around a year, requires an initial assessment and list of questions, a further assessment and list of outstanding questions, further consultations, and a final discussion and adoption of opinion, plus a possible re-examination triggered by a request of the applicant firm. Throughout the procedure, the EMA relies on its Committee for Medicinal products for Human Use (CHMP), which consists of experts nominated by the NRAs

---

[10] See also https://www.ema.europa.eu/en/about-us/what-we-do/authorisation-medicines (last accessed 16 February 2023).

of each member state. But it also builds on a twin committee, the Pharma-covigilance Risk Assessment Committee (PRAC), which deals with the way risks will be minimized if the medicine is authorized and how more informa-tion will be obtained about the medicine's risks and uncertainties. In addition, the EMA also builds on additional members, who offer expertise in particular scientific areas, and on applicant firms themselves, which may be requested to provide data and clarifications on the medicine additional to the evidence initially supplied (European Parliament and Council 2004: arts. 5–15).[11] It is only after this highly inclusive and interactive procedure that the Commission, which has the authority over all centrally authorized medicines, may transform the EMA's recommendations into legally binding decisions. Yet, not even the Commission can act unilaterally. Indeed, it must send its draft implementing decisions to the Standing Committee on Medicinal Products for Human Use, allowing for their scrutiny by member states. Once a favourable position is reached, the draft decision is eventually adopted via comitology procedures (European Parliament and Council 2004: arts. 10, 87).

The experimentalist features of the institutional framework are not lim-ited to marketing authorization, however; they also extend to the post-authorization phase. The creation of a common database noticed by the literature almost fifteen years ago (Sabel and Zeitlin 2008: 285) has, since 2012, evolved into a fully fledged pharmacovigilance system. Based on the observa-tion that adverse drug reactions and 'noxious and unintended' responses to medicines caused around 197,000 deaths per year in the EU, in the early 2010s, the hitherto safety monitoring of medicines (European Parliament and Coun-cil 2001: arts. 101–108, 2004: arts. 16–29) was greatly strengthened. Since the reinforcement of the pharmacovigilance framework and the creation of a dis-tinct committee dedicated to it (i.e. the PRAC), the EMA has been tasked to play an increasingly important role in monitoring medicines' safety across Europe. Once a medicine is authorized for use in the EU, by building on NRAs, firms, doctors, and patients alike, the EMA is expected to constantly moni-tor its safety and take action if new information indicates that the medicine is no longer as safe and effective as previously thought. The safety monitoring involves a number of routine activities. These include assessing the way risks associated with a medicine will be managed and monitored once it is autho-rized, continuously monitoring suspected side effects reported by patients and health-care professionals, or identified in new clinical studies, or reported in

---

[11] For a complete, detailed description of the procedure, see https://www.ema.europa.eu/en/human-regulatory/marketing-authorisation/evaluation-medicines-step-step (last accessed 16 February 2023).

scientific publications, regularly assessing reports submitted by the company holding the marketing authorization on the benefit–risk balance of a medicine in real life and assessing the design and results of post-authorization safety studies that were required at the time of authorization. Importantly for one of this chapter's sub-cases, through 'referral procedures' that can be triggered by a member state or the European Commission in case of concerns about the safety, effectiveness of risk minimization measures, or benefit–risk balance of a medicine, the EMA can also carry out reviews of medicines that were originally authorized via national routes (European Parliament and Council 2010d, e; European Commission 2012f). By design, the pharmacovigilance system thus aims at the rapid detection of changes in relevant information and the correction of initial decisions accordingly, which might range from merely amending the information available to patients and health-care professionals, through restricting the use of a medicine, to suspending it altogether.

In short, the centralized marketing authorization procedure epitomizes the rule-making based on lower-level proposals characteristic of experimentalist governance, just as the post-authorization pharmacovigilance system, strengthened in 2012, embodies the regular reviews and revisions at the heart of it. But to what extent have the experimentalist promises brought by these institutional structures been really honoured? The chapter now turns to this question.

Same Structure, Different Processes, and Trajectories: European Pharmaceutical Markets 1995–2022

Analysis of EU pharmaceutical regulation in action from 1995 onwards reveals a general pattern as well as exceptions to it. For the vast majority of innovative medicines—including the BioNTech and Pfizer COVID-19 vaccine, experimentalist governance has dominated the scene. Thus, to grant these medicines marketing authorization, the Commission has leveraged lower-lever actors like NRAs and firms by employing the experimentalist structure of the EMA. Once authorized, the EMA has constantly assessed implementation experience with the use of these medicines, notably pooling data on suspected side effects from lower-level actors. These reviews have frequently led to revisions of the initial authorizations, most commonly updating the product information that must be provided to doctors and patients. The specific BioNTech and Pfizer COVID-19 vaccine, moreover, demonstrates how experimentalist processes may travel across distinct policy cycles. Despite the very limited period between initial marketing authorization and time of writing (fourteen months), this medicine has experienced eight revisions of its initial authorization, each of them based on reviews of implementation experiences with the vaccine, which prompted extensions of its use to additional categories of population as well as updates of the information on possible side effects.

HES solutions for infusion, however, demonstrate that exceptions to the general experimentalist pattern can, and do, exist. This medicine, which is conventional and thus had initially taken the national authorization route, has seen its marketing authorization revised twice in the 2010s. In 2012–2013, processes were experimentalist. Rule-making greatly relied on lower-level actors in that the Commission followed the EMA's opinion, and the EMA, in turn, built on NRAs, additional experts, and firms. Reviews considered new data, both from novel studies and from additional submissions by firms. This led to major revisions: the use of the medicine became forbidden to certain patient populations. After these experimentalist beginnings, however, processes took a more hierarchical turn. In 2017–2018, reviews geared towards compliance monitoring revealed that HES solutions were still being supplied to forbidden patients. The Commission did not follow the opinion elaborated by the EMA by building on the majority of NRAs therein. This curbed revisions, which entailed strengthened risk minimization measures rather than the outright removal of the medicine from the market. Most recently, the compliance-monitoring provisions set up in the late 2010s have just revealed that HES solutions continue to be used despite the 2018 (and 2013) restrictions. In this example, therefore, experimentalist governance followed a self-limiting pathway as experimentalist origins led to hierarchical governance.

Carrying on with experimentalism, for innovative pharmaceuticals such as COVID-19 vaccines

Looking at the governance actually used to regulate pharmaceuticals in the EU reveals that experimentalism is the general rule. From the creation of the EMA and the introduction of the centralized procedure in 1995 to the present day, the Commission has deviated from the EMA's opinion on marketing authorization in a handful of cases only (Krapohl 2008: 100–102; EUI 17a, EUI 17b; EUI 18; EUI 19; EUI 20; EUI 24a; EUI 25).[12] This is impressive, considering that during the two-and-a-half-decade-long period, the applications submitted

---

[12] The European Commission could not supply the author with a precise figure.

for marketing authorization were 1,569.[13] Rule-making has thus built on lower-level actors because the Commission has employed the architecture of the EMA to leverage NRAs, broader networks of experts, and regulated firms, all of which have a say in the marketing authorization procedure. This also applies to the specific example of the BioNTech and Pfizer COVID-19 vaccine, for which the Commission granted a conditional marketing authorization in December 2020, based on the EMA's positive recommendation, itself built on NRAs, experts, and firms (EMA 2021). The first indicator of experimentalist processes therefore is that rules were not made and imposed from the top, that is, directly by the Commission.

A second indicator that governance processes were experimentalist is that, after having granted marketing authorizations, actors have constantly reviewed implementation experience with authorized medicines. Since the entry into operation of the strengthened pharmacovigilance system in 2012, the EMA has been playing a pivotal role in post-authorization monitoring, in collaboration with NRAs, firms holding marketing authorizations, patients, and health-care professionals. All these lower-level actors have, in particular, participated in studies and reported suspected adverse drug reactions (Santoro et al. 2017). Through this network, the EMA has been keeping up to date the 'EudraVigilance' database, which at the end of 2018 stored around 14.6 million relations referring to more than 8 million individual cases of suspected adverse reactions (Potts et al. 2020: 521). As reported by the former Chair of the EMA's PRAC, a PRAC member, and several EMA officials, during its first six years of activity, the pharmacovigilance system centred on the PRAC reviewed over 26 thousand potential signals. Most of these (around 55%) came from spontaneous adverse reaction data in EudraVigilance, while other potential signals emerged from national reviews, scientific literature, studies, and communications from other regulatory authorities. Through activities of validation, confirmation, prioritization, and analysis, the EMA then filtered the over 26 thousand potential signals initially detected, eventually assessing 453 of them in depth (Potts et al. 2020: 522–523; see also European Commission

---

[13] See the European public assessment reports (available at https://www.ema.europa.eu/en/medicines/download-medicine-data, last accessed 16 February 2023).

This finding is all the more remarkable when considering the organizational changes that occurred within the European Commission during the period analysed. As suggested by the Head of Legal Services of the EMA, the allocation of responsibilities over the pharmaceutical domain has shifted from the Directorate-General (DG) Enterprise and Industry through DG SANCO for Health and Consumers to DG SANTE for Health and Food Safety. This means that within the Commission there are now more experts in the pharmaceutical sector (e.g. biologists)—as distinct from the economic experts of DG Enterprise, who can understand the EMA's opinion and thus no longer 'copy and paste it' into the Commission's decision (EUI 24a).

2017e; HMA and EMA 2019). These considerations apply even more so to the BioNTech and Pfizer vaccine, which actors have put under 'additional monitoring' and have thus reviewed even more intensively than other innovative medicines (EMA 2021: 129). At the time of writing, EudraVigilance contained a total of 582,074 cases of suspected side effects spontaneously reported, 7,023 of which indicating a fatal outcome (EMA 2022a: 5).

Third, and finally, the review of implementation experiences has often led to the revision of the initial marketing authorizations. Thus, the in-depth assessment of 453 potential signals during 2012–2018 has led the EMA to issue an equal number of recommendations for revision, which the Commission has regularly followed. Half of these concerned amendments to the information on the medicine provided to doctors and patients. One-third concerned the inclusion of pharmacovigilance activities and routine monitoring in the periodic safety update reports on the safety of the medicine. In a minority of cases (twenty-nine), the PRAC considered it necessary to recommend changes in the use of the medicine, for example, restricting its use in women planning pregnancy (Potts et al. 2020: 523–524; see also European Commission 2017e; HMA and EMA 2019). Indirectly, these figures thus confirm what was highlighted by several interviewees, namely, that the suspension or revocation of a marketing authorization is nowadays extremely rare (EUI 17a, EUI 17b; EUI 18; EUI 19; EUI 20; EUI 24a; EUI 25). Hard figures aside, it is also worth noting the emphasis that pharmacovigilance leaders put on a 'culture of continuous improvement' (Potts et al. 2020: 528), which resonates with experimentalist governance recursiveness. Periodic revisions have affected COVID-19 vaccines, too (EUI 24b). Indeed, as new data emerged from studies not available at the time of the initial authorization and most of all from experiences after clinical trials, actors revised the marketing authorization for the BioNTech and Pfizer vaccine no less than eight times. These revisions have, notably, extended the vaccine's use to adolescents aged twelve to fifteen years and then to children aged five to eleven years, as well as updated the product information to include myocarditis and pericarditis as side effects and added data on use during pregnancy and breastfeeding.[14]

In sum, analysis of the operation of the EU centralized marketing authorization and post-authorization pharmacovigilance has shown that the architecture centred on the EMA has, indeed, honoured its experimentalist promises,

---

[14] See 'Key developments since authorisation', https://www.ema.europa.eu/en/medicines/human/EPAR/comirnaty (last accessed 16 February 2023).

leading to experimentalist processes that have been both pervasive and resilient. Yet, exceptions to this general rule are possible.

Diverting towards hierarchy, for conventional HES solutions for infusion

In a first phase in the early 2010s, experimentalist governance dominated the regulation of HES solutions for blood infusion. That is, infusion solutions containing hydroxyethyl-starch, which were, until then, frequently used for blood volume replacement; had been approved via national procedures; and were available in all member states. The process started in 2012, when the German NRA triggered a referral, requesting the EMA, and specifically the PRAC, to carry out an EU-level review.

The first indicator that processes were initially experimentalist is that the review of infusion solutions containing HES was requested by the German NRA following three recent studies, which compared HES—which belongs to the class known as 'colloids'—with the other main type of medicines used for volume replacement, called 'crystalloids' (EMA 2013a). The studies showed that patients with severe sepsis treated with HES were at greater risk of kidney injury requiring dialysis and also that in patients treated with HES, there was a greater risk of mortality (Brunkhorst et al. 2008; Myburgh et al. 2012; Perner et al. 2012). The EMA, and specifically its committee responsible for the evaluation of safety issues, thus assessed data from the scientific literature as well as data submitted by the relevant companies including new evidence that became available in 2013 from novel studies and fresh information from firms (EMA 2013a, b). In short, reviews focused more on assessing the performance of lower-level implementation experience than on ensuring compliance.

Far from being unilateral and top-down, moreover, rule-making relied on lower-level actors extensively. Based on the review of available evidence and advice from a group of external experts, the NRAs composing the EMA initially concluded that the benefits of HES no longer justified the risks that had recently surfaced. The EMA thus recommended that the marketing authorization for this medicine be suspended and that 'the suspension should remain in place unless the marketing authorisation holder can provide convincing data to identify a group of patients in whom the benefits of the medicines outweigh their risks' (EMA 2013a: 1–2). Following the PRAC recommendation, some of the marketing authorization holders requested a re-examination, as the procedure allows. The PRAC then analysed and considered 'new evidence that was not available at the time of the initial recommendation, including new studies [and] new information and commitments from companies for additional studies and risk minimisation activities' (EMA 2013b: 1). On that basis, the PRAC partially changed its mind. It confirmed that HES should no longer be used in patients with sepsis or burn injuries or who were critically ill. But it agreed that this medicine could continue to be used in patients with low blood volume caused by acute blood loss, where treatment with alternative infusion solutions (i.e. crystalloids) alone was not considered sufficient and provided that additional risk minimization measures were put in place, for example, that HES solutions were not used for more than twenty-four hours and that patients' kidney function were monitored thereafter (EMA 2013b: 1–2). As HES-containing solutions for infusion had all been authorized nationally, the PRAC recommendation was forwarded to the Co-ordination Group for Mutual Recognition and Decentralised Procedures—Human (CMDh), a body representing member states and responsible for ensuring harmonized safety standards for medicines authorized via national procedures across the EU. This group endorsed the PRAC recommendation, albeit by majority (EMA 2013c). The Commission endorsed it too, making it legally binding throughout the Union (EMA 2013d). Thus, rule-making involved a multitude of actors operating at distinct governance levels.

Finally, these processes led to major revisions. Actors decided that the hitherto widespread HES solutions could no longer be used except in restricted patient populations, insofar as no alternative solutions were sufficient and measures to minimize potential risks in these patients were implemented. In addition to curbing the use of this medicine, actors also decided to update the product information and that further studies on its use in elective surgery and trauma patients be carried out (EMA 2013d).

Yet, a few years later, governance processes turned their back on experimentalism. In 2017, the PRAC initiated a new review of HES solutions for infusion at the request of the Swedish NRA. The review was triggered by results from two drug utilization studies submitted by the relevant firms. These indicated that HES solutions continued to be used in critically ill patients as well as in patients with sepsis and kidney injury, precisely as forbidden by the restrictions introduced in 2013 to reduce risks of kidney problems and death in these patient populations (EMA 2018a). At this stage, reviews thus focused less on appraising the performance of implementation experiences than on verifying adherence to the existing rules.

Rule-making, moreover, came to build less on lower-level actors, specifically the NRAs within the EMA. Based on the monitoring that had revealed lack of compliance with the restrictions introduced in 2013, in view of the serious risks that certain patient populations were exposed to and that alternative treatment options were available, the PRAC concluded that introducing additional measures would have been insufficient. Instead, it recommended the outright suspension of the marketing authorization for HES solutions (EMA 2018a), albeit with the disagreement of the German and another member (EMA 2018b: 67–68). By contrast, the CMDh suggested that HES solutions should remain on the market provided that a combination of additional measures to protect patients be implemented (EMA 2018c: 1). It is worth noting that a few months earlier, such a body—representing member states—had endorsed the PRAC's recommendation, albeit by majority. Indeed, its subsequently divergent position was accompanied by a statement undersigned by CMDh members from no less than twelve states, who denounced that the CMDh position 'goes against the scientifically based recommendations of the PRAC' (EMA 2018b: 64–66).[15] Thereafter, at a meeting of the comitology committee scrutinizing the Commission, some member states raised new questions that they considered had not been sufficiently addressed. They prompted the Commission to refer back to the PRAC (and the CMDh) for further consideration of any possible unmet medical need that could result from the suspension of the authorization and of the feasibility and likely effectiveness of additional risk minimization measures (EMA 2018b: 40). However, the PRAC did not alter its recommendation and nor did the CMDh. At that point, the Commission took a legally binding decision, which deviated from the EMA. Member states, nevertheless, adopted it in comitology (EMA 2018c). In summary, although the Commission did not unilaterally impose its own view on all lower-level actors, it did adopt a decision running counter to the position of most NRAs.

This led to a limitation of revisions. Rather than the categorical suspension recommended by the EMA, actors favoured a mere strengthening of risk minimization measures. These included: a controlled access programme by the companies holding the marketing authorizations to ensure that only accredited hospitals will be supplied with this medicine, warnings in the medicines' packaging and at the top of the summaries of product characteristics reminding health-care professionals that this medicine must not be used in patients with sepsis or kidney impairment or in critically ill patients, and writing directly to health-care professionals to ensure that they are fully aware of the conditions of use of the medicine and the groups of patients

---

[15] See the CMDh divergent positions, https://www.ema.europa.eu/en/medicines/human/referrals/hydroxyethyl-starch-hes-containing-medicinal-products (last accessed 16 February 2023).

that must not receive them due to an increased risk of kidney injury and death. Actors also requested companies marketing HES solutions to conduct a drug utilization study to check whether these restrictions were adhered to in clinical practice and to submit the results to the EMA (EMA 2018c).

In what appears like a dramatic replay, these compliance-monitoring provisions have just revealed that HES solutions for infusion are still being used outside the recommendations included in the product information. Since the further restrictions introduced in 2018 have not been adhered to, the PRAC has once again recommended the suspension of the marketing authorizations for this medicine (EMA 2022b). At the time of writing, it is too early to know how the Commission will choose to proceed, especially since, on this occasion, the CMDh majority position favours that of the PRAC (EMA 2022c). But what can already be appreciated is that, far from assessing the performance of lower-level implementation experiences as distinctive of experimentalism, the reviews that have begun this new policy cycle have focused on compliance monitoring, characteristic of hierarchical governance instead.

Thus, while in the early 2010s, the regulation of HES solutions for infusion was pursued through the experimentalist processes typical of EU pharmaceutical regulation more broadly, in the late 2010s, governance processes became more hierarchical in that rule-making disregarded lower-level NRAs, reviews focused mainly on compliance enforcement, and revisions were modest. But how can this variation in processes and trajectories be explained?

Conditions: Not Polyarchy and Not Just Uncertainty But Also Opposition

Looking at distributions of legal power does not bring the explanatory analysis very far. Although the widespread use of experimentalism is consistent with the multipolar or polyarchic constraints characterizing the whole sectoral regulation, the more hierarchical processes employed to regulate HES solutions in the late 2010s are not. The chapter instead argues that drawing attention to uncertainty as well as opposition helps to explain the pattern found. While actors generally recognize the impossibility of identifying all possible side effects of medicines at the marketing authorization stage, in the HES sub-case, in the late 2010s, the Commission could build on a precedent, which equipped it to know with confidence the best rules beforehand. Equally, the Commission typically seeks consensus with the EMA and the NRAs populating it, not least to facilitate smooth adoption and implementation afterwards.

Nevertheless, in the HES sub-case in the late 2010s, the Commission could rely on a strong coalition of member states led by Germany, which allowed it to deviate from the EMA's opinion and, nevertheless, still see its draft decision approved in comitology. In short, then, functional and political pressures were more influential than legal ones and were far from rival.

Identical, firmly multipolar distributions of power

The EMA is not empowered to take legally binding decisions, which are instead the responsibility of the European Commission, itself constrained by comitology committees composed of member states representatives (European Parliament and Council 2004: arts. 10, 87). Thus, distributions of legal power were polyarchic and equally so in the two sub-cases. What is more, such polyarchic or multipolar constraints were not lifted over time but remained firm.

This common, stable multipolar distribution of legal powers, therefore, cannot explain the variation observed; that is, it is hard to square with the finding that, in the late 2010s, HES solutions regulation took a hierarchical shape, in contrast to its own previous experimentalist experience as well as that of the BioNTech and Pfizer COVID-19 vaccine, themselves exemplifying the sectoral governance more generally. Dissatisfied with distributions of legal power, the chapter now shifts attention to uncertainty, which yields more explanatory value.

Different uncertainty

As the EMA itself explains, regulators have to strike a balance between making new medicines available as early as possible and waiting until sufficient information on a product's safety and efficacy is known.[16] As put by Stefano Marino, Head of the EMA's Legal Services:

> The objective is always to provide a useful medicine. Thus for example if a medicine works only in 10% of the cases or there are side effects, but at the same time there is a need for that medicine and in that moment there are no

---

[16] See https://www.ema.europa.eu/en/human-regulatory/overview/pharmacovigilance/legal-fra mework-pharmacovigilance (last accessed 16 February 2023).

alternative medicines, then this may be, provisionally, the best solution. This is actually the case [. . .] for COVID-19 [. . .] it is a rather complex task.

(EUI 24a)

As the EMA openly recognizes, the challenge is augmented by the limited amount of information that, at the time of marketing authorization, is available from clinical trials. Before a medicine is authorized, evidence of its safety and efficacy is restricted to the results from clinical trials where, no matter how extensive and thorough the trial might be, patients are selected carefully and followed up very closely under controlled conditions. This means that at the time of authorization, a medicine has been tested on a relatively small number of selected patients for a limited length of time. After authorization, however, patients using a medicine may have other diseases and may be taking other medicines. The medicine will also be used in a larger number of patients, raising the possibility that rare side effects could start to be seen only once the medicine is being used. Therefore, certain side effects may emerge only after a given medicine is used in a large number of patients, for a long period of time, and in combination with other medicines.[17] In short, 'due to the recognised limitations of clinical trials, not all potential or actual adverse reactions can be identified and addressed at the time of initial marketing authorisation' (Vandenbroucke 2008; Potts et al. 2020: 521).[18] The connection between such a candid recognition of uncertainty and the reviews and revisions distinctive of experimentalism could not be more evident. Acknowledging the limits of results from clinical trials and the impossibility of fully eliminating uncertainty *ex ante*, pharmacovigilance leaders like the former Chair of the PRAC argue that 'More can be learnt of the safety of a medicine post-authorization. Therefore, continuous and careful monitoring of the safety profile of all medicines throughout their lifecycle is essential in identifying and minimizing risk' (Potts et al. 2020: 521). This is also the official view of the EMA, which states that 'It is therefore essential that the safety of all medicines is monitored throughout their use in healthcare practice'[19] and that 'By continuing to collect information once a medicine is available and taking action in response, regulators

---

[17] See https://www.ema.europa.eu/en/human-regulatory/overview/pharmacovigilance-overview; https://www.ema.europa.eu/en/human-regulatory/overview/pharmacovigilance/legal-framework-pharmacovigilance (last accessed 16 February 2023).

[18] See also https://www.ema.europa.eu/en/human-regulatory/marketing-authorisation/pharmaco vigilance/risk-management (last accessed 16 February 2023).

[19] See https://www.ema.europa.eu/en/human-regulatory/overview/pharmacovigilance-overview (last accessed 16 February 2023).

can continue to protect the public from emerging safety issues throughout a medicine's life cycle, thereby ensuring its safe and effective use.'[20]

If the explicit acknowledgement of uncertainty and the associated need for experimentalist reviews and revisions is typical of EU pharmaceutical regulation in general, this could not be more manifest in the sub-case of the BioNTech and Pfizer COVID-19 vaccine. This example concerns a medicine authorized via the centralized procedure, which, as explained, is compulsory for the most innovative medicines, such as those against cancer and HIV/AIDS and those using biotechnology and gene therapy, and can also be employed for other ground-breaking medicines (European Parliament and Council 2004: recs. 7–9, art. 3). For all too obvious reasons, the development of COVID-19 vaccines was fast-tracked and subjected to an accelerated evaluation, which further heightened the uncertainty outstanding from clinical trials and the associated need for post-authorization monitoring.[21]

By contrast, the second sub-case featured, especially in the late 2010s, lower uncertainty. HES solutions had been authorized through national procedures, which apply to less innovative medicines and to medicines authorized before the creation of the EMA in 1995 (European Parliament and Council 2004: recs. 7–9, art. 3). In the late 2010s, moreover, the Commission could build on the assessment previously carried out by the EMA in the early 2010s (EMA 2013b), as well as its own decision (EMA 2013d). In effect, the decision made by the Commission via comitology in 2018 to keep the medicine on the market whilst, at the same time, reinforcing risk minimization measures was, by and large, a photocopy of the opinion delivered by the EMA in 2013, which the Commission had then followed (cf. EMA 2018c with EMA 2013b, d). In the example of HES solutions, therefore, the Commission was dealing with a medicine that is conventional and that, by the late 2010s, it had already regulated.

Different opposition

Yet, an exclusive focus on functional uncertainty would come at the expense of obscuring political factors, which also contributed to actors' choices. As the literature pointed out, actors, including the EMA, generally 'seek to arrive at

---

[20] See https://www.ema.europa.eu/en/human-regulatory/overview/pharmacovigilance/legal-framework-pharmacovigilance (last accessed 16 February 2023).

[21] See https://www.ema.europa.eu/en/human-regulatory/overview/public-health-threats/coronavirus-disease-covid-19/treatments-vaccines/vaccines-covid-19/covid-19-vaccines-development-evaluation-approval-monitoring (last accessed 16 February 2023).

consensus decisions' (Krapohl 2004: 534; Sabel and Zeitlin 2008: 284). This is confirmed by the Agency itself, which declares that 'most of the time, the committee reaches decisions by consensus'.[22] It is further supported by interviewees like the EMA's Head of the Regulatory Science and Innovation Work Stream, who confirms that it is, indeed, very rare that the Commission does not follow the EMA's opinion because, 'if the Commission has problems, in practice there are quite a lot of exchanges between itself and EMA. Notably, the Commission can ask clarifications on the report sent to it by EMA, before issuing any formal disagreements. In addition, the Commission sits as observer in the EMA committees' (EUI 17b). The search for consensus is also evidenced in the HES solutions example. There, as mentioned, the Commission, prompted by member states, asked the PRAC to consider revising its harsh recommendation (EMA 2018b: 40) in the (unsuccessful) attempt to avoid an overt conflict. The desirability of achieving agreement in order to favour subsequent adoption and implementation makes even more sense when looking at the COVID-19 vaccines, where visible lack of scientific unanimity would have caused even greater distrust in the population than had already been the case. Thus, the endeavour to mould agreement favoured the use of experimentalism.

Nevertheless, in exceptional cases, coalitions were strong enough to allow for hierarchical governance. As noted, in the HES solutions example, even in the early 2010s, the CMDh had endorsed the PRAC's recommendation by majority (EMA 2013c), thus revealing the presence of a resisting coalition which, however, was isolated at the time. A few years later, in the late 2010s, two dissenting members, one of which was German, opposed once again the PRAC's recommendation (EMA 2018b: 67–68). But although Germany remained marginalized within the PRAC, this time, it did manage to tilt the balance within the CMDh in its favour. Thus, as seen, even though the majority view within the CMDh was initially in favour of the PRAC recommendation for an outright suspension of the medicine (EMA 2018b: 64–66), it then embraced a more accommodating approach (EMA 2018c: 1). According to the CMDh itself, this change of majority position—not shared by twelve of its members!—'followed further reflection, in consultation with EU Member States'. On that basis, the CMDh:

Gave further consideration to the place of HES in the clinical practice of some countries, noted that previous risk minimisation measures had some effect,

[22] See   https://www.ema.europa.eu/en/human-regulatory/marketing-authorisation/evaluation-medicines-step-step (last accessed 16 February 2023).

and considered that a combination of new risk minimisation measures would effectively ensure that HES solutions are not used in patients at risk.

(EMA 2018c: 1)

As recalled by the Head of the EMA's Legal Services, 'in the 2018 case in which the Commission deviated from a recommendation by the PRAC, Germany made a lot of noise. I remember receiving a harsh letter from a German professor.' Several other countries eventually followed Germany, Mr Marino adds (EUI 24a). Indeed, as seen, after consultation with member states, the CMDh altered its majority view, which came to coincide with that of the comitology committee, allowing the Commission to escape the otherwise generally undesirable consequences of deviating from the PRAC and most of the NRAs populating it. In this exceptional example, therefore, the presence of a powerful alliance reduced political pressure on the Commission to engage in experimentalist processes.

In summary, rather than the multipolar distribution of legal powers—which did not always prevent the use of hierarchical processes, the generally high but exceptionally low cognitive uncertainty and political opposition explain the variation in governance processes and trajectories found. Nevertheless, if the regulation of pharmaceuticals has been largely replete with political opposition, through which mechanisms did actors stimulate participation and avoid gridlock? The chapter turns now to this last question.

Mechanisms: Stand-Alone Penalty Defaults

If the shadow of hierarchy had played a role in avoiding deadlock, one would see evidence of threats by higher-level authorities to retake control of the regulatory process, imposing on other reluctant parties specific positive rules.[23] Yet, this is not what the available evidence suggests. According to the Head of the Legal Services of the EMA, the sectoral legislation does not provide the Commission with legal instruments to incentivize NRAs within the EMA to overcome impasse, should impasse happen. The interviewee goes as far as to argue that, in fact, there cannot be gridlock within the EMA because procedural time limits are very short and strict. The Chair of an EMA committee, for example, cannot arbitrarily postpone the moment in which decisions have

---

[23] The chapter has not found evidence of either mechanism in the two specific examples analysed in depth (i.e., BioNTech and Pfizer COVID-19 vaccine, and HES infusion solutions). Therefore, this section analyses the role of the two mechanisms in the sectoral regulation more broadly.

to be taken (EUI 24a). Of course, interviewees and the institutions they represent may well have their own interests, thus one should not take their opinions at face value. Nevertheless, looking at the procedure through which the Commission takes decisions in this domain confirms that EU legislation constraints each of the rule-making steps with specific time limits (European Parliament and Council 2004: arts. 5–15). Furthermore, as discussed, the Commission does not decide whether to follow the EMA's opinions unilaterally. Rather, it is 'assisted' by comitology committees of member states (European Parliament and Council 2004: arts. 10, 87). Thus, the Commission could cast a credible shadow of hierarchy over the NRAs within the EMA only insofar as it was backed by member states in comitology, which should not be taken for granted. As the chapter has described, the Commission has usually followed the EMA's opinion. Of course, this does not mean that this route is inevitable. On the contrary, the chapter has taken pains to discuss a sub-case where, for a certain period, actors have chosen an alternative path. But the fact that over the past twenty-five years the Commission has deviated from the EMA's opinions only in a handful of cases out of more than 1,500 suggests that hierarchical rule-making is extremely rare, with the upshot that also the credibility of hierarchical threat is highly questionable.

By contrast, the evidence is supportive of penalty defaults, which induce actors to participate in experimentalist processes by threatening the imposition of negative sanctions such as fines and prohibitions, as distinct from precise positive rules. Especially after its sector inquiry into the pharmaceutical sector (European Commission 2009), the Commission has frequently used its competition law powers to fine pharmaceutical companies, notably for delaying market entry of generic medicines. Thus, in 2013, the Commission imposed a fine of €93.8 million on the Danish Lundbeck and fines totalling €52.2 million on several producers for having agreed to delay the market entry of cheaper generic versions of Lundbeck's blockbuster antidepressant (European Commission 2013d). The same year, the Commission fined Johnson & Johnson and Novartis €16 million for delaying market entry of the generic painkiller fentanyl (European Commission 2013e). In 2014, the Commission imposed fines totalling €427.7 million on Servier and five generics companies for curbing entry of cheaper versions of their bestselling cardiovascular medicine (European Commission 2014b). More recently, in 2020, the Commission fined Teva and Cephalon €60.5 million for delaying entry of a cheaper generic version of their medicine for sleep disorders (European Commission 2020c). In short, pharmaceutical firms have constantly been under the 'Damocles' sword' of negative sanctions arising from general competition regulation.

What is more, threats of negative penalties have not just come from such cross-sectoral regulation.

Higher-level actors have also cast negative threats by leveraging powers idiosyncratic to pharmaceutical regulation. Following a routine inspection in 2012 by the UK NRA that had identified shortcomings by Roche, the Commission asked the EMA to investigate allegations that the company had failed to meet its pharmacovigilance obligations for nineteen centrally authorized medicines (EMA 2012). This was the first case initiated under the so-called 'Penalties Regulation', which empowers the Commission to impose financial penalties for infringement of obligations associated with marketing authorizations granted via the centralized procedure (European Commission 2007d). In consultation with the company, member states, and the Commission, during the period 2012–2014, the EMA developed an initial report (EMA 2014), which it later finalized (EMA 2016). In 2017, the Commission chose to close the infringement procedure without imposing any penalties. This followed a public *mea culpa* of Roche, which fully recognized the findings of the investigation, rapidly remedied the deficiencies, and provided a long-term commitment to enhance its pharmacovigilance activities (EMA 2017; European Commission 2017f). It also took into account that the previously missing information, which Roche then rapidly incorporated into its periodic safety update reports and which the PRAC assessed during 2013–2016, did not have any impact on the benefit–risk profiles of the medicines and thus did not lead to any change to their marketing authorizations (EMA 2013e). But despite the non-imposition of financial penalties in this particular case, the episode nevertheless signals to all pharmaceutical companies—including giants like Roche—that the Commission, with the support of the EMA, is prepared to use financial penalties to support the operation of the distinctively experimentalist pharmacovigilance processes.

In summary, then, the effective functioning of experimentalism did not depend on credible shadows of positive hierarchy. Instead, it was sustained by negative penalty defaults, which stemmed from both cross-sectoral competition and sector-specific regulation.

Conclusion

The pharmaceutical case contributes to four general arguments developed in previous chapters. First, it qualifies findings from electricity and finance (Chapters 2 and 5), confirming the conclusion from the gas and communication domains (Chapters 3 and 4) that, in and of themselves, experimentalist architectures do not necessarily lead to experimentalist processes. In both the sub-cases at hand, the Commission could rely on the multi-level, networked structure provided by the EMA, which brings together national experts and additional stakeholders and offers an institutional framework for recursive reviews and revisions of initial marketing authorizations through pharmacovigilance. For regulating the vast majority of innovative medicines, including the COVID-19 vaccine by BioNTech and Pfizer, actors did engage in experimentalist processes. The Commission built on the EMA opinion—developed in conjunction with NRAs, firms, and stakeholders—to decide on marketing authorizations. Then, it employed the EMA to constantly collect and analyse potential side effects reported by lower-level actors. This regularly led to revisions of the original marketing authorizations, most often updating product information. In exceptional cases, however, actors favoured hierarchical governance instead. This is illustrated by the example of HES solutions for blood infusion whereby, after an experimentalist beginning in the early 2010s, in the late 2010s, the Commission deviated from the opinion put forward by the EMA and most NRAs to suspend the marketing authorization, reviews concentrated on compliance monitoring, and revisions were curbed. Tables 6.1 and 6.2 summarize the governance processes dominant in EU pharmaceutical regulation, distinguishing between the general pattern— also witnessed in the COVID-19 vaccine most used in the Union—and an

Table 6.1 Governance of EU regulation of innovative pharmaceuticals (incl. BioNTech and Pfizer COVID-19 vaccine), 1995–2022

	1995–2022
Rule-making	Out of 1,569 marketing authorization applications since 1995, European Commission almost never deviated from the EMA recommendations, themselves built on NRAs and stakeholders (same for BioNTech and Pfizer COVID-19 vaccine, authorized in 2020)
Monitoring	During 2012–2018, the EMA assessed 14.6 million relations on 8 million individual cases of suspected adverse reactions, reviewing 26,000 potential signals (582,074 cases for the BioNTech and Pfizer vaccine)
Revision	Assessment of potential signals during 2012–2018 led to 453 recommendations for revision, regularly followed by the Commission, mostly amending product information (for the BioNTech and Pfizer vaccines, eight revisions in 2021–2022, notably updating product information) Experimentalist governance

Source: author.

Table 6.2 Governance of EU regulation of conventional pharmaceuticals (HES solutions for infusion), 2012–2022

	Early 2010s	Late 2010s–early 2020s
Rule-making	Commission followed the EMA recommendation, developed with NRAs, firms, and additional stakeholders	Commission deviated from the EMA recommendation, shared by most NRAs
Monitoring	Comparisons of effects of (colloids) solutions containing hydroxyethyl-starch (HES) with alternative medicine (crystalloids) revealed greater risk of kidney injury and mortality	Late 2010s studies showed lack of compliance with 2013 restrictions, as HES still used widely; early 2020s studies revealed same lack of compliance
Revision	2013 major revision, curbing use to restricted patient populations	2018 revisions limited to additional risk minimization measures rather than outright suspension recommended by the EMA[a]
	Experimentalist governance	Hierarchical governance

Note: [a] It is too early to know what the Commission will decide now that, in 2022, the EMA has once again recommended suspension.
Source: author.

exceptional deviation—seen in HES solutions for infusion in the most recent period.

Second, by offering an example of the self-reinforcing trajectory and another one of the self-limiting alternative, pharmaceuticals show that either route is possible. In the BioNTech and Pfizer sub-case, the marketing authorization, originally granted based on the input of lower-level actors such as NRAs, firms, doctors, and patients, has already been revised eight times in the light of reviews of possible side effects reported by the same lower-level actors as well as new data emerging from its use beyond clinical trials. Thus, experimentalist processes have spanned eight policy cycles in just fourteen months, bringing the pace of experimentalism to an arguably extraordinary pace. Conversely, in the HES solutions sub-case, a first cycle of experimentalism was followed by another one of hierarchy in that monitoring became concentrated on compliance enforcement rather than performance review, rule-making took a more top-down shape since the Commission deviated from the opinion elaborated by the EMA and the NRAs composing it, and the revisions so vital to experimentalism were limited. Table 6.3 illustrates the contrasting long-term trajectories of experimentalist governance in the pharmaceutical

Table 6.3 Trajectories of experimentalist governance in EU pharmaceutical regulation, 1995–2022

Issue	Sequence									Trajectory
BioNTech and Pfizer COVID-19 vaccine	Experimentalist governance, late 2020	Experimentalist governance, May 21	Experimentalist governance, July 21	Experimentalist governance, September 21	Experimentalist governance, October 21	Experimentalist governance, November 21	Experimentalist governance, December 21	Experimentalist governance, February 22	Experimentalist governance, February 22	Self-reinforcing
HES solutions for infusion	Experimentalist governance, early 2010s				Hierarchical governance, late 2010s					Self-limiting

Source: author.

domain. This case contributes to the overall more robust evidence for the self-reinforcing trajectory, observed also in electricity, gas, and digital communications (Chapters 2, 3, and 4). At the same time, however, it reminds us that, as also seen in gas (Chapter 3), experimentalism might also follow the opposite, self-limiting path eventually leading to a return of conventional hierarchy.

Third, the pharmaceutical case confirms that regardless of the multipolar distribution of legal powers, actors are more likely to engage in experimentalist processes the greater the cognitive uncertainty and political opposition and vice versa. In the two sub-cases analysed, the distribution of legal powers was the same as the Commission was constantly subject to polyarchic constraints; although the Commission can deviate from the EMA's opinions, it ultimately needs the approval of member states in comitology. But despite the same, firmly multipolar distribution of power, as seen, the two sub-cases experienced variation in governance processes and trajectories. In contrast to experimentalist literature expectations, this finding thus challenges the capacity of multipolar or polyarchic distributions of legal power to prevent, on their own, hierarchical governance, as already suggested in natural gas and electronic communications (Chapters 3 and 4).

By contrast, the chapter explains the variation in governance processes and trajectories by drawing attention to uncertainty as well as opposition. All the medicines authorized via the centralized procedure are, by definition, particularly innovative. This applies even more to the COVID-19 vaccines, which have been developed and approved in record times. As discussed, the EMA is candid about the impossibility of fully knowing in advance all the possible side effects of medicines because the data from clinical trials that is available at the authorization stage is intrinsically limited. The recognized impossibility of fully eliminating uncertainty *ex ante* is precisely what motivates actors such as the EMA to use the pharmacovigilance reviews and revisions extensively. HES solutions, by contrast, is a conventional medicine. What is more, in the late 2010s, the Commission could build on a previous assessment of the same medicine carried out by the EMA as well as on its own decision, which made the regulation of this medicine more familiar. Nevertheless, political factors, too, contributed to actors' choices. The Commission generally seeks consensus with the EMA and among the NRAs therein, not least to facilitate subsequent adoption in comitology. This makes sense, especially for COVID-19 vaccines whereby disagreements at the rule-making stage would have exacerbated citizens' distrust even further. But on HES solutions, in the late 2010s, the Commission could rely on an alliance bringing together several member states under the German leadership, which allowed the Commission to deviate from the EMA and the majority of NRAs therein and nevertheless get its draft decision approved in comitology. In line with all the previous chapters, these findings thus highlight the positive effect of cognitive uncertainty on experimentalism, consistently with experimentalist expectations and at odds with predictions of studies of regulatory networks, which see functional factors—of which uncertainty is a specimen—favouring hierarchical governance instead. These findings also underline the positive influence on experimentalism of political opposition, this time consistently with regulatory networks analyses.

Finally, the chapter permits deeper investigation of the mechanisms underpinning the effective functioning of experimentalist processes. Surprisingly, in the pharmaceutical domain, these processes did not rely on the shadow of hierarchy characterized by threats of specific positive rules. Instead, they hinged exclusively on penalty defaults, which were distinguished by the negative nature of its threats. Otherwise reluctant firms were therefore incentivized via negative prohibitions and fines (or threats thereof), which came from both general competition and sector-specific regulation. This finding, which is summarized in Table 6.4, does not offset the evidence from most previous chapters that, generally, shadow of hierarchy and penalty defaults operate jointly (Chapters 2, 3, and 5). Nevertheless, it does provide an additional demonstration, besides that offered in the digital domain (Chapter 4), that, occasionally, experimentalist governance depends entirely on penalty defaults.

Overall, the chapter thus issues yet another warning against equating experimentalist arrangements with experimentalist processes as the two might not coincide. Despite initial engagement with experimentalist processes in both sub-cases, furthermore, governance subsequently took diametrically opposed trajectories, showing at once that experimentalism might be durable but also

Table 6.4 Mechanisms underpinning experimentalist governance in EU pharmaceutical regulation,[a] 1995–2022

Shadow of positive hierarchy	Negative penalty defaults
None	Prohibitions and fines imposed on several firms through competition regulation for anti-competitive practices, especially after 2009 sector inquiry; since 2007, firms also under threat of sector-specific fines for lack of compliance with pharmacovigilance obligations (i.e. Roche during 2012–2017)

Note: [a] As explained at the beginning of the 'Mechanisms: Stand-Alone Penalty Defaults' section, this table focuses not on the mechanisms supporting the two specific issues analysed but on those underpinning EU pharmaceutical regulation in general.
Source: author.

that it might wither away. The chapter shows that, under the same multipolar distributions of legal power, actors did not use experimentalist structures to their full potential insofar as they were empowered with major coalitions and cognitive confidence. When under greater pressure from both cognitive and political factors, by contrast, they embraced experimentalism. Finally, when employing experimentalist processes, actors did not stimulate participation of otherwise reluctant parties by threatening to impose specific positive rules. Instead, they relied exclusively on threats of negative fines, as typical of penalty defaults.

7

Conclusion

The theme of this study has been the effect of non-hierarchical structures on governance processes and outcomes. The key questions have been: What does non-hierarchical governance mean? Under what conditions are key actors more likely to engage in non-hierarchical processes? Which trajectories capture the evolution of non-hierarchical and hierarchical processes in the long run? What mechanisms aid non-hierarchical processes to overcome gridlock and deliver outcomes effectively?

In response to these questions, the book has conceived non-hierarchical governance as experimentalist governance, contrasted it to hierarchical governance, and distinguished between institutional architectures and actual processes. It has focused attention on three factors: legal factors, namely, distributions of power *de jure*; functional pressures, specifically cognitive uncertainty; and political factors, namely, opposition. It has examined periods encompassing multiple policy cycles. It has distinguished two mechanisms: shadows of positive hierarchy and negative penalty defaults. It has appraised the relationship between experimentalist architectures, processes, and outcomes in five crucial policy domains in the European Union (EU). All host well-developed experimentalist structures that have been present for significant periods but also offer useful variation in factors as well as a variety of mechanisms that can be used to deal with well-entrenched interests. In two, electricity and natural gas, the analysis has covered the period between the late 1990s and the present day. In another two, communications and financial services, the analysis has begun around 2010, and in a final one, pharmaceuticals, it has returned to a longer temporal perspective beginning from the 1990s. The latter three cases allow greater investigation and testing of the arguments developed in the first two empirical chapters.

The effects of experimentalist architectures have been compared across not only policy domains but also couples of sub-cases within each domain. Process-tracing has allowed key actors and their choices on governance processes and supporting mechanisms to be studied. Thus, experimentalist governance has been analysed over time and comparatively across, as well as within, domains.

Experimentalist Governance. Bernardo Rangoni, Oxford University Press. © Bernardo Rangoni (2023).
DOI: 10.1093/oso/9780198849919.003.0008

This concluding chapter relates the findings of the book back to its key questions. It begins by briefly summarizing the central empirical findings. Then, building on the analytical starting point for the study (namely, the contemporary debates on regulatory governance analysed in Chapter 1), it offers an approach to non-hierarchical structures, processes, and outcomes more generally. Finally, the chapter looks at avenues for further research and how the arguments could be tested elsewhere and generalized.

Central Empirical Findings

A first major empirical finding is that, while, in most cases, experimentalist architectures offering the potential for rule-making and revision based on review of implementation experiences with local discretion did lead to corresponding processes in practice, this was not always the case. At times, despite, or even thanks to, the experimentalist structures available, processes involved hierarchical development and imposition of stable rules coupled with compliance enforcement.

Most often, the presence of experimentalist arrangements led to corresponding processes. Thus, in electricity, experimentalist processes stemmed from the active employment from the late 1990s to the present day of the Florence Forum, the European Regulators' Group for Electricity and Gas (ERGEG), and the Agency for the Cooperation of Energy Regulators (ACER). This helped to develop and revise rules on network access and tarification based on the review of the implementation experiences with a variety of approaches conducted by national actors such as national regulatory agencies and transmission system operators. Similarly, in natural gas, the same or equivalent experimentalist arrangements (e.g. the Madrid Forum) were employed to address, through experimentalist processes, the regulation of network tarification throughout the past two decades and the regulation of network access until the early 2000s. The active use of experimentalist structures was not confined to electricity and natural gas, that is, energy. In communications, the European Commission tackled Google's abuse of dominance by requiring the company to develop rules directly itself and then regularly reviewing their performance, which led to revisions of the initially proposed remedies. In finance, thanks to the European Securities and Markets Authority (ESMA), the European Banking Authority (EBA), and the European Insurance and Occupational Provisions Authority (EIOPA), higher-level actors addressed both the regulation of credit rating agencies (CRAs) and of packaged retail investment and insurance-based products (PRIIPs) by leveraging the discretion of lower-level actors, be they national regulators or regulated firms, regularly reviewing implementation experiences and revising the original rules accordingly. In pharmaceuticals, too, the experimentalist network of the European Medicines Agency (EMA) generally led to experimentalist processes whereby initial decisions on marketing authorizations of innovative medicines built on the input of national regulators, firms, and other stakeholders, and such initial authorizations were subsequently revised in the light of extensive post-authorization monitoring. This also applies to the most used COVID-19 vaccine in Europe.

Yet, at times, hierarchical processes were undertaken despite, or even thanks to, experimentalist structures. Hence, in natural gas, the regulation of network access from the mid-2000s onwards featured rules developed and imposed from the top, ignoring the Madrid Forum and then employing the ACER to monitor compliance rather than reviewing performance. In electronic communications, the Commission did not employ the Body of European Regulators for Electronic Communications (BEREC) to review experiences of national regulators and learn from them; instead, it built on the European network to shape national regulators' draft rules in line with its own preferred approach. In pharmaceuticals, to regulate a conventional medicine—hydroxyethyl-starch (HES) solutions—in the late 2010s, the Commission exceptionally deviated from the opinion that the EMA had developed based on its network of national actors, adopting a more top-down decision that limited regulatory revisions and embracing compliance enforcement rather than performance review.

A second key empirical finding is that, while multipolar distributions of legal power were neither necessary nor sufficient for experimentalist governance, both functional uncertainty and political opposition are positive conditions for it. Under conditions of greater cognitive uncertainty and weaker political support, actors favoured experimentalist processes even when equipped with extraordinarily centralized powers. Conversely, under conditions of lower uncertainty and stronger coalitions, actors pursued more hierarchical governance processes in the face of multipolar distributions of power.

Thus, in the communication and financial domains, higher-level actors engaged in experimentalist processes despite the exceptionally centralized powers held by the European Commission in general competition regulation (including against tech giants such as Google) and those held by the ESMA in the regulation of CRAs.

Conversely, the multipolar distribution of powers typical of the EU did not prevent key actors such as the European Commission from pursuing more hierarchical processes when regulating access to natural gas networks from the mid-2000s onwards, electronic communications, or the HES medicines in the late 2010s.

Instead, key actors engaged in experimentalist processes when under greater cognitive as well as political pressure. Thus, in several instances, key actors recognized that they did not know the best rules beforehand and that they could not build on a readily available coalition strong enough to allow the imposition of preferred rules on others. These instances are the regulation of the following sub-cases: electricity network access and tarification; gas network access until the early 2000s and network tarification; Google; CRAs and PRIIPs; and innovative medicines such as the BioNTech and Pfizer COVID-19 vaccine and the conventional HES solutions in the early 2010s.

However, when more confident about the best rules and supported by a strong coalition, key actors opted for more hierarchical processes. Hence, in the regulation of access to natural gas networks after the mid-2000s, electronic communications, and traditional HES solutions in the late 2010s, the Commission was convinced that it knew the best rules already, notably thanks to its own previous experiences. Further, the Commission could rely on the support of other major actors to successfully trump multipolar distributions of power and impose the rules favoured by itself and its own coalition on other recalcitrant actors. In particular, in gas, the Commission built on the support of key national regulators, such as the German and Austrian authorities, to address incumbent firms' resistance. In electronic communications, it leveraged the courts and the BEREC against some reluctant national regulators. And in pharmaceuticals, it allied with a coalition of several member states led by Germany to override opposition by most national regulators.

A third key empirical finding is that, more often than not, experimentalist processes in a given policy cycle led to additional experimentalist processes in the following policy cycle, rather than to their own exhaustion, and therefore to the eventual return to conventional hierarchical governance. Further, such a self-reinforcing dynamic was driven by re-emergences of not only cognitive uncertainty but also required political coalitions.

In two instances, experimentalist processes followed a self-limiting path. In the regulation of access to natural gas networks, after having initially engaged with experimentalist processes in the late 1990s–early 2000s, the Commission shifted towards the development and enforcement of rules in a more hierarchical manner because, by the mid-2000s, it perceived itself as know-ing the best rules and to be supported by some key national regulators already. Similarly in the regulation of HES solutions, in the late 2010s, the Commission reverted to the top-down development of rules, limited revisions, and compli-ance monitoring typical of hierarchical governance. It did so because, by then, it could build on its own early 2010s decision on the same medicine, which reduced uncertainty, as well as a coalition of member states led by Germany, which ensured comitology approval despite deviation from the EMA and most national regulators therein.

Overall, however, the cases in this book provide evidence of experimentalist durability that is more robust. Thus, in electricity, in the period between the late 1990s and the present day, the Commission and other key actors engaged in three cycles of experimentalist processes for regulating network access and in two such cycles for regulating network tarification. Equally, even within a shorter period covering the past decade, the Commission used two cycles of experimentalist processes to tackle the regulation of Google. Pharmaceuticals, finally, bring the pace of experimentalism to unprecedented levels, given that in just fourteen months, the initial marketing authorization for the BioNTech and Pfizer COVID-19 vaccine was revised eight times. In all these cases, far from breaking with it, key actors kept engaging with experimentalism. This was because key actors perceived neither to have reached the definitive rules nor to have moulded enough support to be able to impose rules hierarchi-cally. In turn, this was due to the constant uncertainty and (risked) opposition in Google, the emergence of novel issues demanding new rules and coalitions in electricity, and the open recognition with the BioNTech and Pfizer vaccine that side effects may arise after clinical trials and that decisions reached by con-sensus may help subsequent approval and implementation of decisions over authorized medicines.

Finally, a fourth central empirical finding is that, in most cases, experimen-talist processes were neither exclusively supported by threats of specific pos-itive rules nor just by threats of negative penalties. Instead, most commonly, a mix of shadows of positive hierarchy and negative penalty defaults jointly underpinned experimentalist processes, with no evidence of one mechanism replacing the other.

The book found no evidence of experimentalist processes exclusively sup-ported by shadows of positive hierarchy. In rare cases, instead, experimentalist processes were entirely aided by negative penalty defaults. Thus, in the reg-ulation of Google as well as of pharmaceutical companies like Roche, the European Commission has been inducing recalcitrant firms to develop and revise rules under the threat of fines, sometimes of billions of euros, arising from both general competition and sector-specific regulation.

Yet, in most cases, experimentalist processes were supported by both shadows of positive hierarchy and negative penalty defaults. Hence, in electricity, natural gas, and finance, experimentalist processes were underpinned by threats not only of positive legislation and sector-specific network codes and technical standards but also of negative competition prohibitions, fines, and commitments offered by firms as well as sector-specific sanctions.

It is worth stating briefly the lines of argument or inquiry that the study has not pursued. The book did not claim that the only form of non-hierarchical governance is experimentalist governance. It did not study the possibility that experimentalist processes might anticipate the institutionalization of corresponding architectures or affect their subsequent evolution.[1] Instead, it has focused on the extent and conditions under which experimentalist structures matter for behaviour and policy outcomes. The book did not show that functional and political factors were the sole causes of engagement with experimentalist processes but rather that, in contrast to legal factors, they played significant roles in actors' choices over what type of governance processes to employ. It does not prove definitively that experimentalist processes are always self-reinforcing and never self-limiting but has found more robust evidence of the former trajectory. Equally, it neither claims nor implies that the mechanisms supporting non-hierarchical processes are confined to the shadow of hierarchy and penalty defaults and that these never occur on their own. However, the book does show that these two mechanisms do underpin experimentalist processes and that, typically, they help to deliver policy outcomes jointly.

Overall, the central empirical findings are that cognitive uncertainty and political opposition influenced the use of experimentalist architectures, whereas multipolar distributions of power had little impact. The former two factors played a significant role because of their constraints on the cognitive and political capacity of key actors to develop and enforce rules hierarchically, even when armed with centralized powers. Conversely, when equipped with confidence and coalitions, key actors were able to overcome legal constraints on the exercise of hierarchical authority. Both cognitive uncertainty and political resistance frequently resurfaced as new questions that demanded the identification of fresh rules and the creation of renewed support arose, thus

---

[1] It might well be possible that experimentalist processes emerge before experimentalist architectures are institutionalized. Equally, once set up, such architectures might be revised in the light of experimentalist governance processes.

preventing experimentalist governance from fading away. When employed, experimentalist processes delivered policy outcomes thanks to both shadows of positive hierarchy and negative penalty defaults, which were often mutually compatible rather than mutually exclusive.

A Framework for Analysing Non-hierarchical Architectures, Processes, and Outcomes

The analytical starting point of the book was contemporary debates in regulatory governance that, although having different focal points, deal directly with the relationship between non-hierarchical structures, processes, and outcomes (or parts thereof).[2] The experimentalist literature has documented the widespread institutionalization of non-hierarchical arrangements, such as regulatory fora, networks, and agencies, and has argued that it represents the rise of a novel form of governance that differs in many respects from conventional hierarchical governance (Sabel and Zeitlin 2008, 2010, 2012a). Yet, the actual pervasiveness of experimentalist governance has been questioned (Börzel 2012: 380; Eckert and Börzel 2012: 374–375). The experimentalist literature has further identified the scope conditions for experimentalist governance as strategic uncertainty—in which actors do not precisely know how to achieve their broad goals—and a multipolar distribution of powers—in which no single actor can impose its own view without taking into account those of others (Sabel and Zeitlin 2008: 280, 2012a: 174–176). For their part, explanations of different regulatory structures have suggested that functional demands drive more rather than less centralized arrangements, though political resistance then mitigates their supply (Dehousse 1997; Coen and Thatcher 2008; Eberlein and Newman 2008; Kelemen and Tarrant 2011). Experimentalist advocates have suggested that in the long run, novel forms of governance are more likely to transform conventional ones and be self-reinforcing (Sabel and Simon 2006; Rangoni and Zeitlin 2021). Sceptical observers have countered such a transformative argument by suggesting that experimentalist governance may, on the contrary, lead to an endogenous reduction of uncertainty and thus to its own exhaustion (Eberlein 2010: 70–74). Finally, the shadow-of-hierarchy literature has underlined the hierarchical threats that non-hierarchical governance ultimately requires to deliver policy outcomes effectively (Héritier and Lehmkuhl 2008), whereas the experimentalist literature responds that such

---

[2] For a review, see Chapter 1.

threats, though crucial indeed, are in fact better understood as penalty defaults (Sabel and Zeitlin 2008: 305–309).

The case studies point to the strengths of these literatures. As the experimentalist literature suggests, experimentalist architectures often led to experimentalist governance. Moreover, as also predicted by that literature, uncertainty played a significant role in actors' decisions to engage in experimentalist governance. Yet, so did political factors, supporting the focus on politics of studies of regulatory networks. Empirically, experimentalist processes were mostly self-reinforcing. These were supported both by the shadow of hierarchy and by penalty defaults, in partial consistency with both shadow-of-hierarchy and experimentalist models.

Yet, the limits of these approaches are also exposed. The current experimentalist literature uses a narrow definition of experimentalist governance, centred on experimentalist architecture but underplaying processes. Equally, it gives attention to functional and legal factors but too little to political ones. For their part, analyses of different governance arrangements overlook legal factors and are over-dominated by rivalry between political and functional factors, leaving too little scope for the possibility that the former might also matter and that the latter two might not conflict with one another but, instead, jointly favour non-hierarchical governance. Both the self-reinforcing and self-limiting arguments, moreover, remain largely untested predictions and focus attention exclusively on functional drivers, here, uncertainty. Finally, both the shadow-of-hierarchy argument and the penalty-defaults counterargument suffer from concept stretching in that neither clarifies the boundaries of its chief notion and thus how its claim could be refuted.

Given the foregoing critique, this section suggests the benefits of drawing on contemporary debates in regulatory governance but also seeks to remedy their *lacunae*, thereby developing a framework for analysing non-hierarchical structures, processes, and outcomes. Four elements of the analytical approach can be set out here, responding to the questions raised at the start of the chapter and, indeed, at the start of the book, concerning the nature of non-hierarchical governance, scope conditions, trajectories, and mechanisms.

First, non-hierarchical governance should include actual governance processes as well as non-hierarchical structures. Although the experimentalist literature has hitherto focused most systematic comparative attention on the latter (Sabel and Zeitlin 2010; Sabel and Simon 2011, 2012; de Búrca et al. 2013, 2014; Zeitlin 2015), it acknowledges that structure and behaviour do not always match (Sabel and Zeitlin 2008: 280–281). This must be integrated into analysis explicitly. Indeed, while the experimentalist literature valuably documents a new governance architecture, the case studies show that the role of key actors like EU and national authorities, as well as regulated firms, is also crucial. In particular, key actors do not just respond passively to institutional frameworks; the case studies show that they make decisions on whether, when, and how to use such frameworks. Hence, the decisions of key actors must be considered. Non-hierarchical structures affect but do not automatically determine governance processes. Non-hierarchical governance is not an inevitable force beyond the influence of key actors. Instead, it arises from their decisions. A broader view of non-hierarchical governance offers a better understanding of how non-hierarchical institutions can lead to non-hierarchical processes.

A second aspect concerns the scope conditions for non-hierarchical governance. The book suggests that on their own, legal factors have little impact on the use of more or less hierarchical governance. Using the cases studied, it argues that actors used non-hierarchical governance despite extremely centralized powers. Equally, but conversely, they pursued hierarchical governance notwithstanding legal constraints on the exercise of hierarchical authority. The book therefore contends that legal factors are neither a necessary nor a sufficient condition for non-hierarchical governance. This claim runs counter to arguments of the experimentalist literature, emphasizing the importance of multipolar distributions of power as bulwarks against hierarchical governance (Sabel and Zeitlin 2008: 280, 2012a: 175–176, 2012b: 412; Overdevest and Zeitlin 2014: 26, 43–44; Zeitlin 2016: 1073–1074, 1091–1092).

Instead, the book claims that functional and political factors can lead to non-hierarchical governance even in the face of centralized legal powers, as was the case for the regulation of the North American tech giant in the digital markets and the regulation of CRAs in the financial domain. They have considerable scope to contribute to non-hierarchical governance and even trump centralizations of power seen as inimical to it because they affect key actors' cognitive and political capacities of using such powers to develop and enforce rules hierarchically. Key actors can derive considerable advantages from non-hierarchical governance as it can aid them to learn and create powerful reform coalitions. At the same time, key actors can overcome legal constraints on the exercise of hierarchical governance to impose rules on opponents, if equipped with cognitive resources and supporting coalitions beforehand.

Thus, the book confirms that the experimentalist literature valuably points to strategic uncertainty (Sabel and Zeitlin 2008: 280, 2012a: 174–175, 2012b: 411–412; de Búrca *et al.* 2014: 479, 483; Sabel and Simon 2011: 56, 78, 82; Sabel et al. 2018: 371–372). However, the case studies show that political opposition is also crucial and positively so. This is at odds with the experimentalist discussion, which has not been attentive enough to politics, and when exceptionally acknowledging politics, it has seen it as inimical to experimentalist governance (Radaelli 2008; de Búrca et al. 2013: 782–783). In contrast to the literature on regulatory networks (Dehousse 1997; Coen and Thatcher 2008; Eberlein and Newman 2008; Thatcher and Coen 2008; Kelemen and Tarrant 2011; Thatcher 2011), furthermore, the case studies show that functional factors can be a positive rather than a negative scope condition for non-hierarchical governance. In addition, it shows that far from being necessarily antithetical to political factors, functional and political considerations may row towards the same form of governance. Hence, functional and political factors putting pressure on the relevant key actors must both be considered, and neither of those factors should be assumed to work against non-hierarchical governance.

A third element concerns the pathways along which non-hierarchical governance evolves in the long run. Although the trajectories found empirically do not always map onto the transformative argument put forward by the experimentalist literature (Sabel and Simon 2006), the cases examined in the book lend more robust support that experimentalist processes may be sustainable, thanks to either constant or re-emerging cognitive and political challenges. This claim refines existing ones focusing exclusively on cognitive uncertainty and overlooking political coalitions (Eberlein 2010; Rangoni and Zeitlin 2021). It runs counter to conservative predictions that, by gradually reducing the uncertainty that serves as its own primary fuel, experimentalist governance is destined to wither away (Eberlein 2010: 70–74; Börzel 2012: 381). The long-term trajectories of non-hierarchical governance should not only be claimed but also studied empirically through analysis covering multiple policy cycles.

Finally, the book offers claims on the mechanisms whereby non-hierarchical governance influences policy outcomes, even if actors have notoriously well-entrenched interests, as was the case in the five policy domains. Engaging with the shadow-of-hierarchy and the experimentalist literatures, Chapter 1 distinguished, on the one hand, mechanisms relying on threats of specific positive rules and, on the other hand, those relying on threats of negative sanctions and prohibitions. The cases examined in the book suggest that the shadow of hierarchy does not appear on its own. As for penalty defaults, two examples from the communication and pharmaceutical domains show that this negative mechanism can operate alone. However, the cases in this book provide more robust evidence that this negative mechanism is generally linked with its positive counterpart. Thus, in the electricity, natural gas, and financial domains, key actors induced other reluctant parties to overcome impasse, on the one hand, via threats of legislation and sector-specific network codes and technical standards, and, on the other hand, via threats of competition prohibitions, fines, and commitments as well as sector-specific sanctions. What is more, no obvious temporal pattern in the use of the two mechanisms emerged. Thus, the shadow of hierarchy is far from being the only mechanism underpinning non-hierarchical governance, in contrast to what is implied by that literature (Héritier and Lehmkuhl 2008; Héritier and Rhodes 2011) but in line with research on functional equivalents in the absence of a strong state (Börzel and Risse 2010). However, penalty defaults do not occupy such a monopolistic position either, challenging suggestions in the experimentalist literature (Sabel and Zeitlin 2008: 305–309, 2010: 13–16, 2012b: 413–414; Zeitlin 2016: 1075–1076). In contrast, non-hierarchical governance can deliver policy outcomes, even where reform is especially difficult due to well-established interests, precisely because it can rely on a variety of mechanisms that, far from being incompatible alternatives, can be married to one another.

Thus, overall, the approach used in the study offers a broader view of non-hierarchical governance and relates it to governance processes. It gives greater prominence to the scope for key actors to choose whether, and how, to use institutional frameworks and lead to policy outcomes. It also seeks to integrate political factors involving alliances and opposition as well as cognitive resources and functional pressures. It sees policy outcomes as a result of policy processes in which both positive and negative mechanisms play a significant role.

Testing the Arguments More Broadly

How can the arguments developed from the sectoral cases in the EU be tested to see whether they hold more widely? Three avenues seem open. First, non-hierarchical governance could be conceptualized through frameworks other than experimentalist governance. After all, experimentalist governance is not the only mode of governance distinct from traditional hierarchical governance. A promising contender seems to be orchestration, a conceptual framework that has recently gained attention. It argues that governors can overcome a variety of limits to their capabilities and ultimately achieve their goals by voluntarily enlisting intermediary actors that possess complementary capabilities (Abbott et al. 2015). It would be interesting to probe whether the book's general claims about the relationship between non-hierarchical structures, processes, and outcomes are idiosyncratic to experimentalist governance or else remain valid even if non-hierarchical governance is conceptualized through another theoretical lens.

A second avenue is to examine other policy domains in the EU. In particular, it would seem fruitful to extend analysis from the regulation of markets that was prevalent in this book to other types of regulation such as risk and catastrophe-avoiding regulation in policy domains marked by not only rapid and complex technological changes but also political salience and controversy. Food safety, for instance, is said to be no exception to the widespread institutionalization of the experimentalist architecture in the EU. Yet, recent analysis has questioned the extent to which, in the realm of genetically modified organisms, such architecture has actually led to experimentalist processes (Weimer 2019; Dabrowska-Klosinska 2022). The approach developed in the book would explain the hierarchical route taken by the European Commission in the light of its intolerance to scientific uncertainty as well as its underestimation of the opposition it would have met from member states should it have imposed—as it did—rules from the top. Another promising case could be environmental policy, a vital domain all too clearly associated with unprecedented but, unfortunately, increasingly familiar natural disasters. This domain is said to be well suited to experimentalist strategies, which have been successfully emerging in a number of instances (Overdevest and Zeitlin 2014, 2018; Sabel and Victor 2017, 2022; Zeitlin and Overdevest 2021). Yet, in the promotion of renewable energy, which is central to the sustainable transition, the EU, and particularly the European Commission, have thus far refrained from using such experimentalist strategies (Rangoni 2020: 33–37). These specific examples aside, the broader point is that one way to test the generalizability of this book's arguments would be to look at other regulated sectors in which experimentalist architectures have become institutionalized and distributions of legal powers are as multipolar as characteristic of the EU but which might have experienced different combinations of functional and political pressures, thereby generating further cases.

Finally, a third avenue for expanding the range of cases is to look at major policy domains or issue areas outside of the EU. The United Sates is an obvious case, not least because it seems to feature generally more centralized powers than the EU and thus also a more credible shadow of hierarchy. Conversely, the international plane is especially interesting because of precisely the opposite reason: the notoriously poor centralization of legal powers. However, this clearly does not imply that all actors have the same power *de facto*, that they do not forge alliances to impose rules on others, or that they cannot cast any threat to induce others to participate. Indeed, analysis here would permit further exploration of functional equivalents to the shadow of hierarchy, including penalty defaults at levels—rather than in areas—of limited statehood (Börzel and Risse 2010; de Búrca et al. 2013, 2014: 479, 484; Posner 2015: 221–226). Finally, a promising case for testing the capacity of the book's claims of travelling elsewhere would be to focus attention on China. For all-too-obvious reasons, this appears as an especially unlikely polity for non-hierarchical governance. Yet, studies arguing just the opposite are now flourishing (Heilmann 2008; Bi 2015; Morgan 2018; Zhu and Zhao 2021; Zhang et al. 2022; Wang et al. 2022). These include analyses of the environmental domain (Shin 2017a, b; Drahos 2021; Zhuang and Wolf 2021), whose vital importance is, just as that of China, bound to grow.

Appendix: Interviews

Interview key

BUS = Businesses (companies and trade associations, law firms and consultancies)
EUI = EU institutions (European Commission and European Union (EU) regulatory agencies)
REG = Regulators (national authorities and their European networks)

Acronyms

ACER	Agency for the Cooperation of Energy Regulators
BEREC	Body of European Regulators for Electronic Communications
CEER	Council of European Energy Regulators
EFET	European Federation of Energy Traders
EMA	European Medicines Agency
ENTSO-E	European Network of Transmission System Operators for Electricity
Eurelectric	Union of the European Electricity Industry
PRAC	Pharmacovigilance Risk Assessment Committee

Number	Name	Function(s) and institution(s)/ organization(s)	Date and place of interview	Interview code
1	Dr Guido Cervigni	Head of Market Development at Italian power exchange	Email exchanges, 7/4/2015	BUS1
2	Dr Juan José Alba	Vice-President for Regulatory Affairs at	Brussels, 17/5/2016	BUS2a
3	Rios	Endesa and Chairman Markets Committee of	Florence, 1/7/2019	BUS2b
4		Eurelectric	Email exchanges, 1–5/8/2019	BUS2c
5	Marco Foresti	Market Advisor at ENTSO-E	Brussels, 18/5/2016	BUS3
6	Dr Margot Loudon	Deputy Secretary General of Eurogas	Brussels, 18/5/2016	BUS4

7	Dr Matti Supponen	Policy Coordinator for Wholesale Markets at Directorate-General for Energy of the European Commission	Brussels 19/5/2016	EUI1a
8			Phone, 2/7/2019	EUI1b
9			Phone, 2/8/2019	EUI1c
10	Edith Hofer	Assistant to the Director General for Energy of the European Commission	Brussels, 19/5/2016	EUI2
11	Stephen Rose	Head of Gas Market Design at RWE and Chairman Gas to Power Working Group at Eurelectric	London, 25/5/2016	BUS5
12	Prof. Pippo Ranci Ortigosa	President of Italian Energy Regulatory Authority and Vice-President of CEER	Email exchanges, 26/5/2016	REG1a
13			Email exchanges, 20/6/2019	REG1b
14			Zoom, 1/3/2022	REG1c
15	Tom Maes	Chairman of ACER Tariff Task Force, Vice-Chairman of ACER and CEER Gas Working Group, and Principal Advisor at Belgian regulatory authority	Phone, 27/5/2016	REG2
16	Alberto Pototschnig	Director of ACER	Ljubljana, 9/6/2016	EUI3a
17			Florence, 1/7/2019	EUI3b
18			Phone, 29/4/2020	EUI3c
19			Email exchanges, 8–10/1/2021	EUI3d
20			Zoom, 10/1/2022	EUI3e
21			Email exchanges, 11/2/2022	EUI3f
22	Dr Martin Povh	Officer for Framework Guidelines at ACER	Ljubljana, 9/6/2016	EUI4
23	Thomas Querrioux	Gas Officer at ACER	Ljubljana, 9/6/2016	EUI5

Continued

Continued

Number	Name	Function(s) and institution(s)/ organization(s)	Date and place of interview	Interview code
24	Csilla Bartok	Team Leader for Framework Guidelines and Network Codes at ACER	Ljubljana, 9/6/2016	EUI6
25	Thomas Holzer	Officer for Framework Guidelines and Network Codes at ACER	Ljubljana, 9/6/2016	EUI7
26	Dr	Director of International	Phone 10/6/2016	REG3a
27	Annegret	Relations at German	Phone, 15/7/2019	REG3b
28	Groebel	regulatory authority and Vice-President of CEER	Email exchanges, 24–25/7/2019	REG3c
29	Fernando Lasheras Garcia	Director of Brussels representative office of Iberdrola	London, 23/6/2016	BUS6
30	Mark Copley	Associate Partner for Wholesale Markets at British regulatory authority and Vice-Chair of Electricity Working Group of ACER	London, 24/6/2016	REG4
31	Peter Styles	Chairman of Electricity Committee of EFET	London, 28/7/2016	BUS7a
32			Phone, 9/7/2019	BUS7b
33	Dr Antonio	Manager at BEREC	Phone, 31/7/2019	REG5a
34	Manganelli		Email exchange, 1–2/8/2019	REG5b
35	Dr Diego Valiante	Senior Officer and Team Leader at the Directorate-General for Financial Stability, Financial Services and Capital Markets Union of the European Commission	Phone, 2/9/2019	EUI8

36	Jérôme Le Page	Director for European electricity markets at EFET	Phone, 24/09/2019	BUS8
37	Anonymous	Head of a European company	Amsterdam, 7/10/2019	BUS9
38	Dr Francesco Maria Salerno	Managing Partner of Brussels office of Gianni and Origoni law firm	Skype, 17/10/2019	BUS10
39	Maria Popova	Manager for market supervision and renewable electricity at EFET	Phone, 17/10/2019	BUS11
40	Anonymous	Senior Official at Directorate-General for Competition of the European Commission	Brussels, 2/2020	EUI9
41	Anonymous	Head of a national competition authority	Brussels 2/2020	REG6
42	Anonymous	Head of a national competition authority	Brussels 2/2020	REG7
43	Anonymous	Head of a national competition authority	Brussels 2/2020	REG8
44	Anonymous	Senior expert in policymaking and regulation at a national energy company	Skype, 15/4/2020	BUS12
45	Anonymous	Senior Officer at Directorate-General for Energy of the European Commission	Phone, 8/5/2020	EUI10
46	Volker Zuleger	Head of Market Integrity and Transparency at ACER	Phone 8/5/2020	EUI11a
47			Email exchange, 25/5/2020	EUI11b
48	Anonymous	Senior Representative of EU-level energy trade association	Zoom, 12/5/2020	BUS13a
49			Email exchange, 26–28/5/2020	BUS13b
50	Eleonora Nagali	Policy Officer at Market Integrity and Transparency department of ACER	Email exchange, 26–28/5/2020	EUI12

Continued

Continued

Number	Name	Function(s) and institution(s)/ organization(s)	Date and place of interview	Interview code
51	Joaquín	Commissioner for	Zoom, 29/5/2020	EUI13a
52	Almunia	Competition of the European Commission	Zoom, 9/4/2021	EUI13b
53	Prof.	Chief Competition	Zoom, 29/5/2020	EUI14a
54	Massimo Motta	Economist of the European Commission	Email, 5–8/4/2021	EUI14b
55	Anonymous	Senior Official at Directorate-General for Competition of the European Commission	Zoom, 29/5/2020	EUI15
56	Dr	Director General for	Zoom, 10/6/2020	EUI16a
57	Alexander Italianer	Competition of the European Commission	Email, 5–7/4/2021	EUI16b
58	Dr Matteo Padellaro	Partner at Gianni, Origoni, Grippo, Cappelli and Partners law firm	Phone, 10/6/2020	BUS14
59	Prof. Michele Grillo	Board Member of the Italian competition authority	Zoom, 6/6/2020	REG9
60	Jordi Llinares	Head of Research and Innovation at EMA	Email exchange, 23/7–15/10/2020	EUI17a
61	Garcia		Zoom, 27/11/2020	EUI17b
62	Anonymous	Risk Management Specialist/PRAC Scientific Lead at EMA	Email exchange, 23/7–15/10/2020	EUI18
63	Anonymous	Regulatory Affairs Officer for Pharmacovigilance at EMA	Email exchange, 23/7–15/10/2020	EUI19
64	Anonymous	Academic Liaison for Research and Innovation at EMA	Email exchange, 23/7–15/10/2020	EUI20
65	Anonymous	Senior Official at BEREC	Zoom, 9/10/2020	REG10

66	Anonymous	Senior Official for Credit Rating Agencies at Italian regulatory authority	Zoom, 9/10/2020	REG11
67	Anonymous	Senior Official of Italian financial regulatory authority, seconded to the European Commission	Zoom, 13/10/2020	REG12
68	Anonymous	Senior Official of Spanish telecommunications regulatory authority	Zoom, 16/10/2020	REG13
69	Anonymous	Official at Italian financial regulatory authority	Phone, 28/10/2020	REG14
70	Anonymous	Senior Official at Directorate-General for Communications Networks, Content and Technology of the European Commission	Email exchange, 14–24/11/2020	EUI21
71	Anonymous	Senior Official at Directorate-General for Communications Networks, Content and Technology of the European Commission	Email exchange, 14–24/11/2020	EUI22
72	Anonymous	Senior Official at Directorate-General for Communications Networks, Content and Technology of the European Commission	Email exchange, 14–24/11/2020	EUI23
73	Stefano Marino	Head of Legal Services at EMA	Phone, 16/11/2020	EUI24a
74			Email exchange, 25/2/2022	EUI24b
75	Olga Solomon	Head of Unit for Medicines Policy, Authorization and Monitoring at Directorate-General for Health and Food Safety of the European Commission	Email exchange, 20/11–10/12/2020	EUI25

Continued

Continued

Number	Name	Function(s) and institution(s)/ organization(s)	Date and place of interview	Interview code
76	Anonymous	Head of a Department at German regulatory authority	Zoom, 10/1/2022	REG15
77	Anonymous	Deputy Director General for a Directorate-General of European Commission	Zoom 13/1/2022	EUI26
78	Luis Berenguer	President of Spanish competition authority	Zoom, 18/1/2022	REG16
79	Anonymous	Head of a Department of United Kingdom's telecommunications regulatory authority	Zoom, 21/1/2022	REG17
80	Anonymous	Board Member of Spanish regulatory authority	Zoom, 1/2/2022	REG18
81	Anonymous	Official for telecommunications at Spanish regulatory authority	Zoom, 1/2/2022	REG19
82	Anonymous	Deputy Head of a unit at European Commission	Zoom, 3/2/2022	EUI27
83	Prof. Antonio Perrucci	Vice Secretary General at Italian telecommunications regulatory authority	Zoom, 4/2/2022	REG20

Bibliography

Abbott, K.N., Genschel, P., Snidal, D. and Zangl, B. (2015) *International Organizations as Orchestrators*, Cambridge: Cambridge University Press.

ACER (Agency for the Cooperation of Energy Regulators) (2012a) ACER Public Consultation on Scope and main policy options for Framework Guidelines on Harmonised Transmission Tariff Structures: Evaluation of responses, 5 September.

ACER (2012b) ACER Opinion No. 04-2012: Reasoned opinion on the network code on capacity allocation mechanisms for the European gas transmission network, 4 June.

ACER (2012c) Recommendation No. 04/2012 of the Agency for the Cooperation of Energy Regulators of 9 November 2012 on the network code on capacity allocation mechanisms for the European gas transmission network, 12 November.

ACER (2013a) Recommendation of the Agency for the Cooperation of Energy Regulators No. 05/2013 of 25 March 2013 on a new regulatory framework for the inter-transmission system operator compensation, 3 April.

ACER (2013b) Opinion of the Agency for the Cooperation of Energy Regulators No. 07/2013 of 25 March 2013 on the suitability of long run average incremental costs for the assessment of intertransmission system operator compensation for infrastructure, 2 April.

ACER (2013c) ACER Framework Guidelines on Rules Regarding Harmonised Transmission Tariff Structures for gas, 29 November.

ACER (2014a) Report on the influence of existing bidding zones on electricity markets: Undertaken in the context of the joint initiative of ACER and ENTSO-E for the early implementation of the Network Code on Capacity Allocation and Congestion Management (CACM) with respect to the review of bidding zones, 7 March.

ACER (2014b) ACER annual report on contractual congestion at interconnection points, 1st edn, 28 February.

ACER (2014c) Opinion of the Agency for the Cooperation of Energy Regulators No. 09/2014 of 15 April 2014 on the appropriate range of transmission charges paid by electricity producers, 16 April.

ACER (2015a) ACER annual report on contractual congestion at interconnection points, 2nd edn, 29 May.

ACER (2015b) Opinion of the Agency for the Cooperation of Energy Regulators No. 02/2015 of 26 March 2015 on the Network Code on Harmonised Transmission Tariff Structures for gas, 30 March.

ACER (2015c) Minutes of the 49th meeting of the Board of Regulators, July.

ACER (2015d) Minutes of the 50th meeting of the Board of Regulators, September.

ACER (2015e) Minutes of the 51st meeting of the Board of Regulators, October.

ACER (2016a) ACER request for review of bidding zones, Ljubljana, 21 December, ACER-AP CGC ss 20 16-698.

ACER (2016b) ACER annual report on contractual congestion at interconnection points, 3rd edn, 31 May.

ACER (2017a) Request for a technical report on current bidding zones, Ljubljana, 16 October, ACER-AP-CGC-ss-20 17-501.

ACER (2017b) ACER annual report on contractual congestion at interconnection points, 4th edn, 31 May.

ACER (2018) ACER annual report on contractual congestion at interconnection points, 5th edn, 31 May.

ACER (2020) Decision No. 29/2020 of the European Union Agency for the Cooperation of Energy Regulators of 24 November 2020 on the methodology and assumptions that are to be used in the bidding zone review process and for the alternative bidding zone configurations to be considered.

ACER (2021) 8th ACER report on congestion in the EU gas markets and how it is managed —period covered: 2020, May.

ACER & CEER (Council of European Energy Regulators) (2020) Annual Report on the Results of Monitoring the Internal Electricity and Natural Gas Markets in 2019: Energy Retail and Consumer Protection Volume. October, https://acer.europa.eu/ Official_documents/Acts_of_the_Agency/Publication/ACER%20Market%20 Monitoring%20Report%202019%20-%20Energy%20Retail%20and%20Consumer%20 Protection%20Volume.pdf).

ACT (Association of Corporate Treasurers) (2011) European regulation of credit rating agencies: Brief from the Association of Corporate Treasurers, November.

Albers, M. (2002) 'Energy Liberalization and EC Competition Law', *Fordham International Law Journal* 25(3): 909 945.

Ansell, C.K. (2011) *Pragmatist Democracy: Evolutionary Learning as Public Philosophy*, New York: Oxford University Press.

Ayres, I. and Gertner, R. (1989) 'Filling in the Gaps in Incomplete Contracts: An Economic Theory of Default Rules', *Yale Law Journal* 99: 87–130.

Baldwin, R., Cave, M., and Lodge, M. (2011) *Understanding Regulation: Theory, Strategy, and Practice*, 2nd edn, Oxford: Oxford University Press.

Bartolini, S. (2011) 'New Modes of European Governance: An Introduction'. In A. Héritier and M. Rhodes (eds), *New Modes of Governance in Europe: Governing in the Shadow of Hierarchy*, Basingstoke: Palgrave Macmillan, pp. 1–18.

Beach, D. and Pedersen, R.B. (2013) *Process-Tracing Methods: Foundations and Guidelines*, Ann Arbor, MI: University of Michigan Press.

Bennett, A. and Checkel, J.T. (eds) (2015) *Process Tracing: From Metaphor to Analytic Tool*, Cambridge: Cambridge University Press.

Bi, Y. (2015) 'Experimentalist Approach of Chinese Legislation Model: From Passive Response to Institutional Design', *Theory and Practice of Legislation* 3(2): 141–167.

Bickerton, C.J., Hodson, D., and Puetter, U. (2015) 'The New Intergovernmentalism: European Integration in the Post-Maastricht Era', *Journal of Common Market Studies* 53(4): 703–722.

Black, J. (2010) 'The Rise, Fall and Fate of Principles Based Regulation', LSE Legal Studies Working Paper No. 17/2010.

Blauberger, M. and Rittberger, B. (2015) 'Conceptualizing and Theorizing EU Regulatory Networks', *Regulation & Governance* 9(4): 367–376.

Blauberger, M. and Rittberger, B. (2017) 'A Rejoinder to Tarrant and Kelemen', *Regulation & Governance* 11(2): 223–227.

Bocquillon, P. and Maltby, T. (2020) 'EU Energy Policy Integration as Embedded Intergovernmentalism: the Case of Energy Union Governance', *Journal of European Integration*, 42(1), 39–57.

Boeger, N. and Corkin, J. (2012) 'How Regulatory Networks Shaped Institutional Reform under the EU Telecoms Framework', *Cambridge Yearbook of European Legal Studies* 14: 49–73.

Börzel, T.A. (2010) 'European Governance—Negotiation and Competition in the Shadow of Hierarchy', *Journal of Common Market Studies* 48: 191–219.

Börzel, T.A. (2012) 'Experimentalist Governance in the EU: The Emperor's New Clothes?', *Regulation and Governance* 6(3): 378–384.

Börzel, T.A. and Risse, T. (2010) 'Governance without a State: Can It Work?', *Regulation & Governance* 4(2): 113–134.

Brunkhorst, F.M., Engel, C., Bloos, F., Meier-Hellmann, A., Ragaller, M., Weiler, N., Moerer, O., Gruendling, M., Oppert, M., Grond, S., Olthoff, D., Jaschinski, U., John, S., Rossaint, R., Welte, T., Schaefer, M., Kern, P., Kuhnt, E., Kiehntopf, M., Hartog, C., Natanson, C., Loeffler, M., and Reinhart, K. (2008) 'Intensive Insulin Therapy and Pentastarch Resuscitation in Severe Sepsis', *New England Journal of Medicine* 358: 125–139.

Bulfone, F. (2019) 'The State Strikes Back: Industrial Policy, Regulatory Power and the Divergent Performance of Telefónica and Telecom Italia', *Journal of European Public Policy* 26(5): 752–771.

Cameron, P.D. (2002) *Competition in Energy Markets: Law and Regulation in the European Union*, Oxford: Oxford University Press.

Cameron, P.D. (2007) *Competition in Energy Markets: Law and Regulation in the European Union*, 2nd edn, Oxford: Oxford University Press.

Campbell-Verduyn, M. and Porter, T. (2014) 'Experimentalism in the EU and Global Financial Governance: Interactions, Contrasts, and Implications', *Journal of European Public Policy* 21(3): 408–429.

Cave, M., Genakos, C., and Valletti, T. (2019) 'The European Framework for Regulating Telecommunications: A 25-Year Appraisal', *Review of Industrial Organization* 55: 47–62.

CEER (Council of European Energy Regulators) (2002) 'Establishing the Preferred Tariff Methodology for Intrastate, Cross-Border and Transit Flows in European Gas Markets', CEER paper delivered to the 6th Madrid Forum, 30–31 October.

CEER (2004) Monitoring report 2004 concerning compliance with the Guidelines for Good Third Party Access Practice to Gas Transmission Systems, Brussels.

Coen, D. and Thatcher, M. (2008) 'Network Governance and Multi-level Delegation: European Networks of Regulatory Agencies', *Journal of Public Policy* 28(1): 49–71.

Cohen, J. and Sabel, C.F. (1997) 'Directly-Deliberative Polyarchy', *European Law Journal* 3(4): 313–342.

Council of the European Union (2003) Council Regulation (EC) No. 1/2003 of 16 December 20002 on the implementation of the rules on competition laid down in Articles 81 and 82 of the Treaty, OJ L 001, 4 January.

CRE (Commission de Régulation de l'Énergie) (2008) Report on electricity interconnection management and use, June.

Dabrowska-Klosinska, P. (2022) 'Uniformity, Experimentalism, and the Unfulfilled Promise of Differentiated Integration in EU Regulation of GMOs: Which Way Forward?', Working Paper EUI RSC 2022/11.

De Búrca, G. (2010a) 'Stumbling into Experimentalism: The EU Anti-discrimination Regime'. In C.F. Sabel and J. Zeitlin (eds), *Experimentalist Governance in the European Union: Towards a New Architecture*, Oxford: Oxford University Press, pp. 215–236.

De Búrca, G. (2010b) 'New Governance and Experimentalism: An Introduction— Symposium: New Governance and the Transformation of Law', *Wisconsin Law Review* 2: 227–238.

De Búrca, G. and Scott, J. (eds) (2006) *Law and New Governance in the EU and the US*, Oxford: Hart Publishing.

De Búrca, G., Keohane, R.O., and Sabel, C.F. (2013) 'New Modes of Pluralist Global Governance', *Journal of International Law and Politics* 45(1): 723–786.

De Búrca, G., Keohane, R.O., and Sabel, C.F. (2014) 'Global Experimentalist Governance', *British Journal of Political Science* 44(03): 477–486.

De Hauteclocque, A. (2013) *Market Building through Antitrust: Long-Term Contract Regulation in EU: Long-Term Contract Regulation in EU Electricity Markets*, Cheltenham: Edward Elgar.

De Hauteclocque, A. (2016) 'Article 102 TFEU—Abuse of a Dominant Position'. In C. Jones (ed.), *EU Competition Law and Energy Markets*, Deventer: Claeys & Casteels, pp. 283–375.

Dehousse, R. (1997) 'Regulation by Networks in the European Community: The Role of European Agencies', *Journal of European Public Policy* 4(2): 246–261.

DevStat (2020) Consumer testing services—retail investors' preferred option regarding performance scenarios and past performance information within the Key Information Document under the PRIIPs framework. Final report for Directorate-General for Financial Stability, Financial Services and Capital Markets Union (FISMA), February.

Dewey, J. (1927) *The Public and Its Problems*, New York: Henry Holt.

DNV GL (Det Norske Veritas and Germanischer Lloyd) (2020) Methodology to estimate the impact of a bidding zone reconfiguration on market liquidity and transaction costs: Liquidity and transaction costs, 2020-0379, Rev. 1.

Dorf, M.C. and Sabel, C.F. (1998) 'A Constitution of Democratic Experimentalism', *Columbia Law Review* 98(2): 267–473.

Drahos, P. (2021) *Survival Governance: Energy and Climate in the Chinese Century*, Oxford: Oxford University Press.

Eberlein, B. (2005) 'Regulation by Cooperation: The "Third Way" in Making Rules for the Internal Energy Market'. In P.D. Cameron (ed.), *Legal Aspects of EU Energy Regulation: Implementing the New Directives on Electricity and Gas across Europe*, Oxford: Oxford University Press, pp. 59–88.

Eberlein, B. (2008) 'The Making of the European Energy Market: The Interplay of Governance and Government', *Journal of Public Policy* 28(1): 73–92.

Eberlein, B. (2010) 'Experimentalist Governance in the European Energy Sector', In C.F. Sabel and J. Zeitlin (eds), *Experimentalist Governance in the European Union: Towards a New Architecture*, Oxford: Oxford University Press, pp. 61–78.

Eberlein, B. and Kerwer, D. (2004) 'New Governance in the European Union: A Theoretical Perspective', *Journal of Common Market Studies* 42(1): 121–142.

Eberlein, B. and Newman, A.L. (2008) 'Escaping the International Governance Dilemma? Incorporated Transgovernmental Networks in the European Union', *Governance* 21(1): 25–52.

Eckert, S. and Börzel, T.A. (2012) 'Experimentalist Governance: An Introduction', *Regulation & Governance* 6(3): 371–377.

Egerer, J., Weibezahn, J., and Hermann, H. (2016) 'Two Price Zones for the German Electricity Market—Market Implications and Distributional Effects', *Energy Economics* 59: 365–381.

EIOPA (European Insurance and Occupational Pensions Authority), EBA (European Banking Authority), and ESMA (European Securities and Markets Authority) (2016) ESAs' response to the intention of the European Commission to amend the draft Regulatory Technical Standards (RTS) jointly submitted by EBA, ESMA and EIOPA under Articles 8 (5),10 (2)and 13 (5) of Regulation (EU) No. 1286/2014, ESAs 2016 81, 22 December.

EMA (European Medicines Agency) (2012) 'European Medicines Agency starts infringement procedure to investigate Roche's alleged non-compliance with pharmacovigilance obligations', press release, 23 October.

EMA (2013a) 'PRAC recommends suspending marketing authorisations for infusion solutions containing hydroxyethyl starch', press release, 14 June.

EMA (2013b) 'PRAC confirms that hydroxyethyl-starch solutions (HES) should no longer be used in patients with sepsis or burn injuries or in critically ill patients', press release, 11 October.

EMA (2013c) 'Hydroxyethyl-starch solutions (HES) should no longer be used in patients with sepsis or burn injuries or in critically ill patients—CMDh endorses PRAC recommendations: HES will be available in restricted patient populations', press release, 25 October.

EMA (2013d) 'Hydroxyethyl-starch solutions (HES) no longer to be used in patients with sepsis or burn injuries or in critically ill patients: HES will be available in restricted patient populations', press release,19 December.

EMA (2013e) 'European Medicines Agency finalises review of medicines concerned by Roche pharmacovigilance inspection', press release, 19 November.

EMA (2014) 'Update on infringement procedure against Roche Registration Ltd.', press release, 14 April.

EMA (2016) 'Infringement procedure against Roche—EMA update', press release, 4 July.

EMA (2017) 'European Commission Closes Infringement Procedure against Roche', News, 15 December.

EMA (2018a) 'PRAC recommends suspending hydroxyethyl-starch solutions for infusion from the market: Review finds measures to protect patients have not been sufficiently effective', press release, 12 January.

EMA (2018b) Assessment report: Referral under Article 107i of Directive 2001/83/EC resulting from pharmacovigilance data. INN: hydroxyethyl starch, EMA/171888/2018, 17 May.

EMA (2018c) 'Hydroxyethyl starch solutions: CMDh introduces new measures to protect patients. Medicines to remain on the market provided that training, controlled access and warnings on the packaging are implemented', press release, 17 July.

EMA (2021) Assessment report: Comirnaty. Common name: COVID-19 mRNA vaccine (nucleoside-modified), EMA/707383/2020 Corr., 19 February.

EMA (2022a) COVID-19 vaccines safety update: Comirnaty (BioNTech Manufacturing GmbH), COVID-19 Vaccine Janssen (Janssen-Cilag International NV), Nuvaxovid (Novavax CZ, a.s.), Spikevax (Moderna Biotech Spain, S.L.), Vaxzevria (AstraZeneca AB), 17 February.

EMA (2022b) 'PRAC Recommends Suspending Hydroxyethyl-Starch Solutions for Infusion from the Market', News, 11 February.

EMA (2022c) 'Hydroxyethyl-Starch Solutions for Infusion Recommended for Suspension from the Market', News, 25 February.

ENTSO-E (European Network of Transmission System Operators for Electricity) (2014) Technical report bidding zones review process, 2 January.

ENTSO-E (2018) First edition of the bidding zone review: Final report, March.

ENTSO-G (European Network of Transmission System Operators for Gas) (2011) Response to European Commission consultation on congestion management procedures, April.

ENTSO-G (2012) Network Code on Capacity Allocation Mechanisms: An ENTSOG Network Code for Further ACER Review and Comitology Procedure, CAP291-12, 17 September.

ENTSO-G (2015) Network Code on Harmonized Transmission Tariff Structures for gas ENTSOG's Network Code for Re-submission to ACER, TAR0500-15, 31 July.

ERGEG (European Regulators' Group for Electricity and Gas) (2005) ERGEG Guidelines on Transmission Tarification, Explanatory note, 18 July.

ERGEG (2006) Cover note to ERGEG draft proposal on Guidelines on Inter TSO Compensation, E06-CBT-09-08a, 10 April.

ERGEG (2007a) Regional Initiatives annual report: Progress and prospects, March.

ERGEG (2007b) Coherence and convergence report, July.

ERGEG (2007c) Compliance with Electricity Regulation 1228/2003. Presentation delivered by Mrs Asta Sihvonen-Punkka, Chair of ERGEG Electricity Focus Group, at 14th Florence Electricity Forum, 24–25 September.

ERGEG (2007d) Compliance with Electricity Regulation 1228/2003—an ERGEG monitoring report, 18 July, E07-EFG-23-06.

ERGEG (2008a) The Regional Initiatives: Europe's key to energy market integration, Regional Initiatives annual report, February.

ERGEG (2008b) ERI coherence and convergence report—an ERGEG conclusions paper, February.

ERGEG (2009a) ERGEG principles: Capacity allocation and congestion management in European gas transmission networks, 10 December.

ERGEG (2009b) Congestion management on European gas transmission networks: Recommendations for Guidelines Adopted via a Comitology Procedure, 10 December.

ERGEG (2009c) ERGEG principles: Capacity allocation mechanisms and congestion management procedures. An ERGEG public consultation document, January.

ERGEG (2009d) ERGEG principles: Capacity allocation and congestion management in natural gas transmission networks, An ERGEG evaluation of comments paper, August.

ERGEG (2009e) ERGEG capacity allocation on European Gas transmission networks: Pilot Framework Guideline—Initial Impact Assessment, 10 December.

ERGEG (2010a) Congestion management procedures: Recommendations for Guidelines to Be Adopted via a Comitology Procedure, 8 September 2010.

ERGEG (2010b) Capacity allocation and congestion management in natural gas transmission networks. Presentation delivered by Mr Walter Boltz, Chairman ERGEG Gas Working Group and Head of the Austrian NRA, at the 17th Madrid Gas Forum, January.

ERGEG (2011) Monitoring report 2010 on capacity allocation mechanisms and congestion management procedures at selected interconnection points, February.

ESMA (European Securities and Markets Authority) (2015a) Guidelines and Recommendations Guidelines on Periodic Information to Be Submitted to ESMA by Credit Rating Agencies, 23 June.

ESMA (2015b) ESMA's supervision of credit rating agencies and trade repositories: 2015 annual report and 2016 work plan, 5 February.

ESMA (2017a) ESMA's supervision of credit rating agencies, trade repositories and monitoring of third country central counterparties: 2016 annual report and 2017 work programme, 3 February.

ESMA (2017b) Guidelines on the validation and review of credit rating agencies' methodologies, 23 March.

ESMA (2018) 'ESMA fines five banks €2.48 million for issuing credit ratings without authorisation', press release, 23 July.

ESMA (2020) 'ESMA fines Scope Ratings €640,000 for failings in covered bonds ratings', press release, 4 June.

ESMA (2021a) Questions and answers implementation of the Regulation (EU) No. 462/2013 on Credit Rating Agencies, 29 July.

ESMA (2021b) 'ESMA fines Moody's €3.7 million for conflicts of interest failures', press release, 30 March.

ESMA SMSG (Securities and Markets Stakeholder Group) (2020) Advice to ESMA: Response to the ESAs joint consultation paper concerning amendments to the PRIIPs KID, 13 January.

ESMA, EBA, EIOPA, and Joint Committee of the ESAs (European Supervisory Authorities) (2018) Joint consultation paper concerning amendments to the PRIIPs KID: Draft amendments to Commission Delegated Regulation (EU) 2017/653 of 8 March 2017 on key information documents (KID) for packaged retail and insurance-based investment products (PRIIPs), 8 November.

ESMA, EBA, EIOPA, and Joint Committee of the ESAs (2019) Joint consultation paper concerning amendments to the PRIIPs KID: Draft amendments to Commission Delegated Regulation (EU) 2017/653 of 8 March 2017 on key information documents (KID) for packaged retail and insurance-based investment products (PRIIPs), 16 October.

ESMA, EBA, EIOPA, and Joint Committee of the ESAs (2020) Annex to letter ESA 2020 19—draft final report following consultation on draft regulatory technical standards to amend the PRIIPs KID (NOT APPROVED) concerning amendments to Commission Delegated Regulation (EU) 2017/653 of 8 March 2017 on key information documents (KID) for packaged retail and insurance-based investment products (PRIIPs), 30 June.

ETSO (European Transmission System Operators) (2001) Co-ordinated use of power exchanges for congestion management, final report, April.

ETSO (2002a) Co-ordinated use of power exchanges for congestion management in continental Europe: Market design and role of power exchanges, open discussion paper, Draft, February.

ETSO (2002b) Co-ordinated congestion management: An ETSO vision, April.

ETSO (2002c) Outline proposals for a co-ordinated congestion management scheme based on the ETSO vision, September.

ETSO and Europex (Association of European Energy Exchanges) (2004) Flow-based market coupling, a joint ETSO–EuroPEX proposal on cross-border congestion management and integration of electricity markets in Europe, interim report, September.

ETSO and Europex (2008) Development and implementation of a coordinated model for regional and inter-regional congestion management, interim report, April.

ETSO and Europex (2009) Development and implementation of a coordinated model for regional and inter-regional congestion management, final report, January.

Eurelectric (Union of the Electricity Industry) (2004) Contribution to the 11th Electricity Regulatory Forum, April.

Eurelectric (2005) Improving interconnection capacity allocation, position paper, August.

European Commission (1992a) Commission proposal for a council directive concerning common rules for the internal market in electricity, COM(91) 548 final, 24 February.

European Commission (1992b) Commission proposal for a council directive concerning common rules for the internal market in natural gas, COM(91) 548 final, 24 February.

European Commission (1998a) Commission report on the state of liberalization of the energy markets, COM (1998) 212, Bull. 4-1998, point 1. 2.82.

European Commission (1998b) Commission first report on harmonization requirements with regard to Directive 96/92/EC, COM(1998) 167, Bull. 3-1998, point 1. 2.107.

European Commission (1999) Second report to the Council and the European Parliament on harmonization requirements: Directive 96/92/EC concerning common rules for the internal market in electricity, COM(1999) 164 final, 16 April.

European Commission (2000) State of implementation of the EU Gas Directive (98/30/EC). An overview, state of play by the end of May 2000, prepared by Directorate-General for Energy and Transport, European Commission.

European Commission (2001a) Proposal for a regulation of the European Parliament and of the Council on conditions for access to the network for cross-border exchanges in electricity, OJ C 240E, 28 August.

European Commission (2001b) Commission staff working paper: First benchmarking report on the implementation of the internal electricity and gas market, Brussels, 3 December, SEC(2001) 1957.

European Commission (2003a) 2003/796/EC: Commission decision of 11 November 2003 on establishing the European Regulators Group for Electricity and Gas, OJ L 296, 14 November.

European Commission (2003b) Proposal for a regulation of the European Parliament and of the Council on conditions for access to the gas transmission networks, COM(2003) 741 final, 10 December.

European Commission (2003c) Commission recommendation of 11 February 2003 on relevant product and service markets within the electronic communications sector susceptible to ex ante regulation in accordance with Directive 2002/21/EC of the European Parliament and of the Council on a common regulatory framework for electronic communication networks and services, OJ L 114, 8 May.

European Commission (2004) Third benchmarking report on the implementation of the internal electricity and gas market, draft working paper, 1 March.

European Commission (2005) Report from the Commission: Annual report on the implementation of the gas and electricity internal market, COM(2004) 863 final, 5 January.

European Commission (2007a) Commission staff working document accompanying the communication from the Commission—inquiry pursuant to Article 17 of Regulation (EC) No. 1/2003 into the European gas and electricity sectors (final report), SEC(2006) 1724, 8 January.

European Commission (2007b) Communication from the Commission to the Council and the European Parliament: Report on the experience gained in the application of the Regulation (EC) No. 1228/2003 "Regulation on Cross-Border Exchanges in Electricity", COM(2007) 250 final, 15 May.

European Commission (2007c) Communication from the Commission—inquiry pursuant to Article 17 of Regulation (EC) No. 1/2003 into the European gas and electricity sectors (final report), COM(2006) 851 final, 10 January.

European Commission (2007d) Commission Regulation (EC) No. 658/2007 of 14 June 2007 concerning financial penalties for infringement of certain obligations in connection with marketing authorisations granted under Regulation (EC) No. 726/2004 of the European Parliament and of the Council, OJ L 155, 15 June.

European Commission (2009) Communication from the Commission: Executive summary of the pharmaceutical sector inquiry report, 8 July.

European Commission (2010a) Commission Regulation (EU) No. 774/2010 of 2 September 2010 on laying down guidelines relating to inter-transmission system operator compensation and a common regulatory approach to transmission charging.

European Commission (2010b) Commission staff working document accompanying document to the Commission regulation establishing a mechanism for the compensation of transmission system operators for the costs of hosting cross border flows of electricity and a common regulatory approach to transmission charging, (COM(2008) xxx final) (SEC(2008) xxx). Brussels, SEC(2010) XXX final.

European Commission (2010c) Public consultation on credit rating agencies, 5 November.

European Commission (2011) Frequently asked questions: Legislative proposal on credit rating agencies (CRAs), MEMO/11/788, Brussels, 15 November.

European Commission (2012a) European Commission Directorate General for Energy: Invitation to start the procedure on a Framework Guideline on Rules Regarding Harmonised Transmission Tariff Structures for gas, ENER B/JAV/TH/tj s(2012) 913468, Ref. Ares(2012)789016 – 29/06/2012, Brussels, 29 June.

European Commission (2012b) Commission staff working document executive summary of the impact assessment accompanying the document Commission decision amending Annex I to Regulation (EC) No. 715/2009 of the European Parliament and of the Council on conditions for access to the natural gas transmission networks, draft, Brussels.

European Commission (2012c) Commission staff working document impact assessment accompanying the document Commission decision amending Annex I to Regulation (EC) No. 715/2009 of the European Parliament and of the Council on conditions for access to the natural gas transmission networks, draft, Brussels.

European Commission (2012d) 2012/490/EU: Commission Decision of 24 August 2012 on amending Annex I to Regulation (EC) No. 715/2009 of the European Parliament and of the Council on conditions for access to the natural gas transmission networks, OJ L 231, 28 August.

European Commission (2012e) Commission Delegated Regulation (EU) No. 447/2012 of 21 March 2012 supplementing Regulation (EC) No. 1060/2009 of the European Parliament and of the Council on credit rating agencies by laying down regulatory technical standards for the assessment of compliance of credit rating methodologies, OJ L 140, 30 May.

European Commission (2012f) Commission Implementing Regulation (EU) No. 520/2012 of 19 June 2012 on the performance of pharmacovigilance activities provided for in Regulation (EC) No. 726/2004 of the European Parliament and of the Council and Directive 2001/83/EC of the European Parliament and of the Council, OJ L 159, 20 June.

European Commission (2013a) Framework Guidelines on Rules Regarding Harmonized Transmission Tariff Structures for gas, ENER B/JPATH/os s(2013)410004, Brussels, 15 March.

European Commission (2013b) Commission Regulation (EU) No. 984/2013 of 14 October 2013 establishing a network code on capacity allocation mechanisms in gas transmission systems and supplementing Regulation (EC) No. 715/2009 of the European Parliament and of the Council, OJ L 273, 15 October.

European Commission (2013c) New rules on credit rating agencies (CRAs)—frequently asked questions, MEMO/13/13, Brussels, 16 January.

European Commission (2013d) 'Antitrust: Commission fines Lundbeck and other pharma companies for delaying market entry of generic medicines', press release, Brussels, 19 June.

European Commission (2013e) 'Antitrust: Commission fines Johnson & Johnson and Novartis € 16 million for delaying market entry of generic pain-killer fentanyl', press release, Brussels, 10 December.

European Commission (2014a) Speech: Statement on the Google investigation, SPEECH/14/93, Brussels, 5 February.

European Commission (2014b) 'Antitrust: Commission fines Servier and five generic companies for curbing entry of cheaper versions of cardiovascular medicine', press release, Brussels, 9 July.

European Commission (2015) Commission Regulation (EU) 2015/1222 of 24 July 2015 establishing a guideline on capacity allocation and congestion management, OJ L 197, 25 July.

European Commission (2016a) Commission Delegated Regulation of 30 June 2016 supplementing Regulation (EU) No. 1286/2014 of the European Parliament and of the Council on key information documents for packaged retail and insurance-based investment products (PRIIPs) by laying down regulatory technical standards with regard to the presentation, content, review and revision of key information documents and the conditions for fulfilling the requirement to provide such documents, Brussels, 30 June, C(2016) 3999 final.

European Commission (2016b) Intention of the Commission to amend the draft Regulatory Technical Standards jointly submitted by EBA, ESMA and EIOPA under Articles 8 (5), 10 (2) and 13 (5) of Regulation (EU) No 1286/2014, FISMA. C.4/LB/bd/Ares(2016)6926122, Brussels, 10 November.

European Commission (2017a) Commission Regulation (EU) 2017/460 of 16 March 2017 establishing a network code on harmonised transmission tariff structures for gas, OJ L 72, 17 March.

European Commission (2017b) Commission Regulation (EU) 2017/459 of 16 March 2017 establishing a network code on capacity allocation mechanisms in gas transmission systems and repealing Regulation (EU) No. 984/2013, OJ L 72, 17 March.

European Commission (2017c) Commission Decision of 27 June 2017 relating to a proceeding under Article 102 of the Treaty on the Functioning of the European Union and Article 54 of the Agreement on the European Economic Area (AT.39740—Google Search (Shopping)), Brussels, 27 June, C(2017) 4444 final.

European Commission (2017d) Commission Delegated Regulation (EU) 2017/653 of 8 March 2017 supplementing Regulation (EU) No. 1286/2014 of the European Parliament and of the Council on key information documents for packaged retail and insurance-based investment products (PRIIPs) by laying down regulatory technical standards with regard to the presentation, content, review and revision of key information documents and the conditions for fulfilling the requirement to provide such documents, L 100/1, 12 April.

European Commission (2017e) Monitoring safety of medicines for patients: Pharmacovigilance activities related to medicines for human use in the EU, Luxembourg, (COM(2016) 498).

European Commission (2017f) 'Pharma investigations: Commission closes infringement procedure against Roche without penalty', e-News, 15 December.

European Commission (2020a) Commission Recommendation (EU) 2020/2245 of 18 December 2020 on relevant product and service markets within the electronic communications sector susceptible to ex ante regulation in accordance with Directive (EU) 2018/1972 of the European Parliament and of the Council establishing the European Electronic Communications Code, OJ L 439, 29 December.

European Commission (2020b) Letter from Commissioner Mairead McGuiness to ESAs on PRIIPs, (2020)8504351, Brussels, 18 December.

European Commission (2020c) 'Antitrust: Commission fines Teva and Cephalon €60.5 million for delaying entry of cheaper generic medicine', press release, Brussels, 26 November.

European Commission (2021) Commission Delegated Regulation (EU) 2021/2268 of 6 September 2021 amending the regulatory technical standards laid down in Commission Delegated Regulation (EU) 2017/653 as regards the underpinning methodology and presentation of performance scenarios, the presentation of costs and the methodology for the calculation of summary cost indicators, the presentation and content of information on past performance and the presentation of costs by packaged retail and insurance-based investment products (PRIIPs) offering a range of options for investment and alignment of the transitional arrangement for PRIIP manufacturers offering units of funds referred to in Article 32 of Regulation (EU) No. 1286/2014 of the European Parliament and of the Council as underlying investment options with the prolonged transitional arrangement laid down in that article, OJ L 455I, 20 December.

European Commission, ACER, ENTSO-G, and ENTSO-E (2017) Reference paper for the NC Implementation and Monitoring Group, 2 October.

European Daily Electric Markets (2009) 'Set up EU-side master plan for market integration, regulators told', 2 March.

European Parliament (2016) Objection to a delegated act: Key information documents for packaged retail and insurance-based investment products. European Parliament resolution of 14 September 2016 on the Commission Delegated Regulation of 30 June 2016 supplementing Regulation (EU) No. 1286/2014 of the European Parliament and of the Council on key information documents for packaged retail and insurance-based investment products (PRIIPs) by laying down regulatory technical standards with regard to the presentation, content, review and revision of key information documents and the conditions for fulfilling the requirement to provide such documents (C(2016)03999—2016/2816(DEA)), P8_TA(2016)0347, 14 September.

European Parliament (2017) Recommendation for a decision pursuant to Rule 105 (6)of the Rules of Procedure to raise no objections to the Commission Delegated Regulation of 8 March 2017 supplementing Regulation (EU) No. 1286/2014 of the European Parliament and of the Council on key information documents for packaged retail and insurance-based investment products (PRIIPs) by laying down regulatory technical standards with regard to the presentation, content, review and revision of key information documents and the conditions for fulfilling the requirement to provide such documents (C(2017)01473—2017/2602(DEA)), B8-0234/2017, 29 March.

European Parliament and Council (1996) Directive 96/92/EC of the European Parliament and of the Council of 19 December 1996 concerning common rules for the internal market in electricity, OJ L 27, 30 January.

European Parliament and Council (1998) Directive 98/30/EC of the European Parliament and of the Council of 22 June 1998 concerning common rules for the internal market in natural gas, OJ L 204, 21 July.

European Parliament and Council (2001) Directive 2001/83/EC of the European Parliament and of the Council of 6 November 2001 on the Community code relating to medicinal products for human use, OJ L 311, 28 November.

European Parliament and Council (2002) Directive 2002/21/EC of the European Parliament and of the Council of 7 March 2002 on a common regulatory framework for electronic communications networks and services (Framework Directive), OJ L 108, 24 April.

European Parliament and Council (2003) Regulation (EC) No. 1228/2003 of the European Parliament and of the Council of 26 June 2003 on conditions for access to the network for cross-border exchanges in electricity, OJ L 176, 15 July.

European Parliament and Council (2004) Regulation (EC) No. 726/2004 of the European Parliament and of the Council of 31 March 2004 laying down Community procedures for the authorisation and supervision of medicinal products for human and veterinary use and establishing a European Medicines Agency, OJ L 136, 30 April.

European Parliament and Council (2005) Regulation (EC) No. 1775/2005 of the European Parliament and of the Council of 28 September 2005 on conditions for access to the natural gas transmission networks, OJ L 289, 3 November.

European Parliament and Council (2009a) Regulation (EC) No. 713/2009 of the European Parliament and of the Council of 13 July 2009 establishing an agency for the cooperation of energy regulators, OJ L 211, 14 August.

European Parliament and Council (2009b) Regulation (EC) No. 714/2009 of the European Parliament and of the Council of 13 July 2009 on conditions for access to the network for cross-border exchanges in electricity and repealing Regulation (EC) No. 1228/2003, OJ L 211, 14 August.

European Parliament and Council (2009c) Regulation (EC) No. 715/2009 of the European Parliament and of the Council of 13 July 2009 on conditions for access to the natural gas transmission networks and repealing Regulation (EC) No. 1775/2005, OJ L 211, 14 August.

European Parliament and Council (2009d) Regulation (EC) No. 1211/2009 of the European Parliament and of the Council of 25 November 2009 establishing the Body of European Regulators for Electronic Communications (BEREC) and the Office, OJ L 337, 18 December.

European Parliament and Council (2009e) Regulation (EC) No. 1060/2009 of the European Parliament and of the Council of 16 September 2009 on credit rating agencies, OJ L 302, 17 November.

European Parliament and Council (2009f) Directive 2009/65/EC of the European Parliament and of the Council of 13 July 2009 on the coordination of laws, regulations and administrative provisions relating to undertakings for collective investment in transferable securities (UCITS), OJ L 302, 17 November.

European Parliament and Council (2010a) Regulation (EU) No. 1093/2010 of the European Parliament and of the Council of 24 November 2010 establishing a European Supervisory Authority (European Banking Authority), amending Decision No. 716/2009/EC and repealing Commission Decision 2009/78/EC, OJ L 331, 15 December.

European Parliament and Council (2010b) Regulation (EU) No. 1094/2010 of the European Parliament and of the Council of 24 November 2010 establishing a European Supervisory Authority (European Insurance and Occupational Pensions Authority), amending Decision No. 716/2009/EC and repealing Commission Decision 2009/79/EC, OJ L 331, 15 December.

European Parliament and Council (2010c) Regulation (EU) No. 1095/2010 of the European Parliament and of the Council of 24 November 2010 establishing a European Supervisory Authority (European Securities and Markets Authority), amending Decision No. 716/2009/EC and repealing Commission Decision 2009/77/EC, OJ L 331, 15 December.

European Parliament and Council (2010d) Directive 2010/84/EU of the European Parliament and of the Council of 15 December 2010 amending, as regards pharmacovigilance, Directive 2001/83/EC on the Community code relating to medicinal products for human use, OJ L 348, 31 December.

European Parliament and Council (2010e) Regulation (EU) No. 1235/2010 of the European Parliament and of the Council of 15 December 2010 amending, as regards pharma-covigilance of medicinal products for human use, Regulation (EC) No. 726/2004 laying down Community procedures for the authorisation and supervision of medicinal products for human and veterinary use and establishing a European Medicines Agency, and Regulation (EC) No. 1394/2007 on advanced therapy medicinal products, OJ L 348, 31 December.

European Parliament and Council (2011) Regulation (EU) No. 513/2011 of the European Parliament and of the Council of 11 May 2011 amending Regulation (EC) No. 1060/2009 on credit rating agencies, OJ L 145, 31 May.

European Parliament and Council (2013) Regulation (EU) No. 462/2013 of the European Parliament and of the Council of 21 May 2013 amending Regulation (EC) No. 1060/2009 on credit rating agencies, OJ L 146, 31 May.

European Parliament and Council (2014) Regulation (EU) No. 1286/2014 of the European Parliament and of the Council of 26 November 2014 on key information documents for packaged retail and insurance-based investment products (PRIIPs), OJ L 352, 9 December.

European Parliament and Council (2018) Directive (EU) 2018/1972 of the European Parliament and of the Council of 11 December 2018 establishing the European Electronic Communications Code (Recast), OJ L 321, 17 December.

European Parliament and Council (2019) Regulation (EU) 2019/943 of the European Parliament and of the Council of 5 June 2019 on the internal market for electricity, OJ L 158, 14 June.

Europex (Association of European Energy Exchanges) (2003) Using implicit auctions to manage cross-border congestion: 'Decentralised Market Coupling', position paper, July.

Fernández Salas, M., Klotz, R., Moonen, S. and Schnichels, D. (2004) 'Access to gas pipelines: Lessons learnt from the Marathon case', *Competition Policy Newsletter* 2: 41–43.

Ferran, E. (2016) 'The Existential Search of the European Banking Authority', *European Business Organisation Law Review* 17(3): 285–317.

Florence Forum (European Electricity Regulatory Forum) (1998a) Minutes of the 1st meeting, February.

Florence Forum (1998b) Minutes of the 2nd meeting, October.

Florence Forum (1999a) Minutes of the 3rd meeting, May.

Florence Forum (1999b) Minutes of the 4th meeting, November.

Florence Forum (1999c) Towards EU cross-border electricity trade: Regulatory remarks and guidelines on tariffs and congestion, text as amended after the first Florence Working Group of 8 December 1999.

Florence Forum (2000a) Minutes of the 5th meeting, March.

Florence Forum (2000b) Minutes of the 6th meeting, including attached Guidelines on Congestion Management, November.

Florence Forum (2002) Minutes of the 8th meeting, February.

Florence Forum (2003) Minutes of the 10th meeting, July.

Florence Forum (2004) Minutes of the 11th meeting, September.

Florence Forum (2005) Minutes of the 11th meeting, September.

Florence Forum (2007) Minutes of the 14th meeting, September.

Florence Forum (2008) Minutes of the 15th meeting, November.

Florence Forum (2009) Target Model and Roadmap for Capacity Allocation and Congestion Management, Proposed to the 17th meeting, December.

Florence Forum (2012) Minutes of the 22nd meeting, May.

Frontier Economics and Consentec (2004) Analysis of cross-border congestion management methods for the EU internal electricity market. Study commissioned by the European Commission Directorate-General Energy and Transport, final report, June.

George, A.L. and Bennett, A. (2005) *Case Studies and Theory Development in the Social Sciences*, Cambridge MA: MIT Press.

Gerring, J. (2004) 'What Is a Case Study and What Is It Good for?', *American Political Science Review* 98(2): 341–354.

Goldstein, B.E. (ed.) (2011) *Collaborative Resilience: Moving through Crisis to Opportunity*, Cambridge, MA: MIT Press.

GTE (Gas Transmission Europe) (2002) Comments on CEER position paper: Guidelines for Tariff Structure Pertaining to Intrastate and Cross Border Transport and Transit, delivered by Mr Bernard Brelle at the 5th Madrid Gas Forum, 7–8 February.

GTE (2004) 'Entry–Exit System Guidelines', presentation delivered by Jacques Laurelut, GTE Vice-President, at the 8th Madrid Forum, 8–9 July.

Haase, N. (2008) 'European Gas Market Liberalisation: Are Regulatory Regimes Moving Towards Convergence?', Oxford Institute for Energy Studies NG24.

Halfteck, G. (2006) 'Legislative Threats', Bepress Legal Series Working Paper 1122.

Hancher, L. (1997) 'Slow and Not So Sure: Europe's Long March to Electricity Market Liberalization', *Electricity Journal* 10(9): 92–101.

Hancher, L. (1998) 'Delimitation of Energy Law Jurisdiction. The EU and Its Member States: From Organisational to Regulatory Conflicts', *Journal of Energy and Natural Resources Law* 16(1): 42–67.

Haubricht, H.-J., Fritz, W., and Vennegeerts, H. (1999) Study on cross-border electricity transmission tariffs: Prepared by order of the European Commission DG XVII, final report, Aachen, April.

Hauray, B. (2006) *L'Europe du médicament. Politique—Expertise—Intérêts privés*, Paris: Sciences Po Presses.

Hauray, B., Boullier, H., Gaudillière, J.-P., and Michel, H. (eds) (2021) *Conflict of Interest and Medicine: Knowledge, Practices, and Mobilizations*, London: Routledge.

Heilmann, S. (2008) 'Experimentation under Hierarchy: Policy Experiments in the Reorganization of China's State Sector, 1978-2008', CID Working Paper Series No. 172.

Héritier, A. and Lehmkuhl, D. (2008) 'The Shadow of Hierarchy and New Modes of Governance', *Journal of Public Policy* 28(1): 1–17.

Héritier, A. and Rhodes, M. (eds) (2011) *New Modes of Governance in Europe: Governing in the Shadow of Hierarchy*, Basingstoke: Palgrave Macmillan.

HMA (Heads of Medicines Agencies) and EMA (European Medicines Agency) (2019) Report on pharmacovigilance tasks from EU Member States and the European Medicines Agency (EMA), 2015–2018, 10 December.

Hooghe, L., and Marks, G. (2001) *Multi-level Governance and European Integration*, Lanham, MD: Rowman & Littlefield.

Jabko, N. (2006) *Playing the Market: A Political Strategy for Uniting Europe, 1985–2005*, Ithaca, NY: Cornell University Press.

Karkkainen, B.C. (2006) 'Information-Forcing Regulation and Environmental Governance', in G. de Búrca and J. Scott (eds), *Law and New Governance in the EU and the US*, London: Hart Publishing, pp. 293–322.

Kelemen, R.D. and Tarrant, A. (2011) 'The Political Foundations of the Eurocracy', *West European Politics* 34(5): 922–947.

KEMA (Keuring van Elektrotechnische Materialen te Arnhem) and COWI (Christian Ostenfeld and Wriborg Jønson) (2013) Study on entry–exit regimes in gas. By order of the European Commission DG ENER, July.

KEMA and REKK (Regional Centre for Energy Policy Research) (2009) Report: Study on methodologies for gas transmission network tariffs and gas balancing fees in Europe. Submitted to the European Commission, Directorate-General Energy and Transport, December.

Keohane, R.O. (2001) 'Governance in a Partially Globalized World', *American Political Science Review* 95(1): 1–13.

Klop, M. (2009) *Charting the Gaps: EU Regulation of Gas Transmission Tariffs in the Netherlands and the UK*, Oxford: Oxford Institute for Energy Studies.

Knops, H.P.A., de Vries, L.J., and Hakvoort, R.A. (2001) 'Congestion Management in the European Electricity System: An Evaluation of the Alternatives', *Journal of Network Industries* 2(3–4), 311–351.

Kohler-Koch, B. and Eising, R. (eds) (1999) *The Transformation of Governance in Europe*, London: Routledge.

Krapohl, S. (2004) 'Credible Commitment in Non-Independent Regulatory Agencies: A Comparative Analysis of the European Agencies for Pharmaceuticals and Foodstuffs', *European Law Journal* 10(5): 518–538.

Krapohl, S. (2008) *Risk Regulation in the Single Market: The Governance of Pharmaceuticals and Foodstuffs in the European Union*, Basingstoke: Palgrave.

Lindblom, C.E. (1959) 'The Science of "Muddling Through"', *Public Administration Review* 19(2): 79–88.

Lindblom, C.E. (1965) *The Intelligence of Democracy: Decision Making through Mutual Adjustment*, New York: The Free Press.

Lipsky, M. (1980) *Street-Level Bureaucracy: The Dilemmas of Individuals in Public Services*, Cambridge, MA: MIT Press.

London Economics and Ipsos (2015) Consumer testing study of the possible new format and content for retail disclosures of packaged retail and insurance-based investment products. Final report for the Directorate-General for the Internal Market and Services of the European Commission, 8 December.

Lowi, T.J. (2000) 'Frontyard Propaganda'. In C.F. Sabel, A. Fung, and B. Karkkainen (eds), *Beyond Backyard Environmentalism*, Boston, MA: Beacon Press, pp. 70–76.

Madrid Forum (European Gas Regulatory Forum) (1999) Minutes of the 1st meeting, September–October.

Madrid Forum (2000a) Minutes of the 2nd meeting, May.

Madrid Forum (2000b) Minutes of the 3rd meeting, October.

Madrid Forum (2001) Minutes of the 4th meeting, July.

Madrid Forum (2002a) Minutes of the 5th meeting, including Annex II: Recommendations on Guidelines for Good Practice in Relation to TPA Services, February.

Madrid Forum (2002b) Minutes of the 6th meeting, October.

Madrid Forum (2003) Minutes of the 7th meeting, including Annex 1: Guidelines for Good TPA Practice—revised version, September.

Madrid Forum (2008) Minutes of the 15th meeting, November.

Madrid Forum (2011) Minutes of the 19th meeting, March.

Madrid Forum (2015) Minutes of the 28th meeting, October.

Mahoney, J. and Rueschemeyer, D. (2003) *Comparative Historical Analysis in the Social Sciences*, Cambridge: Cambridge University Press.

Mathieu, E. and Rangoni, B. (2019) 'Balancing Experimentalist and Hierarchical Governance in European Union Electricity and Telecommunications Regulation: A Matter of Degrees', *Regulation & Governance* 13(4): 577–592.

Matlary, J.H. (1997) *Energy Policy in the European Union*, New York: St Martin's Press.

McGowan, F. (ed.) (1996) *European Energy Policies in a Changing Environment*, Heidelberg: Physica.

Mennillo, G. and Sinclair, T.J. (2019) 'A Hard Nut to Crack: Regulatory Failure Shows How Rating Really Works', *Competition & Change* 23(3): 266–286.

Midttun, A. (ed.) (1997) *European Electricity Systems in Transition: A Comparative Analysis of Policy and Regulation*, Amsterdam: Elsevier.

Moloney, N. (2015) 'Banking Union and the Implications for Financial Market Governance in the EU: Convergence or Divergence?'. In D. Busch and G. Ferrarini (eds), *European Banking Union*, Oxford: Oxford University Press, pp. 524–563.

Monti, G. (2008) 'Managing the Intersection of Utilities Regulation and EC Competition Law', LSE Law, Society and Economy Working Papers 8/2008.

Monti, G. and Rangoni, B. (2022) 'Competition Policy in Action: Regulating Tech Markets with Hierarchy and Experimentalism', *Journal of Common Market Studies*, 60(4): 1106–1123.

Morgan, K. (2018) 'Experimental Governance and Territorial Development', Background paper for an OECD/EC workshop on 14 December 2018 within the workshop series 'Broadening innovation policy: New insights for regions and cities', Paris.

Myburgh, J.A., Finfer, S., Bellomo, R., Billot, L., Cass, A., Gattas, D., Glass, P., Lipman, J., Liu, B., McArthur, C., McGuinness, S., Rajbhandari, D., Taylor, C.B., and Webb, S.A. (2012) 'Hydroxyethyl Starch or Saline for Fluid Resuscitation in Intensive Care', *New England Journal of Medicine* 367: 1901–1911.

Newbery, D.M. (1997) 'Privatisation and Liberalisation of Network Utilities', *European Economic Review* 41(3-5): 357–383.

Ostrom, E. (1990) *Governing the Commons: The Evolution of Institutions for Collective Action*, New York: Cambridge University Press.

Overdevest, C. and Zeitlin, J. (2014) 'Assembling an Experimentalist Regime: Transnational Governance Interactions in the Forest Sector', *Regulation & Governance* 8(1): 22–48.

Overdevest, C. and Zeitlin, J. (2018) 'Experimentalism in Transnational Forest Governance: Implementing European Union Forest Law Enforcement, Governance and Trade (FLEGT) Voluntary Partnership Agreements in Indonesia and Ghana', *Regulation & Governance* 12(1): 64–87.

Padgett, S. (1992) 'The Single European Energy Market: The Politics of Realization', *Journal of Common Market Studies* 30(1): 53–75.

PCG (Project Coordination Group) (2009a) Minutes of the 5th meeting, July.

PCG (2009b) Minutes of the 6th meeting, October.

PCG (2009c) Minutes of the 7th meeting, November.

Perner, A., Haase, N., Guttormsen, A.B., Tenhunen, J., Klemenzson, G., Aneman, A., Madsen, K., Møller, M., Elkjær, J., Poulsen, L., Bendtsen, A., Winding, R., Steensen, M., Berezowicz, P., Søe-Jensen, P., Bestle, M., Strand, K., Wiis, J., White, J., and Wetterslev, J. (2012) 'Hydroxyethyl Starch 130/0.42 versus Ringer's Acetate in Severe Sepsis', *New England Journal of Medicine* 367: 124–134.

Posner, E. (2010) 'The Lamfalussy Process: Polyarchic Origins of Networked Financial Rule-Making in the EU', in C.F. Sabel and J. Zeitlin (eds), *Experimentalist Governance in the European Union: Towards a New Architecture*, Oxford: Oxford University Press, pp. 43–60.

Posner, E. (2015) 'International Financial Regulatory Cooperation: An Experimentalist Turn?', in J. Zeitlin (ed.) *Extending Experimentalist Governance? The European Union and Transnational Regulation*, Oxford: Oxford University Press, pp. 196–223.

Potts J., Genov G., Segec A., Raine J., Straus S. and Arlett P. (2020) 'Improving the Safety of Medicines in the European Union: From Signals to Action', *Clinical Pharmacology and Therapeutics* 107(3): 521–529.

Radaelli, C.M. (2008) 'Europeanization, Policy Learning and New Modes of Governance', *Journal of Comparative Policy Analysis* 10(3): 239–254.

Ranci, P. (2012) *L'economia e la finanza spiegate ai ragazzi*, Brioschi.

Rangoni, B. (2019) 'Architecture and Policy-Making: Comparing Experimentalist and Hierarchical Governance in EU Energy Regulation', *Journal of European Public Policy* 26(1): 63–82.

Rangoni, B. (2020) 'Electricity Regulation in the European Union: Uniform, Differentiated or Experimentalist?', Amsterdam Centre for European Studies (ACES) SSRN Research Paper No. 2020/07.

Rangoni, B. (2022) 'Experimentalist Governance', in C. Ansell and J. Torfing (eds), *Handbook on Theories of Governance*, 2nd edn, Cheltenham and Northampton: Edward Elgar, pp. 592–603.

Rangoni, B. and Zeitlin, J. (2021) 'Is Experimentalist Governance Self-Limiting or Self-Reinforcing? Strategic Uncertainty and Recursive Rulemaking in European Union Electricity Regulation', *Regulation & Governance* 15(3): 822–839.

Ruester, S., von Hirschhausen, C., Marcantonini, C., He, X., Egerer, J., and Glachant, J.M. (2012) EU involvement in electricity and natural gas transmission grid tarification: Final report, European University Institute, January.

Sabel, C.F. (2004) 'Beyond Principal–Agent Governance: Experimentalist Organizations, Learning and Accountability'. In E.R. Engelen and M. Sie Dhian Ho (eds), *De Staat van de Democratie. Democratie voorbij de Staat*, Amsterdam: Amsterdam University Press, pp. 173–195.

Sabel, C.F. and Simon, W.H. (2006) 'Epilogue: Accountability without Sovereignty'. In G. de Búrca and J. Scott (eds), *Law and New Governance in the EU and the US*, London: Hart, pp. 395–412.

Sabel, C.F. and Simon, W.H. (2011) 'Minimalism and Experimentalism in the Administrative State', *Georgetown Law Journal* 100(1): 53–93.

Sabel, C.F. and Simon, W.H. (2012) 'Contextualizing Regimes: Institutionalization as a Response to the Limits of Interpretation and Policy Engineering', *Michigan Law Review* 110(7): 1265–1308.

Sabel, C.F. and Victor, D.G. (2017) 'Governing Global Problems under Uncertainty: Making Bottom-Up Climate Policy Work', *Climatic Change* 144: 15–27.

Sabel, C.F. and Victor, D.G. (2022) *Fixing the Climate: Strategies for an Uncertain World*, Princeton, NJ: Princeton University Press.

Sabel, C.F. and Zeitlin, J. (2008) 'Learning from Difference: The New Architecture of Experimentalist Governance in the European Union', *European Law Journal* 14(3): 271–327.

Sabel, C.F. and Zeitlin, J. (eds) (2010) *Experimentalist Governance in the European Union: Towards a New Architecture*, Oxford: Oxford University Press.

Sabel, C.F. and Zeitlin, J. (2012a) 'Experimentalist Governance'. In D. Levi-Faur (ed.), *The Oxford Handbook of Governance*, Oxford: Oxford University Press, pp. 170–184.

Sabel, C.F. and Zeitlin, J. (2012b) 'Experimentalism in the EU: Common Ground and Persistent Differences', *Regulation & Governance* 6(3): 410–426.

Sabel, C., Herrigel, G., and Kristensen, P.H. (2018) 'Regulation under Uncertainty: The Coevolution of Industry and Regulation', *Regulation & Governance* 12(3): 371–394.

Santoro, A., Genov, G., Spooner, A., Raine, J., and Arlett, P. (2017) 'Promoting and Protecting Public Health: How the European Union Pharmacovigilance System Works', *Drug Safety* 40: 855–869.

Scharpf, F.W. (1997) *Games Real Actors Play: Actor-Centered Institutionalism in Policy Research*, Boulder, CO: Westview Press.

Scharpf, F.W. (1999) *Governing in Europe: Effective and Democratic?*, Oxford: Oxford University Press.

Schmitter, P.C. and Streeck, W. (1985) 'Community, Market and the State—and Associations? The Prospective Contribution of Interest Governance to Social Order', *European Sociological Review*, 1: 119–138.

Scott, C. (2010) 'Reflexive Governance, Regulation and Meta-regulation: Control or Learning?'. In O. de Schutter and J. Lenoble (eds), *Reflexive Governance: Redefining the Public Interest in a Pluralistic World*, Oxford: Hart Publishing, pp. 43–64.

Shin, K. (2017a) 'Neither Centre nor Local: Community-Driven Experimentalist Governance in China', *China Quarterly* 231: 607–633.

Shin, K. (2017b) 'Mission-Driven Agency and Local Policy Innovation: Empirical Analysis from Baoding, China', *Journal of Chinese Political Science* 22(4): 549–580.

Simpson, S. (2011) '"New" Governance in European Union Policy Making: Policy Innovation or Political Compromise in European Telecommunications?', *West European Politics* 34(5): 1114–1133.

Sørensen, E. and Torfing J. (eds) (2007) *Theories of Democratic Network Governance*, Basingstoke: Palgrave Macmillan.

Solorio, I. and Jörgens, H. (2020) Contested Energy Transition? Europeanization and Authority turns in EU Renewable Energy Policy. *Journal of European Integration*, 42(1), 77–93.

Standard and Poor's (2014) Standard & Poor's Ratings Services Public Comment on Code of Conduct Fundamentals for Credit Rating Agencies, 28 March.

Stern, J.P. (1998) *Competition and Liberalization in European Gas Markets: A Diversity of Models*, London: Royal Institute of International Affairs.

Supponen, M. (2011) *Influence of National and Company Interests on European Electricity Transmission Investments*, Doctoral Dissertations, 77, Espoo: Aalto University publication series.

Svetiev, Y. (2010) 'Networked Competition Governance in the EU: Delegation, Decentralization, or Experimentalist Architecture?'. In C.F. Sabel and J. Zeitlin (eds), *Experimentalist Governance in the European Union: Towards a New Architecture*, Oxford: Oxford University Press, pp. 79–120.

Svetiev, Y. (2014) 'Settling or Learning: Commitment Decisions as a Competition Enforcement Paradigm', *Yearbook of European Law* 33(1): 466–500.

Svetiev, Y. (2020) *Experimentalist Competition Law and the Regulation of Markets*, Oxford: Hart Publishing.

Talus, K. (2011) 'Long-term Natural Gas Contracts and Antitrust Law in the European Union and the United States', *The Journal of World Energy Law & Business*, 4(3): 260–315i.

Talus, K. (2016) *Introduction to EU Energy Law*, Oxford: Oxford University Press.

Tarrant, A. and Kelemen, R.D. (2017) 'Reconceptualizing European Union Regulatory Networks: A Response to Blauberger and Rittberger', *Regulation & Governance* 11(2): 213–222.

Thatcher, M. (2011) 'The Creation of European Regulatory Agencies and Its Limits: A Comparative Analysis of European delegation', *Journal of European Public Policy* 18(6): 790–809.

Thatcher, M. and Coen, D. (2008) 'Network Governance and Multi-level Delegation: European Networks of Regulatory Agencies', *Journal of Public Policy* 28(1): 49–71.

Thatcher, M. (2014a) 'European Commission Merger Control: Combining Competition and the Creation of Larger European Firms: European Commission Merger Control', *European Journal of Political Research* 53(3): 443–64.

Thatcher, M. (2014b) 'From Old to New Industrial Policy via Economic Regulation', *Rivista della Regolazione dei Mercati* 2: 6–22.

Töller, A.E. (2017) 'Voluntary Regulation by the Pharmaceutical Industry—Which Role for the Shadow of Hierarchy and Social Pressure?', *European Policy Analysis* 3(1); 48–80.

Tömmel, I. and Verdun A. (eds) (2008) *Innovative Governance in the European Union: The Politics of Multilevel Policymaking*, Boulder, CO: Lynne Rienner Publishers.

Van der Zwan, N. (2014) 'Making Sense of Sinancialization', *Socio-Economic Review* 12(1): 99–129.

Vandenbroucke, J.P. (2008) 'Observational Research, Randomised Trials, and Two Views of Medical Science', *PLoS Medicine* 5(3): 0339–0343.

Von Rosenberg, H. (2009) 'Unbundling through the Back Door . . . the Case of Network Divestiture as a Remedy in the Energy Sector', *European Competition Law Review* 30(5): 237–254.

Wallace, H., Wallace, W., and Pollack, M.A. (eds) (2005) *Policy-Making in the European Union*, Oxford: Oxford University Press.

Wang, H., Chen, B., and Koppenjan, J. (2022) 'A Refined Experimentalist Governance Approach to Incremental Policy Change: The Case of Process-Tracing China's Central Government Infrastructure PPP Policies between 1988 and 2017', *Journal of Chinese Governance* 7(1): 27–51.

Weimer, M. (2019) *Risk Regulation in the Internal Market: Lessons from Agricultural Biotechnology*, Oxford: Oxford University Press.

Woll, C. (2014) *The Power of Inaction: Bank Bailouts in Comparison*, Ithaca, NY: Cornell University Press.

Zeitlin, J. (ed.) (2015) *Extending Experimentalist Governance? The European Union and Transnational Regulation*, Oxford: Oxford University Press.

Zeitlin, J. (2016) 'EU Experimentalist Governance in Times of Crisis', *West European Politics* 39(5): 1073–1094.

Zeitlin, J. (2017) '*International Organizations as Orchestrators*, Ed. Kenneth W. Abbott, Philipp Genschel, Duncan Snidal, and Bernhard Zangl. New York: Cambridge University Press, 2015, 450p.', *Perspectives on Politics* 15(3): 928–930.

Zeitlin, J. (2021) 'Uniformity, Differentiation, and Experimentalism in EU Financial Regulation: The Single Supervisory Mechanism in Action', Amsterdam Centre for European Studies Research Paper No. 2021/04.

Zeitlin, J. and Overdevest, C. (2021) 'Experimentalist Interactions: Joining Up the Transnational Timber Legality Regime', *Regulation & Governance*, 15(3): 686–708.

Zeitlin, J. and Rangoni, B. (2023) 'EU Regulation between Uniformity, Differentiation, and Experimentalism: Electricity and Banking Compared', *European Union Politics*, 24(1): 121–142.

Zhang, W., Lu, J., Song, B., and Lian, H. (2022) 'Experimentalist Governance in China: The National Innovation System, 2003–2018', *Journal of Chinese Governance* 7(1): 1–26.

Zhu, X. and Zhao, H. (2021) 'Experimentalist Governance with Interactive Central–Local Relations: Making New Pension Policies in China', *Policy Studies Journal* 49(1): 13–36.

Zhuang, H. and Wolf, S.A. (2021) 'Environmental Public Interest Litigation: New Roles for Civil Society Organizations in Environmental Governance in China', *Environmental Sociology* 7(4): 393–406.

Index

For the benefit of digital users, indexed terms that span two pages (e.g., 52–53) may, on occasion, appear on only one of those pages.

Note: Sub-entries under electricity markets, natural gas markets, communications markets, financial markets and pharmaceutical markets pertain specifically to that market but the aforementioned markets also appear as sub-entries under the numerous main entries pertaining to all five of the markets, eg coalitions, cognitive uncertainty, discretion, functional factors etc.